THE
DUKE

THE LIFE AND LIES OF
TOMMY MORRISON

KE

HAMILCAR
PUBLICATIONS
Boston

ISBN: 978-1-949590-52-4

CIP data is available.

Hamilcar Publications
Ten Post Office Square, 8th Floor South
Boston, MA 02109
www.hamilcarpubs.com

On the cover: Tommy Morrison, 1990.

To Mom and Dad, everlasting.

CONTENTS

We are so accustomed to disguise ourselves from other people, that in the end we disguise ourselves from ourselves.
—La Rochefoucauld

Acknowledge thine iniquity.
—Jeremiah 3:13

So many blondes, so little time!
—Tommy Morrison

PART
I

There was pathos, yes, but there was another kind of darkness, the way-
ward American Dream kind, on switchback roads, through knotweed
fields, hard by a Quick Stop or a Sonic. Under a black or starless sky.
Something like that. Why not? After all, Tommy Morrison was trouble
young. Hell, maybe he was born with a shiner. At first his story was saw-
grass or scrubland gothic: Starkweather, Lobster Boy, Karpis-Barker,
whatever. Later, it would be prizefighting, drugs, disease, prison, mad-
ness, perhaps. Morrison came from a broken home. He was a second-
hand son, passed from here to there, from nowhere to nowhere bound,
wherever he would stick. His father was abusive. His mother once beat a
murder charge. Tim, his brother, would spend fifteen years in prison for
rape. And Tommy? His mother first made him use his fists when he was
five years old against a bully at a drive-in movie theater. It was a showing
of The Texas Chainsaw Massacre.

★ ★ ★

ny biographical narrative is bound to raise questions of veracity. The life of Tommy Morrison more so, perhaps, because
of how much of it took place in half-light. Toughman contests, club fights in Wichita and Great Falls, orgies in rattletrap
motels, stints in jail and prison, and night crawling with tweakers from
crash pad to crash pad across the Southeast—by nature, Morrison seemed
drawn to subterranean pursuits. If there is any truth to his claim that
he had been a teenaged enforcer for an organized crime ring, then you
can add illicit activity, fundamentally clandestine, to his list of underbelly
pastimes.

Epistemological questions are also complicated by a series of X-factors.
Yes, Morrison was given to embellishment, lied repeatedly to his wives,
and spent years in the amoral subcultures of low-level crime, boxing,
prison, and drugs, which may have encouraged dissimulation. But he also
suffered from the burnout effect of methamphetamine and, in the early
2000s, he was diagnosed with HIV-related encephalopathy. Combined
with his career as a prizefighter, these afflictions left Morrison, already
given to magical thinking, with a tenuous grip on reality. Although Morrison suffered only three losses in his career, he took debilitating punishment once he stepped up in class. In less than five years, he had been

knocked down at least a dozen times in the ring and took part in several bruising, back-and-forth donnybrooks against Joe Hipp, Carl Williams, Ross Puritty, Razor Ruddock, and, to an extent, George Foreman, who rocked Morrison repeatedly with thudding jabs. What happened against Ray Mercer, Michael Bentt, and Lennox Lewis (Morrison was brutally stopped by each) would have left the American Medical Association, long driven to outlaw boxing because of its deleterious physical effects, wagging its collective finger.

When he was only in his mid-thirties, Morrison was already exhibiting classic signs of pugilistic dementia. Slurred speech, forgetfulness, scattered thoughts, a scanty attention span—Morrison was a cognitive nightmare. He began to scrawl reminders on his hands. His interviews took on a far-out quality. He increasingly suffered from paranoia. It took roughly a year after his HIV diagnosis for him to become a conspiracy theorist. In 1999, his IQ was measured at 78, which placed Morrison on the borderline for mental disability. Anyone who had heard Morrison speak after fights, with his Oklahoma twang, or read his interviews in *KO* magazine and *Boxing Illustrated* knew that he was an eloquent young man capable of expressing himself in complex sentences. By the time he hit rock bottom, a few years after being diagnosed with HIV (a disease he would eventually deny having) that was no longer the case. ESPN interviewed Morrison in 2000, while he was serving out a term in a Texarkana lockup for a variety of drug-related charges. In his orange prison garb, Morrison looked like he had just returned from a weeklong crank binge in Arkansas swampland. He was heavy-lidded, some of his teeth were missing, he spoke haltingly, many of his answers were rote, his hair had thinned into a wispy comb-over. And, as always, he seemed delusional. Name-dropping Sylvester Stallone, while sitting in a lockup no less, was more than just wishful thinking; it was the result of a mind gone irretrievably astray.

When he made his deranged comeback in 2007, Morrison went beyond being a fabulist and an AIDS conspiracist. He became a con artist, one who found the perfect milieu for his hoaxes: boxing, a barely regulated sport that thrives on deception and whose history of corruption cannot be separated from its history of champions.

Because so many of his acquaintances (including family members, professional contacts, and ex-lovers) were of a similar disreputable background, it was difficult to get anyone to talk about Morrison. Which is probably just as well; after all, Tommy Morrison left the world with enough lies to last a lifetime. (As for his partners in denial, the ones who believe Morrison once teleported from danger in a Missouri bar or was a victim of a vast boxing cabal, to go along with a global AIDS conspiracy, they are hardly worth mentioning at all.)

Court records—available online to the public for a nominal fee—will tell you that Morrison had HIV and that he had been on antiretrovirals, off and on, for years. There is no mystery there. The real mystery is why a man would lie to himself so hard and so often that he would wind up killing himself (suicide by denial) at the age of forty-four.

Like so much else in the world of Tommy Morrison, there is no answer to that, much less one that can be considered "true."

★　★　★

"They fuck you up, your mum and dad."
—Philip Larkin

★　★　★

Tommy David Morrison was born in Gravette, Arkansas, on January 2, 1969, to Tim Morrison Sr. and Diana Morrison. Known locally as the "Black Walnut Capital" of America because of its shelling plant, Gravette had barely a thousand residents, but it would only be the first of many sleepy hamlets Tommy Morrison would occupy throughout a tumultuous life.

Tim and Diana married in 1966, two years after their first child, Tim Jr., was born. Morrison Sr., originally from Illinois, was an itinerant construction worker and propane delivery driver, whose rough edges could never be sanded down. Wherever there was work, Morrison would alight. Along the way, it was often whiskey and women; then, whenever he returned home, it was often scattershot rage. When Morrison Sr. suffered an injury to his eye from an accident on the job, he developed a severe case of photophobia. As a result, he taped over the windows in the house, sat in the gloom, bottle in hand, and waited for his hair-trigger temper to catch. "It was like we were living in a cave," Tommy Morrison told *ESPN The Magazine*. "We had to tiptoe across the carpet. Anything that went wrong was our fault. We'd leave the light on in the bathroom, we'd get the shit beat out of us."

★ ★ ★

When Tim Morrison Sr. was a teenager, his brother (named Tommy), died after an accident on a construction site. Tommy had been clearing brush away so that a bulldozer could proceed when the operator accidently dropped the blade on him. Tim Morrison Sr. held his dying brother in his arms; in a fog of grief, he wore the blood-soaked shirt from the accident for days. Then he ran off to California, and when he returned, he brought the dark side with him.

★ ★ ★

Morrison Sr. often dressed entirely in black—like Johnny Cash or a misplaced existentialist—and usually added sunglasses to complete the menacing ensemble. If his sideburns were inspired by Robert Goulet (although his hero was Elvis Presley), then his worldview might have come from Hank Williams. And his cruelty troubled even his younger brother, Troy, who was driven to reveal sordid details to *ESPN The Magazine* in 1998, when it looked like Tommy Morrison was headed for the grave. "He's a very evil man," Troy Morrison said. "He scares me. He had pornography in the house, always by his bed, and in his automobiles. Tommy would be looking at it too, right in front of his mom and dad. You won't believe this, but when I was 14 and my brother Trent was 16, Tim took us to a boxing tournament, and he made us stop at a strip club on the way, and he brought out two strippers in tight outfits, and he said they were for us. He was the devil in the flesh."

And flesh was what drove Tim Morrison Sr. A womanizer without a conscience, Morrison Sr. instilled similar values in his sons, one who would eventually become a convicted rapist, the other a bigamist and the most famous athlete to contract HIV since Earvin "Magic" Johnson. There was nothing out of "Family Circus" or "The Wonder Years" for the Morrisons.

Photographs of Tim Morrison Sr. taken in the 1970s reveal a man of rough good looks, solidly built, sometimes with his shirtsleeves rolled up just past his biceps. He seemed incapable of smiling. By then, he wore a glass eye that lent his gaze a sinister air.

To his tomcatting lifestyle Morrison added verbal and physical abuse, revealing a sadistic streak, usually fueled by liquor, that would eventually lead to tragedy. As a teenager, Troy Morrison saw firsthand the havoc of the Morrison household. "[Tommy's] father would drink, tie one on and beat his mother in front of him. I spent a summer there. I witnessed it."

For her part, Diana Morrison, who took the brunt of the abuse, declined to elaborate on her ordeals. "I'd just as soon not go into that," she told *ESPN The Magazine*. "But, yes, I had broken bones."

★ ★ ★

"Both of his parents drank. He believes his mother is alcoholic and believes his father is not. Knows of no other family member other than his mother, he and his older brother to have problems with dependency issues. He went on to explain he began drinking alcohol at the age of twelve with his parents."
—Valley Hope admissions interview, February 1999

★ ★ ★

In 2000, during an ESPN *Up Close* interview conducted from prison, Morrison would elaborate, in tortured syntax, on his feelings about his father. "Him and I don't have the greatest relationship in the world," he said. "You know, years of seeing him abuse my mother seems like it drove a wedge between he and I's relationship as a father and son. As a business, certain things that we would do, criminal-type things, you know—until I had a son of my own, I started realizing how awful it was for him to subject his own son to do some of the things that we did."

Despite their rift, Morrison inherited from his father a love of boxing and an obsession with Elvis Presley (whose likeness he had tattooed on various parts of his body, including a tooth), but he also acquired a dehumanizing view of women and a taste for alcohol.

The Morrisons lived a nomadic existence: Siloam Springs, Arkansas, where the Riding Club Rodeo took place every year; Noel, Oklahoma, known as Christmas City for its colorful Yuletide postmarks; Sulphur

Springs, Arkansas, home of the Old Spanish Treasure Cave; Decatur, Arkansas, with its annual Homecoming Barbecue; Pawhuska, Oklahoma, distinguished by the Osage County Free Fair.

But the folksy trappings of rural life could not relieve the dark days and nights of the Morrison family. In March 1973 Diana Morrison finally reached her breaking point—she accidentally killed one of her rivals. According to Dawn Gilbert, whose memoir about her relationship with Tommy Morrison came out in 2014, Morrison Sr., his mistress, Donna Faye Shepherd, and Diana were all in the same watering hole in Pawhuska. Diana sat alone at the bar while Morrison Sr. and Shepherd shared a booth. There was the usual taunting from Morrison, with Shepherd chiming in for good measure. It was that extra hectoring voice, perhaps, that proved one turn of the screw too many. Angry, humiliated, and likely tipsy, Diana paid her tab and left the bar, only to return minutes later with a knife she had plucked out of her kitchen drawer. She approached the booth, flashed the blade, and lunged at Tim Morrison Sr., who jerked back at the last instant, avoiding death by mere inches. Her straying husband had been the intended target, but it was Shepherd, seated next to him, whom Diane fatally wounded. Shepherd died on March 4, 1973; she was thirty years old.

In her brush with minor fame over the years—first as the mother of a prominent heavyweight, then as the mother of an outspoken HIV denialist and celebrity train wreck—a span that lasted nearly a quarter century, Diana Morrison rarely broached the subject of Donna Faye Shepherd. Questions from reporters about Shepherd elicited only the tersest of responses from her. It was a grim detail that served as background for several magazine profiles of Tommy Morrison, a reminder of the instability that had produced an athlete who seemed perpetually in extremis. But Diana was never anything but ashamed of what she had done and resentful of how often Tommy Morrison would use her dark past to embellish his life story.

Diana spent six months in jail while awaiting trial. "It was hard on the kids," she said in the ESPN documentary *Tommy*, "and it was hard on me because I didn't know what I was looking at. Well, I knew that if I got convicted what I was looking at. But it turned out different and I thank god for that."

Eventually, Diana was acquitted, but her marriage to Morrison Sr. could not withstand what was essentially a failed murder attempt. They divorced not long after her trial ended.

★ ★ ★

"Oklahomans have always been builders. It is one of our finest qualities, and there is one other quality we Oklahomans have always shared. We are the dreamers. Everything around us all is the result of someone's dream. There can be no builders if there are not also dreamers. We are the wanderers, the gamblers, the builders, the dreamers, and the preservers. We are the cast of a human drama called 'Oklahoma.'"
—from an Oklahoma state tourism film, 1975

★ ★ ★

In 1980, Diana packed up her children (Tim Jr., Tonia, and Tommy) and moved to Jay, Oklahoma, a town with one traffic light and roughly 2,200 inhabitants. Although best known for producing Tommy Morrison, its only boxing champion, Jay is also the self-proclaimed "Huckleberry Capital of the World," and every summer hosts the National Huckleberry Festival.

It was hardscrabble living, spent mostly in trailers, and Morrison bounced around from friend to relative, the proverbial latchkey kid—except he was often away from home for days at a time. "We had kind of a screwed-up life," Diana told the *New York Times* in 1993. "But we all lived through it. Boxing held us together."

Over the years, Morrison would paint a far darker picture of his childhood, one that seemed to presage his disorderly—and sadly limited—future. About his parents and their dysfunctional relationship he rarely restrained himself. "They tried to keep you away from their arguments, but 70 percent of the time you'd be sitting there and he'd come in and she'd be mad and throw a coffee cup at him and . . ." Morrison said, in that same *Times* interview, as if in deliberate counterpoint to an understatement from his mother. "But what do you do? You sit there and you watch it. I had to watch that for a lot of years. I became very withdrawn. I became independent. I started doing things on my own."

But boxing *was* a family affair. "Boxing in my family has been somewhat of a tradition," Tommy Morrison said about how he and his brother, Tim Jr., got started in fisticuffs. "The last five generations on my father's side have all been fighters. My mother and father were always involved in boxing. They always wanted us to be involved in it, and we all started at a very early age."

In 1976 Tim Morrison Sr. formed a ragtag amateur team that included his younger brothers Trent and Troy, and his two sons, Tim Jr. and Tommy. He called it the Wolf Creek Boxing Club. "My parents owned a piece of property in Decatur, Arkansas, and the creek that ran through it was Wolf Creek," Troy Morrison recalls about the organization of the Fighting Morrisons. "I wasn't too crazy about it, but Tommy's dad lived vicariously through all of us because we all boxed. And he wanted to be the coach even though he never put on a pair of gloves in his life, but he wanted people to think he did. And, you know, that was fine. We were kind of self-taught, really. I mean, honest to goodness, we were pretty dedicated. We started out at the Rogers Boxing Club in Rogers, Arkansas, and it was just a long ways to drive over there, so we started our own club there in Decatur and he called it the Wolf Creek Boxing Club."

Tommy Morrison weighed 119 pounds or so in 1981, when he was an amateur on the Arkansas-Oklahoma-Missouri circuit. His brother, Tim, was a few years older and had established himself first as a middleweight and then, a few years later, as a heavyweight. (When Tim turned pro in 1987, his debut came against Oliver McCall, a future world titlist.)

In future interviews, Morrison would claim an amateur record of 202-20, which is as dubious as it is unverifiable. Unless Morrison was adding smokers to his tally, it seems unlikely that he had participated in so many bouts. Were most of these fights unofficial? "Back in the day, the AAU and different [programs] were just kind of coming on, but, no, they were sanctioned boxing events," says Troy Morrison. "We fought in the Springfield Mittens, the Springfield Golden Gloves, Carthage Golden Gloves, Park City—all over the Four State area. There wasn't too many little towns we didn't fight in. Some of them were smokers, Saturday night fights, but a lot of them were tournaments, three-day tournaments."

As for a ledger of over 220 contests, Troy Morrison believes that such a pace was feasible. "I would say it's very, very possible because, let's see, I boxed from '76 to '79, and I had . . . thirty-eight fights," he recalls. "And Tommy started in '76 and he didn't quit for years after that. I started playing basketball, baseball, stuff like that in high school. I said, 'To heck with boxing, this is more enjoyable. I'm getting tired of traveling every weekend to go fight somewhere,' you know. But that little guy started at sixty-five pounds and fought his way on up. He may be counting some of the Toughman contests, too, I don't know. But I would say that it might be a little bit of an exaggeration, but I wouldn't say by much."

★   ★   ★

At some point, Tommy Morrison abandoned amateur boxing to concentrate on teenage pursuits. If Jay could be considered representative of a Middle America wasteland, then Morrison could be typecast as one of its drifting rebels. Although Morrison was a good student and a standout athlete in high school, he had a mutinous streak that would reportedly lead to his being voted "Least Likely to Survive" by his classmates in the high school yearbook. One of the most outlandish stories about Morrison concerns the night he set the high school baseball field ablaze after he was cut from the team. In a 1993 Associated Press profile, Morrison claimed he meant only to scorch an insult about the coach into the grass. Instead, he torched the entire grounds. "But about that time, a big gust of wind comes, burns down the field and the outfield fence," he said. "I think they knew who did it, but they could never prove it."

In keeping with the general air of fiction and fabrication that surrounds him, the ball-field incident may or may not be another instance of ballyhoo, but the fact that Morrison was a true hell-raiser is undeniable. "I wasn't the model citizen," Morrison once said about his years in Jay. As a rowdy teen, he stole car stereos, drank beer, and scrapped whenever he could. "I never started a fight, but it didn't take that much to get me interested," he said. "There'd be parties and the Indians would stand outside and wait for you. Then on the weekends, you'd have to fight their older brothers and cousins. It stopped my junior year—by that time I'd been through pretty much everybody."

Of course, Morrison had a singular edge on nearly all of his school opposition: he had already had a fair number of amateur fights and he was, improbably, a veteran of the barbarous Toughman circuit.

Toughman contests were one of the inexplicable cultural phenomena of the zany 1980s, like Satanic Panic, Moonie weddings, manic televangelists, hair metal—the American panorama Martin Amis referred to as

"The Moronic Inferno." In 1983, even Hollywood tried to cash in on the fad, with the clamorous Dennis Quaid fantasia *Tough Enough*.

In his review of *Tough Enough*, for the *Chicago Sun-Times*, Roger Ebert summed up the allure of this repugnant pseudo-sport: "The genius of Toughman contests is that they combine the violence of prize-fighting, the buffoonery of pro wrestling, the show business of Roller Derby and the chance to see local guys making idiots out of themselves. Given all the energy expended annually in saloon brawls, it was probably only a matter of time until someone found a way to package it."

That someone was Art Dore, a Michigan-based boxing multitasker most famous for guiding super middleweight Murray Sutherland to an IBF championship in 1984. He also worked with comebacking heavyweight Earnie Shavers, who had lost a pair of unsuccessful title shots (against Muhammad Ali in 1977 and Larry Holmes in 1979).

Although Dore was a prominent businessman in Bay City, he had been an amateur boxer in the 1950s and the sport remained in his blood. He worked, variously, as a trainer, manager, and promoter. In 1979, he staged a series of local shows pitting one nonprofessional lout against another in a last-man-standing tournament. Dore explained his Toughman epiphany to Jeff Jacobs of *The Times Herald* (Port Huron): "I've been putting on good boxing shows for a long time and it gets frustrating to see the fans not get interested in two fine lighter-weight amateurs. You put a couple of big heavyweights with little polish in there and they go crazy. So I figured what the heck? We will give the people what they want."

What the people wanted was something like a large-scale roadhouse atmosphere on a Saturday night: blood, beer, and bawdiness. The man-off-the-stool concept was an instant hit among the working stiffs in a Rust Belt state with skyrocketing unemployment. A year later, the Toughman finals drew crowds of more than 30,000 to the gleaming new Silverdome in Pontiac, home of the Lions and the Pistons, triggering a barbaric fad across America. Dore even signed a three-year contract with NBC *Sports-World*, the budget anthology show that also featured second-tier boxing on an almost weekly basis in the early '80s. These barely regulated melees were a grotesque parody of boxing, and that meant exaggerating its lawless mores as well. Oversight was nonexistent; regulations were ignored; weight classes were dangerously broad.

If Dore produced prizefight burlesques, he was also interested in the real thing. Detroit matchmaker Lindy Lindell, who worked for Dore in the 1980s, recalled how Dore tried to parlay his Toughman success into a legitimate boxing venture. "He had Sutherland, who had just won the USBA middleweight title in the Pontiac Silverdome in 1980, and he wanted to have, for the lack of a better term, real professional boxing—to put on shows and to have a stable of his own fighters, most notably, Earnie Shavers," Lindell says. "Shavers only fought once locally, practically a walkover, and other fighters came along, including heavyweight Dave Jaco, from just over the state line in Ohio, and a local lightweight Billy Young—for whom he expressly had shows and for whom I made matches with Young headlining. Young won his fights in good, crowd-pleasing fashion, but by the time he beat Dana Roston in Lansing in 1989, my services were no longer needed."

No sooner did the Toughman concept catch on, however, than disaster struck. By mid-1981, Toughman contests were banned in Michigan, where they began, and, like boxing, became loud targets for moralists and reformers. A rash of injuries that year made headlines across the country, and the death of Ronald Miller in a Johnstown, Pennsylvania, tournament organized by Dore sparked outrage. Miller, twenty-three, was an unemployed ex-Marine at loose ends. "I tried to talk him out of it," his father told the Associated Press. "But he was desperate. He needed the $500. He thought he had a chance, but he was too small."

In less than a month, both the *New York Times* and *Newsweek* published features highlighting the dangers of unregulated combat. *Newsweek* ran a piece on a twenty-one-year-old who had suffered a cerebral hemorrhage in a California tavern, or honky-tonk, where he participated in a "Toughest Cowboy" tournament. The magazine also covered an event in Atlanta and quoted a spectator in attendance. "There was a fight in every corner, and I'm not talking about the ring," said Jay Halpern. "It was the wildest thing I've ever seen. They were throwing chairs, pulling knives, yelling racial slurs at beer vendors, and there were a lot of drunks."

Eventually, ten states would outlaw Toughman tournaments, but they would flourish in the Midwest and the Southeast, where the combination of action, liquor, and round-card girls was irresistible. So, too, was the general air of anarchy. Morrison recalled some of his misadventures in the ring for *KO* magazine. "Well, I've been bit," he said. "I've been kicked.

A lot of karate people get in there. They study karate all their lives, and when you back them into a corner, they raise up their leg and try to kick you in the head. It's instinct. Of course, in the fights that were at bars or fairgrounds, sometimes the referee was someone from out of the crowd, so it was anything goes. In the bigger Toughman contests, the state contests, the rules are strictly enforced."

Only two fighters have emerged from this martial netherworld to reach the money ranks in boxing: Greg Haugen, the future lightweight titleholder, who smacked up loggers in Anchorage, Alaska, and the Pacific Northwest, and Tommy Morrison. (Other prominent figures with Toughman backgrounds include Mr. T, Eric "Butterbean" Esch, Grady Brewer, winner of the reality-television show *The Contender* in 2006, and Christy Martin.) But Morrison did not only participate in "official" Toughman contests, trademarked and branded, he also fought in backrooms/barrooms and county fairs. This is closer to the scenario of *Hard Times*, the Charles Bronson film about an itinerant bare-knuckle scrapper, or the careers of mining camp sluggers such as Stanley Ketchel and Jack Dempsey.

After dropping out of middle school for a year, Morrison lived with his father and joined the Toughman circuit with his encouragement. "The guy I fought that night had hair on his back," Morrison told *ESPN The Magazine* about his Toughman debut. "I'm thinking, 'What am I doing here?' I was thirteen. I didn't even have hair on my balls." Morrison may have been only thirteen years old, but lax oversight and phony ID cards guaranteed his entry into free-for-alls between truck drivers, bouncers, construction workers, farmers, ex-jocks, and day laborers. (A homemade tattoo, a crude depiction of boxing gloves inked into his arm by his mother when he was ten years old, added to the aging effect.) Then it was on the road, in hopes of winning $300 or $500 or, sometimes, more. "I was a lot younger and not nearly as strong as some of the guys I fought. I started when I was 13, and some of the guys I fought were 21," Morrison told *KO*. "At 13, I was about 145 pounds. But I knew how to fight. You just had to survive the first round. They all came out firing in the first 30 seconds, and they're hell. But after that, they can't hold their hands up. Basic boxing skills take over and you just beat the crap out of them. And that was enough to win."

According to Morrison, he won all but one of the Toughman fights in which he competed. All he needed to succeed he had already learned from "Silver Mittens" bouts when he was a scrawny tween and rudimentary training sessions in the backyard, where a duffel bag filled with sawdust and old clothing hung, where his older brother, Tim Jr., would cuff him around during sparring sessions, where the Wolf Creek Boxing Club flourished, raggedly, beneath the wickerwork branches of maples or oaks.

★ ★ ★

There is gloomy video footage of Morrison as a teenager participating in Toughman events. Here he is, impossibly young, in dim lighting, on grainy VHS, calmly hammering some anonymous yokels in blue jeans or a tank top across the ring and into a corner. Morrison looks almost cherubic (mullet notwithstanding), he wears a T-shirt/black cutoff shorts combination, he could be dressed to go to a barbecue or for an afternoon on a dirt bike, but his right cross and his left hook belie his juvenescence.

In a few years, he will be starring in a film opposite Sylvester Stallone, he will be headlining Atlantic City, he will be a millionaire who owns a ranch and a Porsche, he will be one of the biggest crash-and-burn stories in a sport overloaded with them.

★ ★ ★

"I don't know what's the reason that I do the things I do. You've known men who craved drugs or liquor or tobacco. I must have excitement. I crave it and it preys on me until I just step out and get into devilment of some kind."
—Henry Starr

★ ★ ★

Although Morrison would make one disturbing claim after another throughout his public life (many of them unverifiable), perhaps the most shocking is his disclosure that he had been a teenage enforcer for a crime ring in Missouri. "There was a time I used to think that being a faction of an organized crime situation was cool," Morrison told the Associated Press in 2000. "You say, 'Here's the deal, you owe this much money and what do you plan on doing? Get on top of that behavior there, son, and if you don't,

I'm not responsible for what's going to happen to you.' I didn't necessarily always have to be the one to do it, just inform them of where they live, where they hang out, who their friends are, where their kids are."

In her memoir, Dawn Gilbert refuted this story, suggesting that it was Tim Morrison Jr. who, at the behest of his father, had been a collector, using the threat of his fists as encouragement. Although Troy Morrison could not recall ties to an organized crime ring, he acknowledges that Tim Morrison Sr. envisioned himself as some sort of outlaw. "He had this fantasy about . . . he was living, like, in the Jesse James gang or something, and he wanted the Morrisons to be this criminal outfit."

★ ★ ★

A versatile athlete, Tommy Morrison played basketball and football at Jay High School while still walloping truck drivers and bouncers in Toughman competitions on the weekends. As a hard-charging linebacker, Morrison was reportedly good enough to earn a scholarship to Emporia State University. But a brief detour from the varsity gridiron would change his life forever.

While still a senior at Jay, Morrison had been encouraged by his mother to enter the Kansas City Golden Gloves, in hopes of continuing a long-standing family custom of Morrisons participating in this event. Despite the fact that he had not engaged in a regulated amateur fight in years, Morrison agreed. "I'd laid off for about four years to play high school football and hadn't fought in four years on an amateur level," Morrison told *KO* in 1991. "All I did in that time was fight in Toughman contests, which didn't require any training. I got back into boxing in '88. My mother wanted me to fight in the Kansas City Golden Gloves. She talked me into that, and I went up there and fought and won."

After winning the Kansas City title, Morrison went on to the semifinals of the National Golden Gloves, where he lost to Derek Isaman, the standout linebacker for the Ohio State Buckeyes, who would eventually win the tournament and go on to an undistinguished professional career. From there, Morrison entered the Western Olympic trials in Colorado Springs and once again emerged as the winner. That launched Morrison into the Olympic trials, in Concord, California, where he dropped a 5-0 decision to future nemesis Ray Mercer in the quarterfinals.

While Morrison had solid results during that summer of 1988, he had hardly laced on the gloves since he had been thirteen or fourteen years old. This surprise success against a slew of seasoned amateurs suggested a raw but natural talent. It was something Morrison realized as well. "From the time my mom asked me to fight to losing to Mercer was 2½ months," he told *People* magazine. "I started thinking, 'Hey, maybe this is what I ought to do.'"

Amateur tournaments often double as scouting combines and Morrison caught the eye of Douglas Dragert, an Overland Park police sergeant with a background in city-youth boxing programs, and John Brown, the owner of Ringside, a boxing equipment company based in Lenexa, Kansas. "John Brown and I had a dream to get a young heavyweight and groom him," Dragert told the *Kansas City Star*. "At the Golden Gloves, you could see [Morrison] had something because he won and he was out of shape."

For his part, Brown was less enthusiastic. "Tommy was out of shape and could barely go two rounds," he said to the Bonner Springs-Edwardsville *Chieftain* about seeing Morrison fight. "He went three on guts. They were laying on each other. I thought, 'Who cares?'" Despite his misgivings, Brown signed Morrison to a managerial contract and Dragert became assistant trainer.

In the summer of 1988, Tommy Morrison drove his rickety 1983 Ford Ranger roughly 200 miles north to Shawnee, Kansas, past Fairland, Wyandotte, Quapaw, Riverton, Pittsburg, Dry Wood, Pleasanton, Linn Valley, Louisburg, Stillwell. He moved in with an uncle and aunt, only fifteen minutes away from Kansas City. By day he worked in the Ringside warehouse; by night he polished his crude but promising skills. At all times he envisioned fame and a sense of distinction. The small-town boy had the stars within his reach.

Morrison was only a teenager when he put Jay in his rearview mirror, at least for the moment. "There were just too many people that after high school they just wanted to stay in Jay and get a job at 7-11," he told the Kansas City *Examiner*. "I was sad when I left because I knew I would never be back there to live. I was full of mixed emotions, but I honestly knew if I ever wanted to amount to anything I had to get the hell out of there."

He left behind his pregnant teenage girlfriend, as well. His dreams—and his temperament—forced him to ramble on. His daddy might have been proud.

★ ★ ★

"From the time I was a kid, I always knew something was going to happen
to me."
—Elvis

★ ★ ★

He makes his debut on November 10, 1988, in, of all places, the Felt
Forum in Madison Square Garden. Neither John Brown nor Doug Dragert have any experience with professional boxing, so they hire Peyton
Sher, a seasoned jack-of-all-trades, to help develop Morrison. Sher has
been a manager and a promoter in the Midwest for decades. Based in
Overland Park, he is a matchmaker for Don King and, as a freelancer, he
had arranged several early fights for Mike Tyson when Tyson was terror-
izing clodhoppers in upstate New York. In a sport where connections are
almost as important as talent, Sher has the kind of pull that can make a
difference to a minor league outfit.

This is how Morrison, not long removed from smokers and Toughman
scraps in Springfield and Tulsa, finds himself performing in the media capital of the world. His opponent is someone named William Muhammad,
a man who has never fought before and will never fight again. Muhammad is one of the thousands of stuntmen in boxing whose sole purpose
is to provide target practice for young fighters and then tumble at the
right time. These men are often known as "opponents," but that is a
euphemism that softens the brutal reality of their roles in the sordid fight
game. "Opponents" are also known as "tomato cans," "human punching
bags," "smear cases." No other sport places a value on ineptitude the
way boxing does. Opponents are professional losers, without discernible
talent, without professional acumen, without competitive drive, who take
beatings from prospects and contenders on undercards across the country.

From the beginning, 1988, all the way to the bizarre end, 2007, Morrison will share the ring over and over again with opponents, sending them
bouncing off the ropes, off the canvas, off the turnbuckles, like Spaldings.
Under the lights in the Felt Forum, Morrison, who weighs less than 200
pounds, knocks Muhammad out in the first round. The same violent scenario is repeated frequently over the following months. Morrison stops

his next four victims in the first round. It is KO1 in Detroit, KO1 in Oklahoma City, KO1 in Sterling Heights, KO1 in Great Falls. He fights three times in January 1989, spending a total of three minutes and one second in the ring. Finally, in his fifth pro bout, he hears the bell to start the second round and scores a TKO in the fourth of someone named Traore Ali on another detour to New York. Then Morrison is back in Biloxi, Wichita, Kansas City. As a nineteen-year-old, one with a patchwork background, Morrison is not on the fast-track to a world ranking. But his ride is far too slow for Sher. By March, he and John Brown begin to clash over matchmaking. Sher moves on. A few months later he would say, "What you try to do in developing a fighter is put him in with different styles and experience. They're putting Tommy in with experienced fighters, but experienced losing fighters."

★ ★ ★

With Sher gone, John Brown felt he needed to have an experienced hand involved in guiding Morrison. When Brown forwarded a videotape of Morrison knocking over bindle stiffs to Bill Cayton, the stage was set to bring one of the savviest boxing minds of the 1980s to Team Morrison.

Cayton had been co-manager, along with the late Jim Jacobs, of Mike Tyson from the day Tyson turned pro, a future of untold millions awaiting him. From the late 1970s until 1988, Jacobs and Cayton had a stellar record as managers of a few select talents: Wilfred Benitez, Edwin Rosario, and Tyson. Each of them wildly successful; each of them deeply troubled. With Morrison, Cayton would continue the wearying trend of trying to guide volcanic personalities to success.

At the time Cayton entered the Morrison orbit, he was still managing Tyson—but only on paper. In the summer of 1988, when Tyson was in perpetual meltdown mode, he sued Cayton and ultimately forced him to step aside from day-to-day operations. A year and a half later, Tyson would be an ex-champion after being knocked out by a 42-1 underdog named Buster Douglas. Two years after that, Tyson would be serving time in prison after being found guilty of rape.

What Cayton saw in Morrison in those VHS tapes was obvious: a white heavyweight whose aggressive style was a natural extension of his hell-bent-for-leather personality. And then there was that left hook, a hair-trigger blow thrown with both precision and force, a punch that belied the backcountry training regimen of a Toughman contestant whose mother had often worked the corner. "I'd never had anybody train me who knew what they were doing," Morrison told the *Kansas City Star*. "My father has got one eye, and there'd be angles where he'd miss things. We had a heavy bag and a speed bag on the porch, and I lived a couple of blocks from the track where the football field was. That was the extent of my working out."

Intrigued by the raw power Morrison possessed, Cayton signed on as co-manager in April 1989. One of his first acts was to dispatch Kevin Rooney, a Cus D'Amato protege who had trained Tyson for years before also running afoul of the volatile heavyweight champion, to see Morrison. No sooner did Rooney show up in Lenexa than he told the *Kansas City Star* of his plans to overhaul Morrison. "I need to get Tommy to forget everything these clowns taught him so far," said the outspoken trainer in his best New York curbside accent. A strict disciplinarian, Rooney never caught on with Team Morrison, and when Morrison declined to relocate to the Catskills, where the old Cus D'Amato gym still stood, Rooney moved on or was dumped, depending on the source.

According to Brown, the Rooney experiment ended in flames. "Bill Cayton kept wanting Rooney to train [Morrison]. Because Bill Cayton thought everybody from New York was better than everybody else, you know. We were just a bunch of country bumpkins, and we didn't know what the fuck we were doing. So I said, 'OK, Bill . . . send him out.' I think Kevin was around for about two weeks—and I actually kind of liked Kevin, his style and stuff, and again, we were coaching Tommy in the same Tyson style, which I do today to a bunch of guys—but Kevin's ego was so big, I mean, he was just, Kevin's what we call . . . a one-man show, you know. I've had the kid [Morrison] from the amateurs to where he's at now, and you come in here and act like you're a one-man show, it's not going to work, Kevin. 'Well, nobody knows what I know. . . .' So I called Bill and said, 'Get him out of here, because this ain't gonna work; we're gonna come to blows, you know.' It didn't make for harmony in the camp, for damn sure."

Though Cayton added some administrative star power to Team Morrison, his aggressive marketing moves contrasted starkly with his matchmaking strategy. The locales improved—Morrison fought several times in

Atlantic City in 1989, for example—but the opposition did not. In April 1989, Larry Hazzard, chairman of the New Jersey State Athletic Commission, rejected seven dire matches for Morrison before accepting Ricky Nelson, an incompetent former middleweight who had tallied a total of four fights in the previous eight years. By design, Cayton also matched Morrison with ex–Mike Tyson victims, hoping to link the two heavyweights in the public consciousness through some strange mnemonic force. With that nebulous end in mind, Morrison defeated Steve Zouski, Dave Jaco, and Lorenzo Canady—each of whom had been annihilated by Tyson during his meteoric rise as a contender—within six months. If the idea had been to set up a series of flattering comparative performances, then Morrison failed miserably: He went the distance with both Zouski and Canady, whom Tyson had knocked out in a combined total of four rounds, years earlier, before the beatings had accumulated and left them physically debilitated.

But Cayton did reveal his managerial touch by arranging to have the Zouski fight aired on ABC as a swing bout between co-features. John Brown recalled the secret to the Cayton method. "Bill was so tenacious, so, I mean, I talked to the people at [ABC] because after I brought Cayton on board after about seven fights, he got Tommy on ABC. And later I got to know some of those guys, and I asked them, 'how did he do it?' And the ABC guy would tell me, 'Because Bill was such a pest, we arranged it just so he would leave us alone. He would call hour after hour.'"

A trial horse since the late 1970s, Zouski had entered the ring that afternoon having suffered eight stoppage losses in his desultory career, but he survived an early knockdown and forced Morrison to go the four-round distance. It was not exactly the kind of national exposure Cayton had expected.

★ ★ ★

Within weeks of Cayton taking the reins as co-manager, Morrison suddenly became the object of widespread media coverage. Morrison was 9-0 then, his undefeated record built up mostly in the hinterlands, off-TV, and he was as anonymous as any other pug toiling in Wichita or Montana. His abrupt splash in gossip columns and sports pages in the spring of 1989 came because of a suspect revelation: Morrison claimed to be a distant relative of John Wayne. "Well, supposedly he's John Wayne's grandnephew, great-grandnephew," Tony Holden told ESPN. "I don't believe it. But Tommy ran with it. It got him a lot of publicity."

No one could keep the record straight. Thereafter, Morrison found himself misidentified repeatedly vis-à-vis his supposed relation to Wayne: nephew, great-grandson, and grandnephew were the most common appellations. "Amazingly, the media never really checked on it," John Brown told ESPN. "It was a great moniker for him. It was marketable." Stage names, phony backstories cooked up by publicity departments, and "showmances" had largely faded from Hollywood decades earlier and the exotic image, once part of boxing as well, was now relegated to pro wrestling, roller derby, and con artists. "He's no more related to John Wayne than my grandfather from Lithuania," cracked Peyton Sher.

Although the Morrison genealogy chart may not include a bracket for "The Duke," there *is* a family connection to John Wayne. "Here's how that got started," says Troy Morrison. "I have an uncle, my dad's oldest brother, he was a boxer, too, actually was an Army Golden Gloves champion. . . . He went into the military and worked his way all the way to full bird colonel and ended up retiring in Orange County, California, where he met and knew John Wayne." After comparing geographical backgrounds, without drawing direct links, the two men settled on a friendly understanding. "They just said, 'It's likely we're related somewhere.' That's all that was ever said, and that story got bigger and bigger and of course the media, you know, latched on to that big-time. So it's possible; nobody's ever done any DNA testing to say."

Tommy Morrison seemed almost sheepish about his family tree becoming a public commotion. "I guess it is pretty interesting and it does get me some extra attention," he told the *Philadelphia Daily News*, "but once I'm in the ring, it doesn't do too much for me in terms of winning. And that's my No. 1 priority right now. It doesn't mean a whole lot if you've got the name and can't fight. If you're lucky enough to get your foot in the door, you'd better be able to do something with that and that's what I intend to do."

According to Brown, it was Doug Dragert who came up with the nickname during a bull session when Morrison was still an amateur. "I always had a big amateur program in Kansas City and one of my guys who helped me coach was a police sergeant by the name of Doug Dragert, a very funny guy. And so Doug was helping at my boxing gym, so when I took on Tommy, Doug was the first person I brought on to help me. Doug and I trained Tommy for about a year or so and we were in my office one day trying to figure out a good nickname for him, and, Tommy was there also. Tommy said, 'Well, you know, some people have said that they think I might be related to John Wayne because his name was Marion Morrison.' And Doug was a huge John Wayne fan, and he said, 'Yes, that's correct, John Wayne was, I think, from Oklahoma and blah, blah, blah' and that was it. That was the first of it. 'From now on, you're the great-grandson of John Wayne and you're the Duke.'" As with so much of the Tommy Morrison story, there are competing narratives even for something as anodyne as a nickname. Another version is that Morrison swiped the name from his older brother, Tim. (John Wayne, it is worth noting, was born in Iowa and grew up in California.)

Most likely, the John Wayne tie-in, dubious or not, was circulated by Cayton. It was Cayton, along with his partner, Jim Jacobs, who had distributed VHS compilations of a young Mike Tyson pummeling one no-hoper after another in Albany and Latham to reporters in big media markets. It was Cayton who used his boxing-film collection as leverage to gain exposure for his fighters on USA and ESPN. It was Cayton who would get Morrison a segment on *Hard Copy* in 1990. And it was Cayton who understood that Morrison had superstar potential in flyover country. Bolstering that fan base with a possibly dubious connection to an everlasting heartland icon such as Wayne was a shrewd marketing move and one that would keep Morrison a box-office attraction for years.

During his short career, Morrison would draw thousands to Kansas, Oklahoma, Missouri, and Arizona. He wore trunks with an Old Glory motif: red, white, and blue. All American. Salt of the earth. "The Duke."

★ ★ ★

After his seventeenth pro fight—a first-round massacre of Dave Jaco in Jacksonville, Florida—Morrison got the break of a lifetime. Ironically, it would not take place in a ring. Not a real ring, anyway. Morrison was in line for a significant role in *Rocky V*, the latest mediocre Hollywood sequel.

How Morrison got involved in *Rocky V* is just another of the many conflicting stories vying for limited elbow room with veracity. Not surprisingly, the public relations version settles on an inspiring tale of celebrity serendipity. One night Frank Stallone was watching ESPN when Tommy Morrison stepped into a ring and bowled over another softie. Intrigued, Stallone called his brother, Sylvester, and recommended Morrison for the character that would eventually turn into Tommy Gunn.

Several sources point to the industrious Bill Cayton first contacting Sylvester Stallone, possibly via mail and through his preferred medium, VHS tape, and then giving a sales pitch that put Morrison over the top. In 1989 Cayton explained his method to Bernard Fernandez of the *Philadelphia Daily News*: "My purpose was to convince these Hollywood people that it made as much sense to have a real fighter act the part of a fighter as it is for an actor to try to pretend he was a fighter. I got the call from Stallone, saying he wanted Tommy to test for the role. I was elated. I knew he would be selected. Tommy has the makings of a superb actor."

At the time, Sylvester Stallone was holding casting calls for the role and even auditioned Derek Isaman, who had once beaten Morrison in the amateurs. Eventually, Morrison got the part, and, with it, he seemed to step further away from his bleak roots in Oklahoma. "I think about what's happened to me, my good fortune, every day of my life," Morrison said at a press conference before a screening of the film. "Especially when I drive home to Jay. It's a town of two thousand. I started in Toughman contests, and look where I am today."

According to Morrison, he had been a member of the Sylvester Stallone fan club in the late 1970s and was influenced by the first *Rocky* film. "It was a big motivator," he told the *Kansas City Star*. "It made you want to drink the raw eggs and hit on the beef and all that stuff that's actually a little fictional. But it gave me the inspiration."

"Tommy was just what I was looking for," Stallone told Bernard Fernandez. "He's perfect to play the part of Rocky's alter ego. I don't think he'll have a problem with the acting, and he'll do well in the fight scenes because, after all, he's a fighter. He's a very good fighter."

On November 14, 1989, Morrison faced rickety trial horse Lorenzo Canady at the South Mountain Arena in West Orange, New Jersey, with Sylvester Stallone, Burt Young, and the *Rocky* film crew in tow, hoping to catch some violent footage of "Tommy Gunn" in action. But Morrison was flat that night—possibly nervous, as well—and Canady, who had been demolished a few months earlier by Riddick Bowe, survived until the final bell. Scattered boos from a disappointed crowd greeted the unexpected result—after all, they had been expecting a Tinseltown spectacular.

Before filming began, Morrison assured reporters that his focus remained on boxing. "One of our main concerns is making sure it doesn't become an intrusion," Morrison told the Associated Press. "Boxing and acting are two different things. We'll try to keep them far enough apart so I'm not in the gym thinking of lines while I'm sparring." Judging from his performance against Canady, Morrison already seemed disturbed by his approaching C-list status.

With Morrison cast as the rising contender from Oklahoma (no suspension of disbelief required here, a rarity for the *Rocky* sequels), only the role of his championship opponent remained unfilled. Evander Holyfield, then clawing his way to a title shot against future champion Buster Douglas, had refused to play the KO victim for Tommy (Morrison) Gunn. For Holyfield, a Hollywood loss might confuse a public given to believing WCW and WWF kayfabe. Dan Duva, who promoted Holyfield, scoffed at the miscasting. "The thought of Morrison beating up Evander is too fantastic, even for Hollywood," Duva said.

Instead, producers cast a young fighter from Houston named Mike "Mercury" Williams, already a tarnished prospect by then and more than willing to mix up fact and fiction for a payday that did not require an arduous training camp or an uppercut to the jaw. (Williams may have perplexed himself, however, when he signed to face Morrison in a legitimate fight only a few years after playing Union Cane in *Rocky V*.)

Like so many others in the Tommy Morrison orbit, Williams was on the margins: he was a troubled young man who no longer viewed his career as anything but a pickup gig. In *Rocky V*, he is sent hurtling to the canvas like a crash test dummy after Morrison administers an over-the-top beating aided by quick cuts, multiple angles, and thunderous Foley work and sound effects. Today it would probably take CGI to reproduce such violence. And *Rocky V* had plenty of violence . . . and not necessarily the imaginary kind. Two stuntmen—Steve Santosusso and professional wrestler Todd Champion—sued Stallone, Morrison, and the film producers for $20 million after they were both injured during fight scenes. According to reports, Champion wound up with a titanium plate in his head when he suffered a fractured orbital bone. Santosusso, for his part, had his jaw broken.

"For those quick-clip scenes, there were seven or eight guys who were supposed to take punches thrown at 30 percent, one-punch knockout types of things," Morrison told *The Ring*. "A lot of the guys were stuntmen. They would roll with the punch, so it didn't really do anything to them, even though it looked like it knocked the shit out of them. But there were two guys I did it with who just stood there and didn't move their heads at all. I guess they got hurt a little bit. Maybe it was something they thought about doing beforehand. My punches weren't that hard; those stuntmen just didn't do what they were supposed to do. One guy claims that he got his jaw hurt. I find that a little hard to believe. I think it's something those guys had in their back pockets the whole time. After, when they were talking about lawsuits, they tried to say there had been friction on the set between us. I didn't even know the guys. I was just doing what I got paid to do. People will do anything for a little attention."

After its initial splash across tabloids and newscasts, the lawsuit faded from public view, an unmistakable sign of an out-of-court settlement. (Champion returned to World Championship Wrestling, where he formed a successful tag team—The Patriots—with Firebreaker Chip.)

As for the movie itself, *Rocky V* left the Balboa franchise down for the count—until 2006. With the Soviet Union at the tail end of glasnost and the '80s MTV/Sega aesthetic giving way to the gloomy '90s, *Rocky V* was a unique combination of glum and preposterous. Schmaltzy, overacted, poorly scripted, and burdened by an outlandish soundtrack, *Rocky V* was a Golden Raspberry special, earning seven Razzie nominations, including Worst Picture, Worst Actor, Worst Screenplay, and Worst Original Song. In light of what would happen later, however, there is a strange frisson to the film, to seeing the parallels between the character of Gunn, who spirals out of control after tasting fame, and Morrison, whose life began to unravel less than three years after his brush with stardom.

Morrison may not have taken lessons from Stella Adler or Lee Strasberg, but his performance—opposite permanent hams Stallone and Burt Young—certainly outshone film clips of Rocky Graziano or Sugar Ray Robinson. What Morrison accomplished as an actor was negligible, but a role in even a cheesy box-office mediocrity gave him something valuable and, perhaps, deadly: outsized celebrity in the heartland, where his libido had resembled a land spout for years. Now, his sex drive would become a twister roaring across the flatlands.

In addition to his sudden fame, Morrison also credited *Rocky V* with his hulking new physique. "Basically, before I lived off Twinkies and Coke," Morrison told the New York *Daily News* about the positive influence Sylvester Stallone had on his lifestyle choices. "I feel much better about myself physically. These guys were the best trainers in the business, and it was a different kind of training for me. I think I look a lot bigger and I think I look better. I've also reduced my body fat count in my body dramatically. The weight I put on is in the right places instead of just being around the waist."

Stallone, of course, as evidenced by his altered appearance from *Rocky I*—chunky but fit for a heavyweight—to *Rocky IV* and his Rambo franchise—bulging pecs and pop-up vascularity—was undergoing a physical transformation with the help of designer drugs. His metamorphosis paralleled the excesses of the 1980s, and, along with Arnold Schwarzenegger, Stallone became the exemplar of the Genetically Modified Celebrity. But Morrison was an athlete, and his steroid use, calculated to maintain enough bulk to compete as a heavyweight, would come with a deadly price tag. First, it would affect his livelihood; later, perhaps, it would destroy his life. "When we sent [Morrison] to Hollywood to work with Stallone," John Brown recalls, "he was weighing probably about 210, 215. And when he came back, he was weighing about 225 or 230, and you could tell he was muscled up a lot more. And Tom Virgets would tell me that Tommy would get a package from California about once every two weeks and that after he got the package his strength training would always increase. So, I mean, we knew, we highly suspected, that he was on something, but that was all I ever knew about it."

★ ★ ★

Finally, after six months of production work, Morrison, now publicly sporting what appeared to be eyeliner, double-backed to the heavy bag circuit. Blowout wins over Charles Woolard, John Morton, and Mike Acey marked his return from Hollywood the same way he had entered it: with farcical results in the ring. Sylvester Stallone, film premieres, United Artists—these may have been considered Big Time, but Morrison continued a boxing career that was strictly small-scale.

★ ★ ★

Not long after his role in *Rocky V*—and not long after he had begun attracting excessive media coverage—Morrison started to see his name linked, repeatedly, with one of the most derogatory concepts in boxing: that of The Great White Hope.

Throughout most of his career, Morrison declined to make his race an issue. But he was disturbed by the label, aware of its dismissive power, and realized the scrutiny that would accompany it. "It's kind of sad, but to be honest, it's a big advantage being white," Morrison told the *Kansas City Star* in 1990. "There aren't that many white fighters around. But I'd prefer to stay away from that because it's racist to start with. The public will perceive it the way they want to, which is their right."

There was also the fact that Morrison was half Native American; his mother was part Otoe, part Ponca, and she had her own salty opinion regarding the question of race. "Why don't they call him the Great Native American Hope?" she asked Pat Putnam of *Sports Illustrated*. "Or at least half a Great White Hope. It's all so silly."

Of all the so-called Great White Hopes—a designation that stretches back to 1910, when Jack Johnson, the first African American to hold the heavyweight championship, mauled Jim Jeffries in Reno, Nevada, sparking riots and lynchings across the country—only Jess Willard could be considered a success. An oversized cowpoke with limited boxing acumen but plenty of brawn, Willard defeated a dissipated Johnson by knockout in 1915 and put an end to the reign of the most hated sportsman in America.

The first wave of Great White Hopes was assembled by cutthroat promoters eager to cash in on what they saw as a lasting and remunerative fad. They were right. Across the country, roustabouts, wrestlers, ex-soldiers, wranglers, farmhands, and laborers picked up gloves en masse and began thumping heavy bags in barns or out on pasturelands, dreaming of making history or, failing that, a few dollars for a grubstake or a new plow. A gullible public, sympatico with the bigoted principles underlying the Great White Hope crusade, kept underhanded promoters afloat during lean years for boxing, which was still illegal in most jurisdictions.

The key to the Great White Hope movement was a far-fetched and, possibly, interminable endgame. Although Johnson (ironically) drew the color line when he was champion, defending his title against one middling Black fighter named Jim Johnson, his white challengers were bumbling setups. There was little chance that any of these haphazardly chosen aveng-ers would rescue the title from Johnson and return it to the aggrieved and grieving white race. That meant merely marketing a fighter as a potential savior of the heavyweight title was enough to draw paying customers in droves. It was a wish-fulfillment fantasy whose appeal lay mainly in its pursuit. In the days before mass media, advertising a fight was a grass-roots effort spurred by the spinmeisters of the times: fast-talking manag-ers and promoters. They stockpiled burly prospects, created backstories for them, and publicized them with the support of local newspapers. The first Great White Hope Tournament took place on May 26, 1911, in New York City, and its winner, an oversized Minnesota farm boy named Al Palzer, promptly found his true calling as what old-timers referred to as a "chopping block" before his father shot him to death a few years later.

When Johnson fled the country to avoid serving a sentence for violat-ing the Mann Act, he ceded center stage to his pretenders. "From 1912 to 1915, the years of his self-imposed exile, anti-Johnson dogma grew so strong that any white man six feet tall could set up in business as a challenger," wrote John Lardner. Other notable White Hopes of the time included "Iron" Hague, "Bombardier" Billy Wells, Al Kaufman, Frank Moran, Fred Fulton, Sandy Ferguson, and the ill-fated Luther McCarty, the "White Heavyweight Champion of the World," dead at twenty-one after milling for less than a round against Arthur Pelkey.

From the wreckage of The Great White Hope wasteland, there finally emerged Willard, who ensured that the heavyweight title would remain in white hands for the next twenty-two years. After Joe Louis poleaxed James J. Braddock in 1937 to win the heavyweight championship, the most important title in sports slipped almost permanently into posses-sion of African American fighters. (Although Louis drew admiration from all sectors of American society, his extended reign sparked a short-lived revival of Great White Hope talks, with new tourneys to unearth a savior endorsed by Jack Dempsey.)

Only Rocky Marciano, a beloved champion whose photograph would be seen in pizzerias for decades to come, broke the stranglehold of Afri-can American champions. Marciano had a relatively brief reign, however, and it would take decades for another white American to claim a share of the heavyweight title. By then, of course, boxing had degenerated into the Alphabet Soup era, where one sham sanctioning body after another conferred, almost arbitrarily, champion status on a string of middling talents.

By the time Morrison appeared on the scene, it had been more than thirty years since a white American had held the heavyweight championship. (Ingemar Johansson, from Gothenburg, Sweden, held the title briefly after upsetting Floyd Patterson in 1959, and Gerrie Coetzee, a South African who had moved to New Jersey in the early 1980s, had briefly been WBA champion.) Over that period, countless fighters had been labeled White Hopes, including a slew of them during the Muhammad Ali era. At one point or another, fighters as diverse in background and talent as Jerry Quarry, Ron Marsh, Boone Kirkman, Duane Bobick, Chuck Wepner, Scott LeDoux, and even Jim Beattie, who actually starred as the title character in a film called *The Great White Hope*, were labeled as potential saviors, men who would rescue the sacred heavyweight title from Joe Frazier, or George Foreman, or Muhammad Ali.

Not until the early 1980s did the concept reignite. That was when a towering Irishman from Huntington, Long Island, named Gerry Cooney burst onto the scene with a left hook arguably more devastating than the one wielded by Morrison. It was Cooney who provided the blueprint for all future white heavyweights. Where fighters such as Quarry, Bobick, and LeDoux were part of the mix—they fought contenders, considered the risk-reward ratio inherent in a blood sport, and tried to claw their way to title shots by earning rankings—Cooney was the product of a cynical buildup on the part of his management, who matched him with one push-over after another.

In the 1980s, the number of top-notch white fighters could be counted on one hand: Sean O'Grady, Ray Mancini, Greg Haugen, Bobby Czyz, and Vinny Pazienza. And while the proliferation of world titles produced more opportunities for mediocre white fighters to call themselves champions (Murray Sutherland, Don Lalonde, and Darrin Van Horn), none of them set the world on fire. It would take a heavyweight—the embodiment of the American obsession with bigger and better—to do that.

Even as the media criticized Cooney for his bedraggled opposition, his popularity skyrocketed, and his showdown with WBC heavyweight titlist Larry Holmes in June 1982 was an economic blockbuster, earning Cooney a purse of approximately $10 million (roughly $27 million today). The blueprint was clear: Manufacture a deceptive record (preferably accompanied by eye-catching knockouts), raise the expectations of casual observers tuning in on television, and cash in, finally, on a one-time headline fight. In 1995, for example, Peter McNeeley, an inept Boston heavyweight, benefited from such a strategy and earned hundreds of thousands of dollars when he became cannon fodder for Mike Tyson.

"Obviously, people took Gerry Cooney seriously until he got into it with Holmes," Morrison told *KO* magazine in 1991. "Up until that point, people took him very seriously. He got a lot of attention. Had he been a black fighter, he probably wouldn't have gotten that much attention. That's just reality. People are hungry for a white fighter. Maybe I'm him, and maybe I'm not. A lot of people try to tag the 'Great White Hope' thing on you as soon as you start something pretty decent. There's two reasons why I'm against that. Number one is because I think it's racist. Number two is because there hasn't been a Great White Hope that's accomplished anything. I like to think that I'm much better than those Great White Hopes."

Although Morrison received more coverage and bigger paychecks because of his color, he also started at a disadvantage. Boxing is a subculture that specializes in deception, but it also masters paradox. The same qualities that promised Morrison stardom also hindered his development. While an aspiring urban kid may have found himself endangered by his immediate environment—drugs, violence, gangs—he was also likelier to find the structure he needed for a solid foundation in boxing than someone such as Morrison. Until the early 1990s or so, when federal tax cuts reduced state spending, Police Athletic Leagues, prison boxing programs (such as Graterford and Rahway, which produced the likes of Bernard Hopkins and Dwight Muhammad Qawi, respectively), and gyms that doubled as youth centers could be found in city after city.

In contrast, a rural afterthought such as Jay, Oklahoma, lacked the kind of infrastructure necessary for a restless teen to excel at boxing. Instead of training in an organized environment full of relevant equipment and supervised by experienced coaches, Morrison exerted himself on the porch or in his backyard using homespun gear. Compared to Gerry Cooney, Morrison was at a disadvantage even among most Great White Hopes. Cooney had amateur experience that went beyond smokers, Toughman contests, and familial sparring sessions; he came from the New York City region, a boxing hotbed at the time, and he had a veteran handler, Victor Valle, in his corner.

Because Morrison was white, he was viewed as a potential bonanza commodity, and devaluing a commodity by risking it in legitimate fights was out of the question for his handlers. When Ray Mercer left Morrison unconscious in an Atlantic City ring in 1991—a miscalculation Bill Cayton rued until his wild ride with Morrison finally ended—it seemed to justify the prevailing view of Morrison as a fraud. Indeed, Cayton and John Brown never made that mistake—competitive matchmaking—again. Until Morrison signed to face Lennox Lewis, the closest thing to an in-the-ring risk he took was against George Foreman, nearly twice as old as Morrison, and only one fight removed from being hammered by a war-torn Alex Stewart. "He's one of the guys who never reached his full potential," Evander Holyfield told the *Kansas City Star* about Morrison. "He did have the ability to be heavyweight champion. He was definitely a good boxer. Unfortunately, in boxing, skin color derailed him. He got more easy fights in an effort to build him up. It took away that desire to be the best. I saw him fight as an amateur, and he took on everybody. If he would have fought tough opponents on his way up, he would have had the confidence when he got to the big fights."

★ ★ ★

When Kevin Rooney made his exit (or was scrapped), he left Team Morrison in a precarious position. Neither Brown nor Dragert had ever trained a professional fighter before working with Morrison, but the real issue went far beyond the question of experience: Morrison despised Brown. It hardly seemed to matter that Brown had signed him to a contract, had given him a job at Ringside, and had worked hard at helping Morrison streamline his crude technique. If Brown had been overbearing in trying to keep Morrison from self-destructing, it was because he understood the potential stakes at hand. Not even potential riches could bring peace between Brown and Morrison. "I couldn't deal with him because, you know, I'd ask him to work on fundamentals, I'd ask him to pick up the pace, and he'd throw a little fit, and I'd go, 'What is wrong with you?'" Brown recalls. "He and I'd get into arguments, and the next thing you know—in fact, we had to cancel at least two big-money fights because he hurt his lower back trying to throw chairs at me."

Of course, Morrison was not the type to take admonishment (or even advice) without bristling. As a child, he had grown up with little parental supervision, his father set an example (from afar, usually) of unbridled excess, and his tween years spent barnstorming for amateur fights had developed an impulsive, headstrong worldview. And Brown was a grouch with issues of his own. Together, they made an explosive combination. In fact, Brown claims that Morrison once went beyond throwing chairs at him. "I had a million-dollar annuity . . . because I wanted to lock that away so that no matter what happened to him, he would have a million dollars at the end of it," he recalls. "And he came to me, you know, and said, 'I want that million dollars.' And I said, 'I'm not giving it to you. When your career is over it'll be yours.' And he threatened my life. And I said, you know, I thought, this ain't worth that. I said, 'Okay, you can have it.' He reinvested in crazy things."

Their poor working relationship led to Brown yielding his position as trainer. "After Tommy had seventeen fights," he says, "I couldn't train him anymore because, number one, my business was growing at thirty percent a year, I had sixty employees, I had two little kids at home, and if Tommy had been a really good, you know, human being, I could have done it, but he wasn't. He needed constant care, he needed constant supervision, he needed people, you know, watching him all the time and helping him not do stupid stuff. I mean, sometimes, he'd lay out in the sun to get a suntan, and he'd put butter all over his body. So the next thing you know, he's got a terrible fucking sunburn—can't train for a week because of his sunburn. I mean, he did crazy shit like that all the time."

The search was on to get Morrison a trainer, someone who could improve his skill set in the ring and earn his esteem out of it. That job ultimately went to Dr. Tom Virgets, who had even less experience than Brown and Dragert.

While fighters often open their pro careers with unseasoned trainers, it is usually because of ties that date back years. It is not unusual for amateur fighters to turn professional under the guidance of a trainer who had been working with them since childhood, for example, but Virgets came from virtually out of nowhere. A man with deep roots in boxing, Virgets had a love for the sport that had never blossomed into professional involvement until Morrison came along. "I grew up in a family of boxers," he told the *Atlanta Constitution*. "My grandfather and two of his brothers were boxers. They were coached by their father. My father boxed a little while, and I have a brother who boxed."

Virgets had earned a Ph.D. in Exercise Physiology from the University of Alabama. Although Virgets began his academic career as a wrestling coach at the University of Tennessee at Chattanooga, he went on to become the boxing coach of the Virginia Military Institute from 1979 to 1984. He held the same position at the U.S. Naval Academy for a few years before becoming the Athletic Director at West Georgia College. It was at West Georgia that Brown first connected Morrison to Virgets. In 1989, Brown had taken Morrison, still flabby despite having more than a dozen fights, to Virgets for a consultation about nutrition and high-tech training. "He was a little fat boy," Virgets told the *New York Times* about his meeting with Morrison. "He had 23 percent body fat and weighed 209 pounds. Tommy's idea of breakfast was Twinkies and a Coca-Cola."

Virgets focused mainly on diet and conditioning at first. Because Virgets, even in his late thirties, was as fit as any fighter his weight, he often participated in the drills he devised for Morrison, which acted as a form of bonding. Then Virgets moved on to physical strength, making Morrison bigger and stronger. "Tommy's strength is an asset where it used to be a detriment," he told the Kansas City *Examiner* in October 1991, roughly a year after taking over as trainer. "It used to be that in sparring sessions, Tommy would be getting pushed around and controlled inside. It was embarrassing. Now his incline bench is 370 pounds, and he can bench press 400 pounds. He's very strong for a heavyweight boxer, but he can be stronger, and he'll be stronger."

These comments are intriguing, considering how forthcoming Morrison would later be about his steroid use, which likely began in the late 1980s, around the time *Rocky V* went into production, when his weight went from a range of 211 to 215 pounds to 221 to 223 in the early 1990s. Virgets entered the ring with Morrison for the first time on January 11, 1991, the night James Tillis crashed to the deck in less than a round. For that fight, Morrison weighed a career-high 227 pounds. Virgets always denied any involvement with steroids and, in fact, insisted that Morrison was clean, two assertions difficult to comprehend coming from a man who is currently the Director of Physical Education at the United States Naval Academy.

When asked whether it made more sense to go with an established trainer rather than with Virgets, Morrison gave a thorny response to the Passaic *Herald News.* "That couldn't be further from the truth," he said. "And that's only because most other fighters believe that, and they continue to go to those people that have been around a long time. But you never heard of Kevin Rooney till Tyson came along. You never heard of Richie Giachetti before Larry Holmes. And I guarantee you that two years from now, Tommy here will have people knocking at his door because of what I do. I know that. It's always the fighter, anyway, that brings the recognition."

Still, the fact remained that Morrison was surrounded by amateurs, with only Cayton having a proven track record. In addition, Morrison was far removed from the gritty boxing mainstream. He trained in a suburban health club, where there would be no opportunities to learn from other fighters via observation, no opportunities for impromptu sparring sessions with visiting pros, none of the informal lessons that go on every day at a professional gym.

"I don't like being around a lot of other fighters because then there is too much stuff going on," Morrison said about his unusual setup. "I like to be in a situation where I can concentrate, where it's just him (the trainer) and I, which is basically what Tyson did when he trained back when he was still with Kevin Rooney. Because that's the way Rooney trains his fighters; he schedules them. Like this one at two o'clock, the next one at three-thirty, this one at five, and so on, giving all his time to the one fighter at that particular time. I think it's a disadvantage to have like five people in there boxing and one trainer bouncing around trying to hit every fighter."

While Morrison might have been right about the methods employed by Rooney, he was missing the substance of the situation. Rooney had been a fair professional fighter (and a New York State Golden Gloves champion), Rooney had been a disciple of the idiosyncratic but sage Cus D'Amato, Rooney worked out of a bustling gym in the Catskills, where amateurs, trainers, and budding pros congregated. Occasionally, legendary champions such as José Torres and Floyd Patterson dropped by unannounced. As he trained for most of the 1980s, Tyson was surrounded by boxing. This is an ambiance that cannot be reproduced among squash players, deadlifters, or dance-aerobics enthusiasts, in a climate-controlled environment, scrubbed squeaky-clean by Spic-and-Span or Ajax.

★ ★ ★

By early 1991, Morrison had built a record of 25-0, and Las Vegas odds-makers refused to post lines on his fights, citing the woebegone nature of his competition. The Great White Hope stigma, accentuated by fighting so often in boxing hinterlands, made it difficult for bookies and sports-writers to take him seriously as a rising contender, but it was the feeble quality of his opposition that made him a joke to insiders and outsiders alike. Even Mike Tyson, still the most buzzworthy athlete in the world despite having lost his title to Buster Douglas, publicly disparaged Morri-son. "He's a little twerp," Tyson said. "I know his type from when I was in reform school, in the boys home. He's the type of kid I used to pick to blow-dry my underwear."

But Team Morrison compounded the air of humbuggery by continuing to match "The Duke" as objectionably as possible. Neither Mike Acey nor '80s holdover James "Quick" Tillis survived past the opening round against Morrison. The same would be true of his next opponent.

On February 19, 1991, Morrison battered a desolate Pinklon Thomas, who was so far gone from drug abuse and beatings that he told reporters during a prefight conference call that they would all be "bombfounded" by his performance. A short-lived heavyweight titleholder just a few years earlier, Thomas looked like he was in his mid-forties when he answered the bell against Morrison. Heroin abuse had hollowed him out and left him sallow. He had lost four of his last five matches and had been a profes-sional fighter since 1978. *Tuesday Night Fights*, a boxing series aired on the USA Network, broadcast the mismatch live from the Kemper Arena in Kansas City. Wearing a strange camouflage ensemble, Thomas might have stepped out of a Nintendo console, except he was slower and less agile than the 2D characters onscreen. Within a minute, Thomas was cut above his right eye, and he shook, shuddered, and stumbled as Morrison strafed him with lead rights and hooks to the body that made him wince. As soon as he sat on his stool between rounds, Thomas quit, emphatically. "The kid can punch," Thomas said after the fight. "He's the Great White Hope, and I'm glad for him. I prepared, but he came on strong." Thomas would need thirty-eight stitches to close his wound.

Meanwhile, Morrison could no longer check his libertine impulses. He had by now assembled a rowdy entourage, men who would feel comfortable sleeping with beer helmets on, and they shared not only drinks and pranks with Morrison but women as well. In the wake of *Rocky V*, Morrison had become what his co-manager John Brown called a "Bimbo Magnet." This was a far less PC era, in a far less PC environment. Even so, Brown was guilty of understatement. "According to Tom [Morrison] and Virg [Tom Virgets], his life in Kansas City was truly a 'wild' one," Dawn Gilbert wrote. "Supposedly, he participated in drugs and orgies on a near-nightly basis."

With two children already from two different women, Morrison decided a vasectomy was the perfect solution to facilitate his sexual excesses. And his sexual excesses were both riotous and notorious. "There are some stories about Tommy and Westport that are legendary," John Brown told the *Kansas City Star*. "Tommy and his entourage would get into a limo and load it up with women, and they'd all take turns with them."

Nearly every bar in Westport saw Morrison and his crew in action, and they had no shortage of willing accomplices. They were everywhere, with their Western belts, their Aqua Net hair, fringed jean jackets, star-crossed eyes, darkened slightly by mascara.

★ ★ ★

"I was the guy your parents warned you about in high school. I was a rebel."
—Tommy Morrison

★ ★ ★

Nearly everyone who knew Morrison agreed that most of his problems during his Kansas City days were sparked by alcohol. In the future, Morrison would use cocaine, meth, Adderall, Special K, and marijuana, and while he dabbled in ecstasy and cocaine in the early 1990s, it was liquor that fueled his temper. Tom Virgets once offered an anecdote (with a postscript) to the *Kansas City Star* about how Morrison gave away a $1,500 bankroll while en route to a casino in Atlantic City. He handed the money out, piecemeal, to homeless people on the streets along the way. "That was Tommy," Virgets said. "That wasn't one time I saw him do this. It was time and time again. He couldn't pass 'em up. But if he was drinking, he was liable to kick 'em."

Morrison was the kind of drunk who would pick fights in public, shave the eyebrows of his sleeping buddies, and reject outright the concept of a designated driver. He could also become violent when under the influence. In a 2016 deposition, Dawn Gilbert, under oath, recalled a night when a drunk Morrison slashed a woman in Kansas City. "I can remember there was one girl that he had an altercation with at a bar, and I can't think of her name. The story was—I wasn't there, obviously, but I think it was before I met him, he had a broken beer bottle and held it to her neck and cut her, and I remember him telling me he was going through court proceedings while . . . while we were together, and I believe he settled out of court in that matter."

As John Brown remembers it, the woman was a stripper who eventually emerged looking for redress based, in part, on professional considerations. "She called me up and she said, 'Look, I need plastic surgery, it's going to cost about $12,000, and Tommy Morrison should pay that,'" Brown recalls. "And I said, 'Oh, God, I agree with you,' because I'm sitting here thinking she hadn't filed aggravated assault charges or anything, you know. So I go to Tommy and I say, 'Tommy we need to pay this girl,' and he goes, 'Oh fuck her, I'm not paying her anything. Fuck that bitch.' By that time we weren't talking a whole lot anyway, so Tony Holden was his consultant kind of guy, so they decided they weren't going to pay her. I went back and told her, 'I'm sorry, but they're not going to pay you. I suggest you get a lawyer,' and she did, and I think they ended up settling for $100,000."

★ ★ ★

April 19, 1991. The Convention Center, Atlantic City. Finally, Morrison makes his move. He winds up on the undercard of the Evander Holyfield–George Foreman pay-per-view extravaganza. In only his second scheduled ten-rounder, Morrison faces Yuri Vaulin, one of the first wave of Russian fighters to emerge after the fall of the Soviet Union. A southpaw with textbook moves and a limited threshold for pain, Vaulin befuddles Morrison early before being stopped by a body attack in the fifth round. After the fight, Morrison blames his poor showing on an unusual affliction for a prizefighter. "I looked terrible stumbling around trying to catch that guy because, afterward, it was found that I had Compartment Syndrome in both legs," Morrison told the *Springfield News-Leader*. "The legs were fine when I fought at 205–209 pounds, but as I gained weight, it became a factor. I have to go after a guy. I simply couldn't pursue." In fact, this is likely the first public sign that Tommy Morrison is abusing steroids.

★ ★ ★

Morrison undergoes surgery on his legs and accepts one more walkover bout (a first-round TKO over someone named Ladislao Mijangos on June 27, 1991) before his first real test against a world-class fighter: "Merciless" Ray Mercer, the ex–Army sergeant who had outpointed him at the Olympic Trials three years earlier.

★ ★ ★

In late 1991, Ray Mercer was in possession of the WBO heavyweight championship, a trinket that elicited snickers from some but, like other sanctioning body titles, generated wages for fighters that could not be earned any other way. Everyone knew that Evander Holyfield was the only champion that mattered, but billing Mercer–Morrison as a clash for something other than a ranking was a useful marketing tool for promoters.

For half a million dollars, Morrison would have to face a crude but dangerous banger in Mercer, the 1988 gold medalist in Seoul, a man with a Samsonite chin and freakish durability. It was a risk Bill Cayton thought worth taking. "It's the right fight at the right time," Cayton told *The Ring*. "Ray Mercer is a good opponent. He has credibility. I believe it will catapult Tommy into worldwide recognition."

While a victory over Mercer would launch Morrison into the top-money ranks, it would also mitigate some of the "White Hope" criticism that pursued him like Furies. Nearly thirty haphazard opponents had fallen head over heels at his feet; now Morrison would have a chance to prove that he could bowl over a genuine contender.

Since turning professional in 1989, Mercer had amassed a 17-0 record, but his performances were uneven. In his previous fight, Mercer had been baffled by a flabby Italian named Francesco Damiani before scoring a one-punch KO in the ninth round. A ripping uppercut from out of the blue left Damiani, a 1984 Olympian, on his hands and knees, blood pouring from his freshly broken nose. Five months earlier, Mercer had exited the ring with a split lip and a hideously swollen jaw after outpointing erratic Bert Cooper in a twelve-round war aired by CBS. Worse, perhaps, Mercer had barely eked out a split decision over ex–cruiserweight champion Ossie Ocasio, a fighter who had once challenged Larry Holmes for the heavyweight crown . . . in 1979.

Even with Mercer struggling at times—all the while solidifying a reputation for partying that might have made Morrison proud—the leap from six-rounders and blowouts of ghostly figures such as James Tillis and Pinklon Thomas to a hard case such as Mercer turned out to be too wide for Morrison. Rarely had Bill Cayton miscalculated so badly. Before the fight, Marc Roberts, manager of Ray Mercer, seemed dumbstruck. "I don't know why Cayton took this fight," he said. "Maybe he's senile." And John Brown, who understood that Morrison was still an unfinished product, disagreed with Cayton about his matchmaking. "When he lined up the fight with Ray Mercer, we were all against that," Brown recalls. "We said, 'you know, Mercer is not the right guy, Mercer is a rock,' you know, and he said, 'Oh, Mercer has gotten old, he probably can't take a punch anymore and Tommy'll knock him out.' And we were like, 'Bill, I don't think so. You can't hurt Mercer with a truck.' And that's exactly what happened."

Not only was Mercer battle-tested, but he was also bitter at the lack of esteem he had received from the press since turning pro after the Olympics. "What do I have to do to get some recognition, some respect?" he sneered before the fight.

There were other "smart money" issues as well. Mercer was an angry man entering the ring that night. Despite his gold medal, despite his status as the WBO champion, there was near parity in the purse splits, with Mercer receiving only $50,000 more than Morrison, the challenger. That, of course, led to what was unspoken but generally acknowledged: the race factor. "I hate it," Mercer told the *Morning Call* a few days before the fight. "Tommy's been getting all the hype, and people have been saying to me, 'It's racism, it's only because he's white,' and I've been saying 'no.' But now that I found out about the money, what else could it be? That's the country we live in. It always needs a Great White Hope. But what can I do? I just gotta suck it up this time."

As an Olympic gold medalist, Mercer, in contrast to Morrison, had gathered an experienced team around him for his run at heavyweight glory. He had signed an exclusive promotional contract with Top Rank, hired Marc Roberts as his manager, and trained under the shrewd eye of Hank Johnson, who had been the boxing coach of the 1988 U.S. Olympic team. Although he was slow, plodding, and one-dimensional, Mercer could maximize his potential backed by seasoned operatives. And this professional foundation allowed him to see his upcoming showdown with Morrison with appropriately cynical eyes. "I'm Tommy's stepping-stone," he said. "If he beats me, he should go all the way to the top. I'm thirty years old and most of my critics say I'm at the end of my career. It would be impossible for me to lose this fight and come back and get another title shot. But he won't beat me."

To Morrison, Mercer appeared overconfident. "I know he thinks he can walk into the ring and knock me around," he told the Kansas City *Examiner*. "But he's going to be in for a rude awakening."

★ ★ ★

According to reports, Morrison breaks camp before the Mercer fight to see 38 Special in concert.

★ ★ ★

October 18, 1991. In his return to the Convention Center in Atlantic City, where he had struggled against Vaulin on the Holyfield–Foreman undercard six months earlier, Morrison believes he is finally ready to leave his small-time roots behind. "This is the fight I've been working for the last three years," Morrison said at a press conference. "This is a chance to legitimize myself as one of the top heavyweights in the world. After we win this fight, a lot of good things are going to happen."

An expectant crowd of more than 8,000 (as well as a healthy pay-per-view audience) gathers to watch a boxing rarity: two young, undefeated heavyweights go head-to-head. For most of the first three rounds, Morrison pummels Mercer. Left hooks, uppercuts, body shots, right crosses—one multipunch blitz after another. "I know he's gonna come out smoking for the first four, five rounds," Mercer had told *The Ring* a few months earlier. "But he hasn't been past six rounds, and he's going to be getting hit. While he's attacking, I'll be attacking. And he'll say to himself, 'Wow, this ain't worth it.'" Soon, Mercer is bleeding from a split lip, his face begins to puff, and he must be reconsidering his prediction.

It seems inconceivable that Mercer can withstand such abuse for long, and, in fact, he does not. By the fourth round, Morrison is already decelerating; the late nights are catching up to him, the All-American girls in mom jeans and halter tops are catching up to him, the tomato cans he has been knocking over for years are catching up to him, the steroids are catching up to him. And now Ray Mercer is catching up to him. Late in the third round, Mercer begins to move a little, which is not his strength, naturally, but he is elusive enough to keep Morrison at bay. By circling Morrison, he also creates space to land a few of his own punishing blows. During clinches, Morrison, who has never gone more than six rounds, gasps for air. But Morrison still rattles Mercer with slashing combinations, the same shots that sent Dave Jaco airborne, left Jesse Shelby teetering, torpedoed Lorenzo Boyd. They do not have the same effect on Mercer, a professional who is looking for a million-dollar fight, not just enough cash to keep the repo man away for another month or two.

After a bruising fourth, Morrison, who has taken a pair of hard rights from Mercer, returns to his corner breathing like a man who has just been rescued from a riptide. Between rounds, Tommy Virgets urges him to relax and pace himself, but there will be no time for Morrison to act on his advice.

When the bell rings to start the fifth round, it will mark the beginning of the end for Morrison. Almost immediately, Mercer is on top of him, landing a chopping right that spins Morrison around and leaves him leaning against the ropes in his own corner for a moment. Sensing wounded prey, Mercer, now energized, pounces.

If Eadweard Muybridge had made a motion study of those final seconds, he would have marveled, perhaps, at how Morrison, unconscious, eyes shut, seemed suspended in midair for an instant even as Mercer landed his final crippling shots. Indeed, the only thing that appears to keep Morrison vertical is the whirlwind created by the punches themselves.

As Mercer attacks, Morrison, who has rarely been hit in the ring, tries to cover up in his own corner, but he is overwhelmed. The barrage begins with a right hand, a left, and a thudding right to the body. From that point on, the violent finale is inevitable. Planting his feet for maximum leverage, Mercer batters a defenseless Morrison with arcing blows. An overhand right leaves Morrison sagging, and his physical responses from subsequent blows resemble those of a man suffering from myoclonus.

The crowd at ringside is a mix of terror and euphoria. Referee Tony Orlando is late in trying to halt the battering. New Jersey State Athletic Commissioner Larry Hazzard has bolted out of his seat and onto the ring apron in hopes of stopping a manslaughter-in-progress. Finally, after a final screaming left hook that distorts his features, Morrison collapses, hitting the canvas face-first, his left arm draped over one of the ropes. In his first match against an opponent who has not been culled from the Kenny Last, Dusty Trunks, and Willie Getup ranks, Morrison has failed catastrophically.

★ ★ ★

Later, Tommy Virgets would explain how Morrison seemed to come undone all at once. "I was well aware that he was having trouble relaxing," Virgets told *Boxing Scene*. "He took an overhand right that didn't hurt him, but it shocked him. In a big bout like this, there is an anxiety level that you have to control. Tommy did have it under control for a while, but then he went a little bit over his threshold. He ended up taking a lot of shots."

To an extent, Morrison agreed with his trainer. "I was amazed that Ray was able to take the shots I gave him," he said. "What I didn't realize was that even though he was taking a beating, Ray was relaxed the whole time. And there I was, tense, throwing punches like crazy, going a mile a minute. Well, you saw what happened. I ran out of gas."

John Brown has his own take on the Mercer disaster. "It was sad that Tommy did his typical non-100 percent training," he says. "And I heard later that he was taking some drugs at the time—something which . . . to this day I don't know what it was, ecstasy or something, one of his gang members told me. And so Tommy was good for about four rounds and then he just dissipated."

From Jay, Oklahoma, Morrison was finally nearing the bright lights he had attained only in the celluloid fantasy of *Rocky V*. Is it possible that he had overreached? Is it possible that he knew that stardom—in the ring— was beyond his grasp? Is that what rattled his nerves? Was he really just a hell-raiser from what had once been known as Indian Territory—a haven for misfits and outlaws? An ex–Toughman contestant with a good left hook but nothing more? A Great White Hope along the slapstick lines of Boer Rodel, Al Palzer, Duane Bobick? Did this hick think he could reach rarified heights via Great Falls or Wichita?

Morrison has strayed far away from Oklahoma. Maybe too far. The stars out here, seemingly within shooting distance of the Atlantic Ocean, are illusory, they are light-years away and may already be dead.

After he is revived and led to his corner, a glassy-eyed Morrison sits on his stool, bobbing and weaving. "The fight's over, Tommy," the ringside doctor tells him. "The fight's over."

★ ★ ★

"You see, fear is a fighter's best friend. You know, but it ain't nothing to be ashamed of. See, fear keeps you sharp, it keeps you awake, you know, it makes you want to survive. You know what I mean? But the thing is, you gotta learn how to control it. All right? 'Cause fear is like this fire, all right? And it's burning deep inside. Now, if you control it, Tommy, it's gonna make you hot. But, you see, if this thing here, it controls you, it's gonna burn you and everything else around you up. That's right, you know?"
—Rocky Balboa

★ ★ ★

The rehabilitation project—a boxing staple—began a few months after Morrison had been stopped by Mercer. Physically, Morrison was cleared by doctors following a battery of neurological exams. To recuperate mentally from the crushing knockout, Morrison spent a leisurely month in Jay, which, as far as exposure and media were concerned, made Kansas City look like Los Angeles.

Back in his childhood haunts, Morrison did some of what he called "soul searching" and postponed an early return to the gym. He also dwelled on his loss to Mercer. In an interview with *KO* magazine, Morrison did his best to put a positive spin on his defeat. "I was in a state of shock," he said. "But believe it or not, I was also feeling a huge release of pressure. I wasn't happy about losing, of course, but I was glad the fight was over. I no longer had to be perfect. I had a loss on my ledger. Oddly, that made me feel good. It's a lot of pressure when you're undefeated."

As for the nightmare sequence that ended the fight? "I was fresh meat laying on the ropes because the ref had his head in his ass. Not only do I not want to see the KO, I don't have to see it. Every time I step out the front door, people tell me all about it. There was even an item on TV recently that said Mercer's knockout of me was the eighth-most-dramatic knockout of all time. Well, at least I made history, sort of."

Four months later, Morrison returned to the ring, this time at the Las Vegas Hilton. His opponent was Bobby Quarry, the least-accomplished of the Fighting Quarrys and a man who would soon be serving time in Folsom on a variety of charges. He would also make headlines when he joined his brothers, Jerry and Mike, as a brain-damaged casualty of boxing. With a record of 10-10 entering the fight, Quarry was just another of the hapless, hopeless, and helpless that Morrison had been upending like shabby ten pins in a Bowl-A-Rama since his career began. In fact, it was something of a surprise to see the Nevada State Athletic Commission greenlight such an outrageous mismatch. That hardly mattered to fans of "The Duke." His brutal dispatching of Quarry (KO2) wound up drawing the highest ratings in the twelve-year history of ESPN boxing.

As Morrison continued his comeback, the grim world in which he had traveled all of his life materialized. His brother, Tim, was arrested on serious charges. On February 28, 1992, Tim Morrison met a twenty-seven-year-old woman at a Holiday Inn party in Joplin, Missouri. He was in town to referee an amateur boxing tournament ("The Battle of the Bad") at the Hammond Trade Center. He made sure to name-drop his brother, Tommy, and how Tommy had costarred with Sylvester Stallone in *Rocky V.* After the party broke up, Morrison insisted on driving the woman to her hotel. Instead, he burned rubber onto an isolated off-road a few miles away and raped her. "I crawled over to the side of the ditch, and I threw up, and I threw up, and I urinated," the woman testified. "I felt so dirty that I just curled up into a ball, hoping he would leave me there."

Less than a year later, Tim Morrison was found guilty of one count of forcible rape. During his career, Morrison acted as something of a gate-keeper for his brother, losing to a slew of future Tommy victims: Aaron Brown, Dan Murphy, Tim Tomashek, Wimpy Halstead, and Tui Toia. Tim Morrison was an "opponent," the same kind of unskilled body that his brother had spent years abusing. By the time Tim Morrison lost his appeal and shuffled through the gates of Jefferson City Correctional Center in 1994, he had already been knocked out more than a dozen times. His final record, 14-25-2, is one of painful futility, and he was winless in his last thirteen fights. He would spend the next fifteen years in prison.

Between February 16 and May 21, Tommy Morrison (who had now set up training camp at the Virginia Military Institute) scored four crushing knockouts similar to those from his pre-Mercer days. In the longest fight of that destructive stretch, Morrison stopped Oklahoma rival Wimpy Halstead in the fifth round. Halstead was a chatty circuit fighter, barnstorming across the Great Plains against bumpkins straight out of the pumpkin patch since 1980. Whenever Halstead fought a heavyweight with even a modicum of ability, however, he found himself counting atoms on the ring canvas. For years, he had been trying to goad "The Duke" into a rumble, and he finally got his wish after beating Tim Morrison via unanimous decision in December 1991. Years earlier, Halstead had claimed that Morrison had fled the state—like an outlaw who had been posted by a dead-shot marshal—instead of facing him for local bragging rights.

On a pay-per-view card aired from Caesars Palace in Las Vegas, and headlined by Thomas Hearns–Iran Barkley II, Morrison sparred with Halstead at half-speed for the first four rounds before lowering the boom in the fifth. Pasty, balding, and fighting on short notice, Halstead was the epitome of the palooka, even if he was delusional about his own success against local yokels. Usually the fraternal type, Morrison showed minimal interest in sportsmanship after scoring the stoppage. It could have been more than personal enmity that drove Morrison to sympathize half-heartedly with his defeated opponent after the fight. Yes, Halstead was a jackass, but he also represented the lost future Morrison might have had in Oklahoma—if he had stayed in Jay—fighting every few weeks at the Park Plaza Hotel or the Trade Winds Central Inn. Fringe pros like Halstead made little money, found no glory in the grubby environs of low-level fighting, earned just a line or two in the back pages of *Boxing Illustrated* or *The Ring*. Even with the Mercer loss on his record, Morrison believed in his own glittering destiny: top billing on marquees, back-page headlines, million-dollar paydays, the heavyweight championship of the world. That night against Ray Mercer? That night he saw the black lights for the first time? That night was just a bleak detour to a momentary nowhere, and Wimpy Halstead was nothing more than the past Tommy Morrison had been trying to escape since the day he left home as a teenager in search of his destiny.

★ ★ ★

In his first significant fight on the way back to stardom, Morrison faced tough but limited Joe Hipp on *Wide World of Sports*. Born on a reservation in Browning, Montana, and a member of the Blackfeet Nation, Hipp was a plodding southpaw whose career ascension resembled, in some ways, that of Morrison—minus the magazine covers and the slick Hollywood hoopla. Bob Arum, head of Top Rank, put his cultivated sense of bad taste to gauche use to publicize this Saturday afternoon dustup, even going so far as to bill the promotion "The Cowboy vs. The Indian: The Shootout." At a poolside press conference to announce the fight, Morrison and Hipp, dressed like castoffs from the set of *Dances with Wolves*, rode in on horses to greet the local media, and the Echo Sky Singers played "honor drum songs" for the occasion.

Over the years, Hipp had built up a statistically impressive record on the margins of the sport, boxing in Eugene, Oregon; Fife and Yakima, Washington; Gardnerville, Nevada; and Butte, Montana. He was 24-2 when Top Rank Promotions signed him to serve as a future KO victim for Tommy Morrison. It was a move that nearly backfired. Normally portly, Hipp had scaled as high as 246 pounds for one of his fights, but against Morrison, he trimmed down to 223. "I've worked really hard for this fight," Hipp told the *Reno Gazette-Journal*. "I know how important it is and what it means to me. I've worked hard for fights, but nothing like this. I've been here [in Reno] for close to three months. I haven't seen my family for a long time. The reason I haven't is Tommy. I take that in the ring with me."

Like many journeymen weary of toiling in high school gyms, hotel ballrooms, and bingo halls, Hipp saw his first significant fight as a springboard to success. Waiting for that opportunity was a brutal way to make a living. In 1995, the *Great Falls Tribune* published a list of the injuries Hipp had incurred since turning pro at the Lane County Fairgrounds in Eugene, Oregon, in 1987: a broken jaw, a broken cheekbone, some broken ribs, a broken orbital socket, a fractured wrist. He also had some bone chips removed from his elbow. In the cruel terminology of boxing, Hipp was a fighter who "busted up:" he was susceptible to swelling, cuts, and bruises. Against Morrison, whose destruction at the hands of Mercer raised questions about his own durability, Hipp was preparing to initiate skirmishes from bell-to-bell in hopes of outlasting him. Morrison knew he would be in for a brawl. "I think he's going to come right out and initiate the action," he told the *Reno Gazette-Journal*. "That's what I'm going to do, too. It could be over after the first couple of rounds. He possesses punching power, but my speed will be the big factor in the fight."

It was a painful game plan. On June 27, 1992, at Bally's Hotel and Casino in Reno, Nevada, Morrison took on his toughest test since the Ray Mercer fight. Hipp absorbed one combination after another over the first three rounds—including a thumping jab that repeatedly landed—and seemed hard-pressed to survive more than another round or two. But in the fourth, he drove Morrison back with a clumsy flurry. A follow-up left-right staggered Morrison and sent him wobbling to the ropes. Although Morrison fired back and lasted out the round, the ghost of Ray Mercer seemed to be hovering in the dry Reno air. That was something Hipp had calculated before the fight. "It wasn't that long ago," Hipp said about the nightmare KO Morrison had suffered. "It's in the back of your memory. I hope I can jog a few memories for him."

When Morrison flattened Hipp with a roundhouse right in the fifth round, it looked like the natural order of things had been restored: "The Duke" would score an impressive KO on national television and vault back into the title mix. But Hipp staggered to his feet, survived the round, and began rattling Morrison with inelegant but effective combinations. Across rounds six, seven, and eight, Hipp cut Morrison above the right eye, split his lip, and drove him into retreat, an odd sight, considering how Morrison spent most of his time in the ring on the attack.

For the first time in his career, Morrison was milling past the sixth round, and his troubles were compounded by the fact that his jaw and his right hand had both been broken earlier in the fight. Between rounds, John Brown consulted with Team Morrison physician Brent Koprivica on whether the fight should be stopped. "Dr. Koprivica told me that if Tommy could continue taking the pain, the jaw would probably not sustain any more damage," Brown said after the bout. Continue taking the pain? Morrison had absorbed beatings from his father as a child, once took a baseball bat to the skull from his brother during a sibling scrap, fought in Toughman tournaments before he could even shave. Pain was a constant presence in his life, from beginning to end.

For most of the ninth round, Hipp continued outworking a weary Morrison, and an upset seemed inevitable. Then, from out of nowhere, Morrison landed a ripping uppercut that sent Hipp stumbling. Now energized, Morrison followed up with a cuffing sequence of blows before a roundhouse right, a left hook, and another uppercut left Hipp, in distress, splayed out on the canvas. Hipp managed to stagger to his feet before the count of ten, but referee Vic Drakulich peered into his bruised and puffy face (Hipp had suffered a broken orbital bone), saw the glazed look in his eyes, and stopped the contest.

Finally, after thirty-three fights, Morrison had faced adversity in the ring and had come through. "Each time I got hit on the jaw, I felt it separate more," Morrison recalled after the fight. "This is what boxing is all about. I think I erased some questions about what happens to Tommy Morrison after four or five rounds." Because of the injuries he had suffered during the fight, however, Morrison was unable to capitalize on his electrifying win over Hipp. He had his jaw wired shut after surgery. "He'll be on liquids four to six weeks," Bill Cayton told the *Reno Gazette-Journal*. "The earliest he'll begin training is four months. He's the toughest fighter I've ever seen. If he can only learn not to get hit. The punch that broke his jaw . . . he should've never been hit. It was a sucker punch."

Morrison returned to the ring in December, stopping sad, sad Marshall Tillman in the first round. After rising from an early knockdown, Tillman was sent head over heels, like a tumbler, by a left to the ribs. When his body came to a stop, he remained on the canvas, in obvious distress, for the full count. That night, instead of fighting on national television again, Morrison was an ESPN preliminary to junior flyweight champion Michael Carbajal. He also had to share billing with a teenage Oscar De La Hoya, whose superstar future was what Morrison had coveted ever since he had been a teenager but would never achieve.

Even after six months, however, the Hipp KO still reverberated, and HBO accepted Morrison as a co-feature for a card headlined by George Foreman, whose popularity had actually increased since he had lost a title challenge to Evander Holyfield in 1991. Promoter Bob Arum had visions of matching Foreman and Morrison in a pay-per-view extravaganza that would generate millions. If both men won, they would meet in June.

★ ★ ★

For Morrison, his premium cable debut would come against an '80s relic—Carl "The Truth" Williams, who had once gone fifteen close rounds with Larry Holmes for the heavyweight title in a losing effort. That was in 1985, when NBC still aired fights during prime time. A few years later, Williams made a commotion of sorts by getting steamrolled in less than a round by a marauding Mike Tyson. Since then, Williams had been languishing on the ESPN circuit, alternating wins and losses in Atlantic City and unraveling physically with every match. He was going nowhere fast. Past his prime and aware of his encroaching status as a stepping-stone, Williams seemed fortunate, at age thirty-three, to receive a significant payday on a high-profile card. Even Williams sensed that. "By the odds," he said, "I shouldn't be here. I should be finished, blowing away in the wind. I'm with the contenders. This one could put me over the hump."

There was an air of inevitability about the fight when Williams disrobed to reveal a pudgy physique nearly devoid of muscle tone. In the grunge era, Williams seemed wildly out of place, like Crockett and Tubbs decked out in fuchsia at a Soundgarden concert. But Williams was once a top contender, and he had come within a round or two of winning the heavyweight title as a young man based out of White Plains, New York. Like all fighters whose futures were now behind them, Williams remembered the past and what it had promised him. Nearly all fighters eventually reach this point. In a few years, so would Tommy Morrison.

"The Truth" entered the ring as a 5-to-1 underdog, but the only figure that mattered to him was his $150,000 purse, a sum he had not come near since early 1989, when Mike Tyson had annihilated him. Behind that $150,000 was the possibility of more—$250,000 or even $500,000—if he could defeat Morrison. This is the prime mover for all fighters on the downslide: the possibility of generating a potential future from fight to fight. Morrison, for his part, would earn $400,000, a solid figure for a man whose signature win had been over Joe Hipp only seven months earlier.

A crowd of nearly 6,000 gathered at the Reno-Sparks Convention Center in Reno, Nevada, mainly to see Foreman, "The Punching Preacher," in the main event. Not many had expectations for the semifinal, and when Morrison leveled Williams with a trip-wire left hook in the first round, the pay-per-view extravaganza against Foreman was all but guaranteed.

Again, Morrison floored Williams with a whipping hook, this time in the third round. "The Truth," whose poor defense and weak chin had worsened as he aged, appeared ready for smelling salts. As wobbly as he had been in the third round, and as stiff as he had looked since the opening bell, Williams somehow managed to survive the fourth, when Morrison, noticeably slowing down, landed a crashing right to the jaw.

In the fifth, he left Morrison on the brink of catastrophe. A little over a minute into the round, Williams landed a short right cross to the temple that caused a delayed reaction in Morrison. Suddenly short-circuited, "The Duke" turned away from Williams and dropped to his knees, skidding into a neutral corner. He took the mandatory eight count from referee Mills Lane on the canvas, rising at nine, and the fight resumed. Almost immediately, Williams landed a right uppercut that shook Morrison, who ducked low on the inside, looking for a safe zone. But Williams landed another cuffing blow to the head, and Morrison dropped again. With the three-knockdown rule in effect, Morrison was only one more trip to the canvas from losing a jackpot payday against George Foreman in excess of $1.5 million. Although he took more hooks and rights from Williams, Morrison survived the remainder of the round and returned to his corner, looking befuddled.

Both men plodded through the next two rounds. In the eighth, however, Morrison accelerated, rocked Williams with a left hook, pinned him against the ropes, and unleashed a volley that compelled Mills Lane to intervene. Once again, Morrison had been forced to rally in an unexpected shootout. Punch Stat statistics had Williams outlanding Morrison 280-196 at the time of the stoppage. The result left his management team searching for answers. But were they asking the right questions?

A concerned Bill Cayton hinted at the reason Tommy Morrison struggled in certain fights. "Let's put it this way," he said. "Tommy Morrison makes Mike Tyson look like a monk." Comparing Morrison to a convicted felon (who entered his title fight against Trevor Berbick suffering from gonorrhea) for years hell-bent on self-destruction was an awkward if revealing moment. Tommy Morrison was a debauchee seemingly incapable of being satiated.

Despite removing him from Kansas City, despite forcing him to train on military bases, despite subjecting him to perpetual lectures, Brown, Cayton, and Virgets could not constrain Morrison from a lecherous outlook that belied its prosaic surroundings: This was not a man pursuing his pleasures in Los Angeles hot spots or swanky shindigs in Fifth Avenue penthouses. Instead of Manhattan, New York, it was Manhattan, Kansas. In Westport, Morrison roistered from bar to bar night after night. There were long hours with the bottle and reportedly a few short ones with cocaine. But it was women that Morrison indulged in most. "I blame nobody but myself for my situation," Morrison told the *Boston Globe* in 1996. "For three years, I was an animal. I partied every night. I had a different woman every night. I was afraid to be alone because when I looked in the mirror, I didn't like what was looking back at me." Insatiable, indefatigable, and incautious, Morrison would romp his way out of more than one win over his career.

Years later, after everything had come crashing down on Morrison, his co-manager, John Brown, could only bemoan the lack of discipline "The Duke" showed during a short-lived prime. "I gave Tommy a hard time almost every day because I wanted him to get up and run," he said. "If he was going to have sex, have it with one woman a day, not five, to not drink or take drugs, and to train five days a week so we could become successful."

Morrison himself, long after he had been diagnosed with HIV, would joke about a chaotic sex life on par with that of Mötley Crüe or Ratt. "There are a lot of beautiful women in Kansas City who need to be thanked for helping me stay conditioned for years," he told Elizabeth Merrill of the *Kansas City Star*.

But even Morrison thought about cutting back on his extracurricular activities when Top Rank Promotions announced his next major fight. It would take place on June 7 and cap a pay-per-view card from "The Biggest Little City in the World," Reno, Nevada. Tommy Morrison would be squaring off against "Big" George Foreman. After beating Williams, Morrison was asked in the ring if he wanted to fight Foreman. "Not only yes," he responded, "but hell, yes!" Now, he would get his chance.

★ ★ ★

By 1993, George Foreman was six years into his improbable comeback and on the verge of folk-hero status. His thrilling April 1991 loss to Evander Holyfield—when Foreman tried to regain the heavyweight championship he had last held almost twenty years earlier—did nothing to diminish the storybook overtones of his return. In fact, he was more popular than ever. He was still a few months away from starring in his own short-lived sitcom (imaginatively titled *George*) and years from hitting the mother lode in the form of "The Lean, Mean Grilling Machine," soon to be ubiquitous in households across America. At the moment, he was a ratings magnet for HBO, earning $5 million per appearance for fighting the likes of Jimmy Ellis, an ex–football player, and Pierre Coetzer, a pallid South African whose frangible skin made a Dutch Masters box look like a Mosler safe.

But Foreman and Morrison had something in common. For a while, both men were part of the boxing fringes, far, far away from the marquee of Madison Square Garden or the neon glitz of Las Vegas. In 1987, when Foreman first decided to moonlight from his day job as a preacher, he was considered little more than a curiosity by networks and boxing power brokers alike. That left Foreman on the margins of a marginal sport during the early stages of his comeback, scuffling on the tank-town circuit before finally popping up on the USA Network and the casino scene. (Accompanying Foreman on his barnstorming tour in 1987 and most of 1988 was Rick "Elvis" Parker, ex–pool hustler, ex–magazine crew impresario, ex–rock promoter, and future murder victim. Parker was also a drug-addled psychopath and the personification of the boxing dark side. In a few years, he would perpetuate cons involving former contender and Hollywood irregular Randall "Tex" Cobb and NFL lineman Mark Gastineau. In 1995, one of his own fighters, Tim "Doc" Anderson, would pump his plump body full of bullets in an Embassy Suites room.)

Between televised engagements, however, there were fights in Springfield, Missouri (with Tim Morrison losing on one of the undercards); at the Sheraton in Orlando; out in Galveston, Texas, where Foreman knocked out an ex–light heavyweight named J. B. Williamson; at the Casa Royal Hotel in scorched Bakersfield, California. Some of these fights were shady, both in their design and in their execution. On May 21, 1988, Foreman appeared on a card in Anchorage, Alaska, which was organized as a benefit for Missing Children of America, that wound up with the charity owing $8,000 when the night was over. To add to the chicanery, the promoter disappeared and stiffed the preliminary fighters. Foreman, however, received his paycheck. And while Foreman often acknowledged that his competition was weak (AP: "George Foreman Beats Another Unknown Boxer"), some of his fights went beyond poor matchmaking. More than once, Foreman took on—and poleaxed—pratfall artists connected to the shifty Parker, including Tim "Doc" Anderson and Frank Lux, who used one of his aliases, "Frank 'Gator' Williams," when he collapsed against Foreman in Alaska. Then, in 1999, the *Miami Herald* published a bombshell exposé about arranged fights that mentioned Tex Cobb, Frans Botha, Eric "Butterbean" Esch, and . . . Foreman. When the *Herald* contacted Foreman about a doubtful second-round KO of a journeyman named Tony Fulilangi, "Big George" shrugged it off nonchalantly. "That happened to me all the time," he said. "If they're getting a whuppin', it's up to them to decide if they want to continue."

Although Morrison had been flogging stiffs for years, none of his fights appeared fixed. Indeed, his opposition was so harmless that rigging outcomes could only be considered redundant. What Morrison shared with Foreman was the subterranean milieu, an amoral netherworld where fraud was never far from the murky surface. Eventually, Foreman would leave that netherworld behind; Morrison, on the other hand, would be haunted by it for the rest of his life.

With the exception of Evander Holyfield, Foreman, now forty-four, had never faced any real danger in the ring during his second act. A washed-up Gerry Cooney, nearly a decade removed from his heyday, could still bang with his hook but was pulverized in less than two rounds. And Alex Stewart left Foreman grotesquely warped at the final bell of a ten-round struggle, looking more suitable for the pages of *Fangoria* than for *Boxing Illustrated*, but that had been, more or less, an accident, a rare case of routine matchmaking nearly backfiring. So averse was Foreman to the possibility of competition that his promoter, Bob Arum, publicly upbraided him more than once. No matter how much Foreman was criticized, his modus operandi never changed, even when he won the heavyweight title in 1994. At that time, Foreman was desperate to fight newly crowned champion Michael Moorer, who seemed emotionally frail, and was willing to sue the WBA (based on age discrimination) to force the bout.

In Morrison, he found a pay-per-view opponent who had not only shown a wobbly chin but had also been the subject of several news features about anxiety and stage fright. That Foreman accepted a bout with Tommy Morrison suggests just how much Morrison had slipped since the

Mercer disaster: He was now considered safe enough for one of the most prudent fighters in the sport. Oddsmakers immediately installed Foreman as a betting favorite.

In his best salesman voice, Foreman promoted his fight with Morrison on the basis of risk to life and limb. "Tommy Morrison is a puncher who can make you scream," Foreman said, mostly with a straight face. "I will try not to get hit. I didn't want to fight Tommy Morrison. When Morrison fought Carl 'The Truth' Williams, I didn't like what I saw. I want to stay away from punchers." As usual, Foreman was stuck in PR mode, his default setting; almost nothing he said during his second life in boxing had any relation to the concept of truth. That was another trait he shared with Morrison. According to Peyton Sher, who was working with Foreman for the fight, "Big George," in private, was not nearly as worried about Morrison as he made it seem, and his lax training camp, set up in St. Lucia, proved it. "I sent him three sparring partners down to that island, and they sat around for a week and did nothing for their $1,000," Sher said. "He thinks going for walks is how you train. All I know is, if George wants to fight, as soon as he connects, it's over. But it may not happen."

For his part, Morrison played up the generation gap and even threw in a personal bit about hero-worship. "I was in high school when he made his comeback," Morrison said. "I went to Springfield, Missouri, to see him fight. I love the man to death. Everybody loves him. I'm sorry I'm gonna have to spank his butt."

Although Morrison promised a violent outcome against Foreman, John Brown may have given a hint at their strategy when he turned to Jerry "Ace" Miller for pointers. Miller, who had guided John Tate to a short-lived reign as WBA heavyweight titlist in the late 1970s, had also trained several Olympians, including Bernard Taylor and Johnny Bumphus. "Ace is widely respected as being a genius at teaching pro boxers the lost art of defense," Brown told the *Kansas City Star*. "Tommy needs help in that area." In late February, Morrison traveled down to Tennessee for a few training sessions with Miller.

Brown also arranged for Morrison to spar in public, hoping to ease his stage fright. "The whole objective is to get out in front of crowds," Tommy Virgets said. "The more he's in front of a crowd, the less anxiety he will have. Today he didn't spar as well as he has in closed sessions."

In preparation for a tune-up, Morrison went a few rounds with Derrick Roddy and Brian Scott at Bannister Mall in Kansas City, also home to JC Penney and Sears.

To ensure that the often-distracted Morrison would focus on the dangerous task at hand, Virgets, Brown, and Cayton again set up camp at the Virginia Military Institute, where Virgets had once been a boxing coach. At VMI, Morrison could limit distractions—to an extent. "It's just like being in prison," he said. "I live boxing every minute. That's what I need." Of course, his "prison" stint included the occasional conjugal visit.

Against Foreman, he would be the closest he had ever been to being in top condition. Top Rank Promotions billed the fight as "The Star-Spangled Battle," and more than 12,000 spectators jammed the Thomas & Mack Center in Las Vegas to see two KO artists slug it out in mid-ring. It never happened. Although Morrison promised bloodshed during the buildup to the fight, it was soon clear that his public statements were decoys, of sorts, meant to keep Foreman from considering another, altogether more footloose strategy. From bell to bell, Morrison scurried around the ring in hopes of minimizing contact with Foreman, twenty years older and thirty pounds heavier. At times, Morrison even turned his back on his lumbering opponent and fled, outraging the crowd. When Morrison stopped momentarily to plant his feet, he would run off quick combinations before sidestepping out of range. More than once, he landed his thunderous left hook, but Foreman shivered and swayed but never collapsed.

Late in the fight, Morrison seemed so gassed and ragged that a single pinpoint shot might have capsized him. Foreman, however, could not deliver that shot. After twelve rounds of Foreman plodding and Morrison fleeing, the unpopular decision went to The Duke. At the post-fight press conference, the usually avuncular Foreman was pitiless towards Morrison. "If I ever turned my back and ran, they would have told me I should have never been a boxer," Foreman said. "When I hit Tommy Morrison, he fell into my arms like he wanted to call me daddy. I couldn't knock him out in the twelfth round after he had come all that way. I felt sorry for him."

When Morrison had his hand raised in victory at center ring, he was jeered by a crowd expecting more Tommy Gunn and less Running Man, but he was also lambasted by the media. *Newsday* reporter Wallace Matthews, writing for *Boxing Illustrated*, even scored the bout for Foreman and all but accused Morrison of cowardice. "Having been not outfought but outrun by a man half his age who refused to stand and fight," Matthews wrote, "there was enough ammunition for Foreman to make the case that he had been robbed."

That was only one voice of many that rose to discredit Morrison, who had just notched the biggest win of his career but failed to impress the cynical press. Michael Katz of the New York *Daily News* wrote: "Morrison may have won the meaningless 'WBogus' heavyweight title last night, but he did not win many fans at Thomas & Mack arena against a man twenty years older."

"I wasn't impressed at all with Morrison," Kevin Rooney told *Boxing Scene*. "Morrison won the fight. He showed me he was smart, but Foreman had nothing. He just followed the guy around the ring. Morrison did what he was supposed to do, although he really should have knocked out George. In my eyes, his stock did not go up because of this fight."

In response to his hecklers, Morrison offered a sociological defense, of sorts. "If I was black or Hispanic, I wouldn't get any criticism," Morrison told the Associated Press. "Because I'm white, people expect so much more out of me. That's a little unfair, but life isn't fair."

Looking back nearly thirty years later, Morrison–Foreman stands out as more than just a tepid heavyweight fight. Both men landed jolting blows, with Morrison teeing off repeatedly with overhand rights and isolated hooks, and Foreman jarring Morrison again and again with a jab that might have punctured a Humvee. Throughout his career, Foreman had been branded as having a suspect chin, and this bizarre assertion continued even after the pastings he took from Evander Holyfield and Alex Stewart. No matter what the skeptics said about Morrison—about his iffy pedigree, about his fugazi record, about his White Hope quality, about his Ray Mercer catastrophe—one legitimate thing, beyond question, was his crippling left hook. And George Foreman was bombarded by them for nearly thirty-six minutes. True, Morrison seemed to take something off his blows for the sake of speed and mobility (running off multipunch combinations before darting away from return fire), but at times he dug into the canvas and shot hooks that seemed to ricochet off Foreman. Another heavyweight would have toppled from these punches; Foreman, as he had against Holyfield, as he would against Michael Moorer, remained upright. Whatever his limitations, Foreman was no walkover, and Morrison had beaten him, with a few rounds to spare.

"The key was giving him head movement," Morrison told *Boxing 93*. "I watched the films and saw that good head movement kept him from punching. When I moved my head a lot, George had to creep in a little further than usual to throw. And when he'd creep in—pow—my jab would hit him. It frustrated the piss out of him."

In boxing, some wins make you look bad, and some wins make you look good. Revisionist history is often only one or two fights away for a boxer. When Foreman went on to win the genuine heavyweight championship of the world in his next start by flattening the undefeated Michael Moorer, it made Morrison shine in retrospect. Of course, by then, Morrison was already trying to pick up the pieces of his career all over again.

With the win, Morrison collected a bastard heavyweight title (the WBO version, which Morrison had been unable to wrest from Ray Mercer in 1991) and earned the biggest purse of his career—somewhere in the range of $2 million. His stop-and-go strategy put a momentary dent into his reputation as a thrill-maker in the ring, but beating Foreman vaulted him into the mix with the biggest names in the division: Riddick Bowe, Lennox Lewis, Evander Holyfield. Facing Morrison was a risk—he still had a pulverizing left hook—but his status as a box-office draw meant he was worth millions in a pay-per-view setting, and his vulnerabilities gave top heavyweights a decided advantage. Bowe and Lewis, in particular, were eager to tangle with Morrison, now more in demand than he had been as an undefeated Hollywood bit player.

He also enhanced his star appeal to his preferred demographic: women. While not exactly out of circulation when training for Foreman, Morrison took his camp seriously—in his fashion. That meant consulting with Ace Miller, sequestering himself at an Air Force Academy base, possibly injecting more steroids. Beating Foreman meant a celebration was in order, and, for Morrison, part of celebrating meant gang bangs, trios, trains, toilet-stall romps. Some of it, most of it, probably all of it—in the raw and without regret.

Morrison bar-hopped and bed-hopped through the blue hours in Westport accompanied by a famished entourage eager to split the leftover spoils from associating with a genuine local hero. Even with fame and money, Morrison was less than discriminating about his cravings. According to an article in the *Kansas City Star*, Morrison was not above partying in a seedy hot-sheets motel, where registered guests comprised an informal listing of select lowlife in "The Paris of the Plains."

The *Star* quoted a former motel night manager about the comings and goings of Morrison, a heavyweight title claimant who had just added millions to his bank account. "We were surprised to see him," said the night manager. "Why would he be in a place like that, with such scuzzy trash? The place was a whorehouse with drugs. I don't know that he did drugs, but I know the girls did."

His sordid lifestyle—which also included liquor and, yes, drugs—galvanized his management team. In fact, if Bill Cayton, John Brown, and Tommy Virgets agreed on anything, it was that Morrison had to remain busy to keep him from spontaneous human combustion. This is something even Morrison realized.

★ ★ ★

If ever there was a time for a fighter with certain attributes (as well as certain limitations) to excel, it was the early 1990s. Mike Tyson, Evander Holyfield, and George Foreman were all household names (as was Buster Douglas, for most of 1990, at least) and HBO had a seemingly bottomless budget to air matchups featuring champions, contenders, and prospects— including Tommy Morrison. In the 1990s, the heavyweight title remained big business. There were still enough boxing fans, mostly holdovers from the Ali era and the 1980s renaissance, whose memories included a dominant heavyweight champion. In Mike Tyson, they had a larger-than-life figure who embodied the sporting ideal of "The Baddest Man on the Planet."

When Tyson dropped out of the title picture, first while rebounding from his shocking February 1990 KO loss to Buster Douglas in Japan, and then by a rape charge that would lead to a prison stint of nearly three and a half years, the heavyweight division plunged into a remunerative confusion. The early '90s Gold Rush was partly spurred by the expansion of pay-per-view, which delivered a far superior viewing experience than its uncomfortable predecessor, closed-circuit television. Instead of leaving the house to attend a rowdy theater where a giant screen offered inferior sound and image (and, often enough, neither), boxing fans could now watch a quality production from their La-Z-Boys, beer cans in hand and pretzels on the coffee table. That meant more substandard fights were offered to the consumer than in the closed-circuit era, when only sure-shot matchups merited the financial outlay of a city-by-city production.

For years the title had been in the hands of Don King, seemingly in permanent possession of his destructive charge, Tyson, but King lost control of the division when Douglas severed ties with him. In what should have been an afterglow period for Douglas—who had, after all, scored one of the most fabled upsets in sports history—King worked hard both publicly and privately to overturn the result in Japan. Tyson, he claimed, had been the victim of a long count when he had floored Douglas in the eighth round. "The first knockout obliterated the second knockout," King squawked. "Tyson won."

Although King also promoted Douglas, he saw Tyson as a long-term cash cow and Douglas as merely a one-hit wonder. The result of this calculation: Douglas sued King to break their promotional contract.

While Douglas pursued other offers, King eventually settled for a payout, but the legal contretemps broke his stranglehold on the division. The heavyweight title, now up for grabs, sparked endless litigation, record purses, political maneuvering, and general chaos. The title—and all of its receipts—slipped further away from King when Evander Holyfield, promoted by Main Events, stopped an apathetic Douglas in three rounds on October 25, 1990. Although Holyfield was a reasonably popular champion, he was not considered indestructible, and when his title reign ended after just three successful defenses, the heavyweight division opened up even more, a lucrative sinkhole, precipitating a mad scramble for pay-per-view dollars. Every manager, promoter, and network schemed on behalf of a fighter to earn a toehold (even if only a pinky) in a division that remained headline material.

Riddick Bowe, who outpointed Holyfield for the championship on November 13, 1992, dumped his WBC title into a trash bin during a press conference a few weeks later, allowing his top contender, Lennox Lewis, to claim it without a fight. Bowe was more interested in soft touches than he was in making a mandatory defense against the man who had stopped him in the amateurs. Now, at least by the haphazard standards of the sanctioning bodies, there were two heavyweight champions. And a startup fourth organization—the off-brand WBO, based in Puerto Rico—began to gain acceptance among the perpetually self-interested scurrying in the dark corners of the fight racket, giving a sport struggling to maintain cultural relevance a confusing total of three championship claimants by 1993.

The big men of the '90s exemplified what sportswriter Richard Hoffer wrote in his book *A Savage Business*: "Heavyweight fighters, for all the excitement they bring to the sport, are the most unreliable performers in the game. They suffer amazing breakdowns under pressure, react unpredictably in times of crisis, and require unorthodox and sometimes hysterical motivation just to endure, let alone achieve. They're all headcases."

The '90s cast of characters included misfits, malcontents, and malefactors. There was Douglas, of course, who ultimately came to view his shocking win over Tyson as a golden parachute payment. Overweight and undermotivated, Douglas dropped the title in his first title defense, a one-punch KO loss to Evander Holyfield that earned Douglas a certain amount of humiliation to go along with a $24 million check. In a few years, Douglas would balloon to more than 300 pounds and slip into a diabetic coma.

Even Ray Mercer, who had left Tommy Morrison flat on his face in 1991, had seen his career implode. First, he dropped an embarrassing decision to a geriatric Larry Holmes in 1992; then he found himself on trial after being indicted for trying to bribe Jesse Ferguson during a points loss in February 1993.

As champion, Holyfield went on to make a trio of weak title defenses (decisions over aged George Foreman and Larry Holmes bookended a TKO of Bert Cooper, a last-minute substitute with a history of substance abuse) before losing to Riddick Bowe. Like his predecessor, Bowe decided on a pair of fights against pitifully overmatched opposition. Unlike Holyfield, however, Bowe had no interest in discipline. His waistline expanded—Bowe infamously designed a house with a kitchen in the bedroom—until he dropped the title to Holyfield in a rematch a little over a year after winning it. This was the infamous "Fan Man" fight, when a daredevil sailed into open-air Caesars Palace and crashed the ring, mid-round, in a paraglider, causing a near-riot. Everything surrounding the heavyweights verged on lunacy.

In 1994, the mixed-up Michael Moorer outpointed a sickly Holyfield, who retired with a heart ailment that would eventually be "cured" by a faith healer named Benny Hinn.

So psychologically fragile was Moorer that George Foreman, who picked his opposition as carefully as a man defusing a bomb, chased him down by writ. And Foreman, after beating Moorer in 1994, refused to defend his newly acquired championship against anyone resembling a quality contender.

On the margins stood WBO titleholders such as Michael Bentt, Herbie Hide, and enigmas like Oliver McCall and Frank Bruno. A troubled journeyman who would eventually suffer a nervous breakdown in the ring, Oliver McCall upset Lennox Lewis on September 24, 1994, bringing a piece of the championship back into the hands of Don King. Later, King would disdainfully recall the man who had rocketed him back into the big time. "What's the name of that junkie I got?" he told the *New York Times*. "Oh, yeah, Oliver McCall, the junkie. I cleaned him up for that fight, dechemicalized him, and detoxified him. I fired him up that night, singing 'Yankee Doodle Dandy.' Nobody could have beat him."

After years on the outside of the heavyweight title picture, King had already begun plotting for the return of Mike Tyson, who was scheduled to be released from prison in March 1995. Indeed, every boxer weighing over 200 pounds began counting down the days when Tyson, still the most controversial athlete in the world despite not having practiced his trade in years, would be released from prison. That included Morrison, who had been thinking of Tyson since Bill Cayton entered the picture.

★ ★ ★

A month after beating Foreman and raising his profile back to its *Rocky V*, pre-Mercer level, Morrison was a signature away from landing the windfall Bill Cayton and John Brown had envisioned when they first combined forces to steer a roughneck teenager from Jay, Oklahoma, population 2,000-plus, through the nebulous world of professional boxing. On July 5, Frank Maloney, who managed WBC heavyweight champion Lennox Lewis, announced that he was close to an agreement for a fight between Morrison and Lewis. A few days later, Lewis canceled his proposed September title defense against his British rival Frank Bruno. Finally, on July 14, the fight was officially announced: Tommy Morrison would face Lennox Lewis in a partial unification bout that would net him at least $7.5 million. Morrison would defend his WBO title in an August walkover against TBA (to be announced) at the Kemper Arena in Kansas City, and then he would square off against Lewis in November at The Mirage in Las Vegas. It was an astonishing parlay. Throughout the entire decade of the 1990s, the height of the pay-per-view era, only a handful of fighters would earn such a significant sum: James "Buster" Douglas, Evander Holyfield, Mike Tyson, George Foreman, Riddick Bowe, Oscar De La Hoya, Felix Trinidad, and Lennox Lewis.

For Tommy Morrison to find himself among the highest-paid fighters in the world, alongside supernovas such as Tyson and Holyfield, was more than just a dream come true; it was a powerful reminder that boxing was a world of smoke and mirrors. Maybe it was too powerful a reminder for Morrison, maybe Morrison was overwhelmed by the intensity of the spotlight that would now shine on him. In less than a week, Morrison announced that the Lewis fight would be pushed back to early 1994, at his request. After his tune-up in Kansas City on August 30, Morrison would defend his title against another designated victim on October 29. Then he would meet Lewis in March.

From the beginning, there was something peculiar about this decision. Deferring a $7.5 million purse (in 1993, no less, when such a sum is the equivalent of nearly $15 million today) struck observers as more than just questionable. And the pragmatic reasons Morrison gave for making such a curious move convinced few skeptics. "I requested to have it a little bit later," Morrison told *The Ring*. "I'm still playing catch-up to the Riddick Bowes and Lennox Lewises, who came from the Olympics and turned pro with experience. I came right from the Toughman contests. I'm playing catch-up, but I'm closing in."

On the surface, Morrison may have had a point. But Lennox Lewis was not a dominant titlist. Following his showstopping KO of Donovan "Razor" Ruddock on October 31, 1992, Lewis had been unimpressive in a pair of defenses against generic opposition. If ever there was a right time for Morrison to challenge Lewis, it was in 1993, before somebody else came along and toppled the talented but inconsistent Englishman. Indeed, in less than a year, Lewis would be an ex-champion, suffering a TKO at the hands of Oliver McCall. "I was hoping to fight two more times before I faced Lewis," Morrison told the Associated Press. "I'm really excited about this schedule. I believe it gives us the proper preparation to face an opponent of Lewis's caliber."

Later, a simmering Bill Cayton would disavow any role in Morrison choosing what would ultimately prove to be a disastrous course. A tune-up for a fighter barely capable of adhering to a disciplined training camp was one thing, but a second tune-up was a code-red alert. "I absolutely do not want Tommy to take this fight," Cayton told the *Philadelphia Daily News* before Morrison faced Michael Bentt on October 29. "Too much is at stake to put himself at risk now. But there are some people around Tommy who are telling him otherwise, and he's elected to listen to them. I only hope it turns out all right."

His co-partner, John Brown, concocted some stagey quotes for the media, but they were transparent. "The great part of this fight being in March. . . . It gives the fight a chance to build to a great crescendo," Brown said. "These are two of the most popular fighters in the world. We'll be able to pay these guys what they're worth." How much more did he think a Lewis–Morrison fight would be worth? The fifty-fifty split with Lewis guaranteed Morrison one of the top three or four purses in all of boxing in 1993. And how could anticipation for the fight be built by matching Morrison with undetermined opponents who would be hand-picked not for their ability but their lack of it? After all, Morrison became a viable commodity by defeating George Foreman, one of the most popular athletes in America, not by drubbing another belly flopper on ESPN.

And then there was the possibility of Morrison losing. According to some reports, undefeated Frans Botha was the favorite to face Morrison on August 30. Botha was slow, crude, and hittable, but he was no pushover, and in a few months, after Morrison had sidestepped him, he would win the vacant IBF heavyweight title by outpointing Axel Schulz in Germany.

All the hard work of publicizing and maneuvering Morrison to this very point—a staggering payday and an outside chance to win an established heavyweight title—would now be delayed in favor of a bumbling series of events.

As late as August 8, three weeks before the first scheduled title defense, an opponent had not been named, which underscored just how careful Team Morrison had to act to preserve their Lennox Lewis showdown. Indianapolis club fighter Anthony Wade had been mentioned as a possibility, but Top Rank finally decided on a blatant gimmick that would backfire spectacularly: Morrison would have a rematch, of sorts, with his *Rocky V* opponent, Union Cane, this time without a director or choreographer involved. "Mercury" Mike Williams was the opponent.

★ ★ ★

Just how lightly regarded the WBO title was during its early days was reflected by the fact that Morrison, who had just defeated one of the most famous athletes in America, was defending it on ESPN for one-tenth of the purse he had earned against Foreman less than three months earlier. (And, of course, a fraction of what he would have received against Lennox Lewis.) But the Kemper Arena in Kansas City was not the Thomas & Mack Center in Las Vegas. The glitz factor was not just lacking—it was nonexistent. And while a crowd of nearly 10,000 "Duke" supporters, rowdy and ready for action, would eventually gather, they would end the night jeering and hurling debris into the ring.

By the early '90s, nearly all major title fights aired on HBO, Showtime, or pay-per-view. As the '80s boxing boom receded, with its supercharged legends—Duran, Leonard, Hearns, Hagler, Mancini, Arguello, Pryor, Holmes, even Tyson—now fading memories or, worse, sad parodies of themselves, the networks cut back on fight cards across the board. Yet here was Morrison defending his ersatz heavyweight title on a network that aired the Canoe World Championships, monster truck shows, fly-fishing competitions, and "Surfing Pipeline Masters." It was a title fight against TBA until just three weeks before the opening bell, and when the opponent—Williams—was finally announced, the whole event morphed into a pop-postmodernist prank.

More than any other major promoter, Bob Arum relied on novelty acts and tacky stunts. Arum once broadcast Evel Knievel trying to shoot himself over Snake River Canyon in a homemade rocket ship that went haywire seconds after liftoff. Then there was the infamous Muhammad Ali–Antonio Inoki fiasco in Japan, a boxer-wrestler extravaganza so dull and buffoonish it was a wonder that the referee did not break kayfabe and declare it a double disqualification halfway through its torturous fifteen rounds. Arum's idea to reach a crossover audience for pay-per-view shows in the late-1990s was to stick an obese Toughman slugger named Butterbean—aka "King of the Four-Rounders"—and a Playboy model on undercard after undercard in separate farces. With Morrison–Williams, alas, Arum would outstrip himself in the Waterloo department.

Despite the big-top atmosphere surrounding a promotion inspired by a Hollywood gimmick, Mike Williams played it straight at the opening press conference. "That movie was pretend," Williams said about sharing the screen with Morrison in 1990. "That's what Tommy is, a pretender.

That's why doing the movie was easy for him." It had been years since Williams was considered worth quoting by newspapers, yet here he was denigrating Morrison as a fake fighter. "The only place Tommy can beat him is in the movies," added Bob Jordan, who managed Williams until a few minutes after Williams pulled his notorious vanishing act.

A former National Golden Gloves champion, Williams was once a talented heavyweight with a physique straight out of the glossy pages of *Flex* or *MuscleMag*. In the late 1980s, Williams had made instant headlines by reportedly dropping Mike Tyson during a sparring session, a story that carried more than just a whiff of ballyhoo. Whether the Tyson knockdown was a fable or not, Williams blossomed as a prospect for a few years, but unexpected losses to Tim Witherspoon and James "Buster" Douglas—by KO—crushed any title ambitions he might have had. Inactivity and a lack of focus plagued Williams thereafter. But even for a fighter, Williams was erratic. Rumors about drug use had dogged him for years, and his meltdown in Kansas City seemed to confirm that his instability transcended a mere lack of professionalism. Just hours before the main event, in his dressing room, an agitated Williams balked not only at facing Morrison but also at providing a urine sample. He balked hard. No amount of coaxing, cajoling, or coercing could convince Williams to uphold his contractual obligations that night. "The situation in the locker room was unbelievable," Arum told the Associated Press. "Williams's wife was in tears, pleading with him to take the test and fight. It was a bad scene."

Even with Top Rank representatives offering to sweeten the pot, Williams remained desperately adamant. In no time, Williams was pacing Genessee Street on a late August evening, trying to hail a cab. While he waited for his ride to arrive, Williams was approached by a reporter who asked him about the nixed urine test. "Don't even bring that up," Williams snapped. "I don't do drugs." Then he ducked into his taxi and drove off into the night.

"The official word is Mike turned yellow and left," Bob Jordan told the Associated Press after the fight. "He said he pulled a muscle in his back, and we had two doctors check him out, and they could not find an injury. His wife said there's nothing wrong with him. I was his manager. He's a bum."

Such was his reputation for whimsicality that Williams had been eyed with suspicion by Top Rank for more than a week, ever since he had no-showed a recent press conference to hype the fight. On Friday morning, desperate matchmakers thumbed through their Rolodexes in search of a standby. They should have updated their contacts. On short notice, Top Rank, possibly at the suggestion of John Brown, managed to produce Tim Tomashek, a pasty Midwest circuit fighter with a 31-10 record and a bonhomie entirely at odds with the desperate situation in which the promoters found themselves.

After working the day shift at a ShopKo distribution center in Green Bay, Wisconsin, Tomashek boarded a flight to Kansas City on Saturday afternoon, willing, if not precisely able, to play eleventh-hour challenger to a bastardized version of the heavyweight championship. When he arrived, he learned that Williams was not yet AWOL and that the Tommy Gunn–Union Cane rematch was on schedule. As late as Sunday evening, Tomashek had called his mother and told her he would not be fighting but would receive free entry to the card and would become a spectator instead of a participant. That all changed, however, in the dressing room, when Williams suffered his meltdown. Top Rank officials searched the crowd with barely an hour to spare, and Tomashek, beer in hand, jumped into action. Off he went in search of his gear, $40,000, and a brief Warholian fame.

To make matters worse for Top Rank, already reeling from losing its main event, Tomashek was a joker, and his quips underscored the ludicrous nature of the event. "It's like a movie," Tomashek said, "but I ain't Rocky. I'm uglier." In response to questions about his conditioning, Tomashek offered this doozy that culminated in a non sequitur: "Did I train? I do have that step-climber machine. I used that a couple of times. I really didn't train. Green Bay has no boxing, so I have to fight on an Indian reservation."

The crowd that had gathered at the Kemper Arena saw little sporting in what they figured was a bait-and-switch, one with comic overtones only to those who may not have paid for a ticket. Tomashek may have been the everyman given an impromptu chance to pursue glory, but the original main event had been built around a phony *Rocky* story line; a real one was implausible. And his "Common Joe" look went a little too far. His nickname, "Doughboy," as reflected by his slack physique, was both goofy and apt, and his happy-go-lucky outlook did not vanish once he entered the ring.

When the opening bell rang, Tomashek was ready to mug, caper, and grin. He patted Morrison on the head, remonstrated to the referee, spun behind Morrison and covered his eyes with his gloves, played to the increasingly restless crowd, and, occasionally, threw an inelegant combination.

Meanwhile, Morrison, fighting in low gear, landed rights and hooks in close, leaving Tomashek battered and bleeding by the end of the third round. As if in response to the echoing boos filling the arena, Morrison accelerated in the fourth, finally dropping Tomashek with a barrage of punches near the end of the round. Although Tomashek beat the count and made it to the bell, he returned to his corner resembling a man who had been sideswiped by an eighteen-wheeler. The ringside physician was aghast. While Tomashek protested, the doctor halted one of the strangest title defenses in heavyweight history. Instantaneously, the furious crowd began hurling cups into the ring.

As Morrison returned to his corner, barely registering his TKO victory amidst the jeers, he seemed sheepish, even slightly embarrassed. "I didn't know I was fighting what's-his-name till I got out there," Morrison said after the fight. "It wasn't difficult. I'm a skilled fighter. I performed as best I could. This guy was basically in there to survive." For years, his lack of competition had raised red flags among the newshawks of Midtown Manhattan, then his frightening loss to Ray Mercer had convinced many that he was nowhere near ready for the big time. But this situation, like an outtake from *Diggstown*, seemed to solidify the feeling that he was nothing more than an oddity. Indeed, the entire ESPN broadcast was solid midway material—all it needed was a carny barker and a platform for the Human Blockhead.

"It was a sad night," Morrison would later tell the *Philadelphia Inquirer*. "I didn't have to fight at all. We could have canceled the whole show. But there were 10,000 fans there, and they wanted to see me. I wasn't proud of it, but I did what I had to do."

Following his headline win over Foreman with a nationally televised omnishambles only stonewalled his quest for legitimacy. Less than three weeks after Morrison had stopped Tomashek, the WBO announced that it had retroactively deemed the fight a nontitle affair. For his part, Tomashek went on to *Late Night with David Letterman* and local-hero status in Green Bay.

And Morrison? Morrison was headed for disaster.

★ ★ ★

Despite the gap in talent and accomplishments, Tommy Morrison and Mike Tyson shared similar career paths. Bill Cayton matched Morrison against several early Tyson victims with similar violent results. He made sure Morrison got repeated exposure on ESPN. And, most important, aware that Morrison, like Tyson, had a self-destruct setting liable to activate at any moment, Cayton made sure to keep Morrison occupied. That meant isolating Morrison in the gym as often as possible, away from the temptations the real world offered and training for a fight. Morrison was one of the busiest boxers of the late '80s and early '90s, and he, too, realized that an overloaded schedule meant less time for debauchery. Less time, however, still meant too much time for a man who thought each day should have a twenty-fifth hour.

★ ★ ★

For Tommy Morrison, March 1994 seemed light-years away. His scheduled showdown against Lennox Lewis—and the $7.5 million purse that would accompany it—seemed fraught with potential obstacles. His lax training for the scotched Mike Williams bout, combined with increased partying, made his entire team nervous. And when Morrison insisted on going through with his second tune-up, this time against a virtually anonymous neophyte named Michael Bentt, not even Bill Cayton could put a positive spin on the situation. "Tommy is fighting Bentt because he wants it, not I," he told writer Bill Gallo. A few weeks earlier, Lewis had guaranteed the lucrative Morrison matchup by stopping a tougher-than-expected Frank Bruno at National Stadium in Cardiff, Wales, but betting on Morrison to keep his end of the bargain was no sure thing. Not that Bentt was considered much of a threat as a heavyweight. Indeed, Bentt, with only eleven professional starts under his belt, was an off-the-board proposition whose stop-and-go career had taken place mostly on the margins.

Because Bentt had been knocked out in his pro debut and was full of misgivings about his profession, he was considered something of a head case. To some, however, it was Morrison whose psyche was brittle, and this weakness was compounded by a lifestyle that could deplete an athlete physically as well as mentally. Bentt himself doubted that Morrison had the nervous system to compete full throttle. "When Tommy punches, he doesn't breathe," Bentt said before the fight. "He gets tighter the longer the fight goes. He starts to panic."

In the New York *Daily News*, Michael Katz reported that Team Morrison was worried about more than just the haphazard training, the elbow-bending, and the never-ending cavalcade of women. "They also were concerned Morrison did not want to fight Lewis straightaway because he was not confident," wrote Katz, "that he insisted on having two tune-ups."

A few weeks before Morrison faced off against Bentt, Lewis had struggled against the limited Frank Bruno, whose stiff movements in the ring often made him resemble a Ray Harryhausen model in slow motion. This muscle-bound style allowed Bruno to build up a lead on the scorecards before his fragile chin gave way, as was its habit, in the eighth round. Lewis looked so vulnerable against Bruno that even Morrison must have regretted his decision.

As far as Morrison delaying the Lennox Lewis fight, Bentt also felt it was a sign that Morrison lacked confidence. "He's questioning himself," Bentt said. "He's questioning whether he's good enough."

Once upon a time, Michael Bentt was certainly considered good enough. He had won the New York Golden Gloves Open Championship four times and the United States Open Heavyweight Championship three times. He missed making the 1988 Olympic team by losing a narrow decision to Ray Mercer, the same man who had prevented Morrison from representing America in Seoul. When Bentt finally signed a professional contract, it was for a $60,000 bonus and a chance to fight for Emanuel Steward and the legendary Kronk Gym in Detroit. After being knocked out in his pro debut, however, Bentt began to drift away from boxing. He was already twenty-nine years old by the time he answered the opening bell against Morrison, and his 10-1 (5 knockouts) record was a short list of what the cynics and coldhearted referred to as "tomato cans." At a prefight press conference, Bentt said he was ready to fight to the death, to which Morrison sourly responded: "He'd better buy a casket."

Bill Cayton, however, did not sound nearly as confident before the fight. "I don't know which Tommy will show up," Cayton told the *Philadelphia Inquirer*. "He has all the talent in the world, but I honestly don't know if he's hungry enough to be a great fighter." In the end, his uncertainty was justified. That Morrison was less dedicated in training for Bentt than he was for George Foreman was no surprise, but that Morrison would surpass the apathy he had shown for the aborted Mike Williams fight was hard to believe.

"The night before he fought Michael Bentt, Tommy was at a concert drinking beer," Trent Morrison told ESPN. "No professional athlete that is up for a big fight is going to be drinking beer at a concert the night before he gets in the ring."

Somehow, Morrison–Bentt was an off-the-boards matchup, recalling the days when Vegas books refused to post odds on fights involving "The Duke." But Michael Bentt was not a man who had ever thought of himself as an opponent. Nor did the industry itself. Even as he prepared for his dark-horse challenge, Bentt had backing from established professionals, including veteran manager Stan Hoffman and, most important perhaps, ace motivator Eddie Mustafa Muhammad. The wide-open heavyweight division was made for someone like Bentt (as it had been for Morrison), who merely had to keep his name in the news with pickup fights and wait for a phone call for a title opportunity. When that opportunity came, all Bentt had to do was win. In the early to mid-1990s, the post-Tyson era, such ordinary talents as Oliver McCall, a geriatric Larry Holmes, Herbie Hide, a geriatric Foreman, Bruce Seldon, Frans Botha, and Henry Akinwande would all capitalize on the chaos of boxing politics and own a sliver of the heavyweight title.

On October 29, Morrison squared off against Bentt at the Civic Center in Tulsa, Oklahoma, a state without a boxing commission. With HBO televising the card, Morrison would earn $1.5 million for his efforts; Bentt would take home $135,000, a solid purse for a man expected to be smacked around the ring like a shuttlecock. And no one anticipated that outcome more than Morrison. An overconfident Morrison sauntered to the ring to the rollicking sounds of "Bad to the Bone" by George Thorogood and the thunderous cheers of thousands. He sported a Jay Bulldogs baseball cap, and beneath his black robe, he wore a Tulsa Oilers hockey jersey, a local touch that further endeared him to an already smitten crowd.

Across from him stood a man with fewer than a dozen professional fights, dressed in white and gold—his old Kronk colors—nonchalantly chewing bubble gum until referee Danny Campbell gave the final instructions. When the opening bell rang, "The Duke" shot out of his corner, fully prepared for an early shower and a raucous afterparty. The early shower was all he got.

He opened with a measured pursuit as Bentt circled to the left, away from one of the most dangerous weapons in boxing: a left hook that had for years kept Morrison from being the small-town washout so many thought he would be. Despite his sound strategy, however, Bentt mistakenly stood his ground for a moment, which allowed Morrison enough time to unleash a hook that staggered him into the ropes. From the beginning of his career, Morrison had always shown a nasty killer instinct, and when he saw Bentt wobble, he charged right in, whipsawing both hands in a blur. And while Morrison would later claim that Bentt flattened him with a lucky shot, the video proves otherwise: The right hand that left him disoriented was the last blow in a combination calculated to catch Morrison between punches. Bentt was cognizant while under assault. He kept his guard up as Morrison flurried and waited for an opening. When another left rocked him again, he recovered and redoubled his focus. At one point, Bentt even shoved Morrison back, in hopes of creating space for return fire. Because his hooks were compact and his right hand was thrown from the shoulder, Bentt was eventually able to beat Morrison to the trigger.

A cracking right stunned Morrison, and a follow-up barrage dropped him to his knees. Although Morrison beat the count, he wore a sleepy look on his face that hardly inspired confidence among the shocked spectators. When the fight resumed, Bentt stormed out of a neutral corner and decked Morrison again with a left hook and a right to the forehead that practically bounced him off the ropes. Again Morrison climbed unsteadily to his feet, looking even foggier than he had after his first tumble. Just as he had been against Carl Williams, Morrison was on the verge of losing via the three-knockdown rule. This time, however, Morrison would not rally. As Bentt closed in on him, like a heat-seeking missile, Morrison threw a pair of desperation blows, in hopes of delaying the inevitable, but they had no effect on the man who could not inspire him to forgo longneck beer bottles, strippers, and a concert. Bentt tore into Morrison, sent him retreating helter-skelter across the ring with a barrage of rights, and landed a final concussive left uppercut that dumped him onto the canvas.

After Campbell officially stopped the fight, he helped an unsteady Morrison back to his corner, where his forlorn seconds sat him on his stool for the ringside physician to examine. It might as well have been a postmortem for the career of Tommy Morrison. Losing was not necessarily fatal—it was how Morrison lost. He had been demolished, humiliated, in one round by an unheralded fighter whose spotty pro career had convinced oddsmakers to take the night off. In his previous fight, Bentt had earned $5,000 for a ten-rounder on ESPN. Before that, he had been living without a telephone because he could not afford another monthly expense. Until Bentt crushed Morrison, his career apex had been a stint as a sparring partner for Evander Holyfield.

Morrison had suffered the kind of defeat that virtually disqualified him from being mentioned as a credible future opponent for any top heavyweight. Riddick Bowe, Lennox Lewis, Evander Holyfield—it would be impossible to convince the public that Morrison could threaten any of them. He also became a laughingstock in the sports pages for blowing $7.5 million and a shot at an established heavyweight title in a matter of roughly ninety seconds. "I warned against Morrison taking this fight," said manager Frank Maloney, whose client, Lennox Lewis, was probably tearing his dreadlocks out in handfuls. "He should have been wrapped in cotton wool before taking this fight. But now he's been exposed."

Cayton and Brown also rued the move. "We had no business taking this interim fight," Brown told the *Kansas City Star*. "Tommy was the one who wanted to take it." And Cayton again pointed to mysterious figures who had been whispering to Morrison. "Tommy was ill-advised by people outside of his camp. I was violently opposed to this fight."

Post-fight, Morrison seemed to agree with some of the harsh assessments lobbed at him. First, he tried to put a rational spin on his shocking loss. "He was the better man tonight, and I made a mistake," Morrison told the press after he had finally cleared his head. "In the heavyweight division, you can't make mistakes. I got a little careless and stayed in the middle too long. When you are in the middle, the punches come right down the pipe, and I zigged when I should have zagged. I felt that I needed the additional experience to prepare myself for bigger fights that are ahead, and I think tonight showed that we did need that experience."

Then came the distressing admission. "I second-guess my skills at this point," he said. Even against Ray Mercer, Morrison had shown talent; against Bentt, he was nothing but a stuntman, justifying the taunts and whispers that had followed him since he began his career. He was just a hayseed from the willowy grasslands, he was just a D-list Hollywood wannabe, he was just another rope-a-dope Great White Hope, not good enough to have earned his catchpenny fame, playing that strange boxing skin game that no one had seen for years.

He had wants, fears, dreams, all the same.

★ ★ ★

"The Lord can give, and the Lord can take away. I might be herding sheep next year."
—Elvis

★ ★ ★

This, it seems, is the long beginning of the end. Two months after losing to Bentt, Morrison is arrested for assault. He is in Iowa City, Iowa, for some reason. He is drunk, and Tommy Morrison has always been a bad drunk. At the Country Kitchen restaurant, 2:20 a.m., he blindsides a college student, William Strout, for staring at him. "It was a sucker punch," Iowa City Police Sergeant Craig Lihs tells the Associated Press. "He taps the guy on the side of the head and knocked him clear out of the booth. The kid never saw him. The kids were eating and studying for finals. They were looking at him and saying he was in the movie *Rocky V*." Morrison is arrested for public intoxication (he had a blood alcohol level of 0.24) and simple assault. He posts his $260 bond and returns to Kansas, more than 300 miles away. A few days later, he is named "Pinhead of the Week" by the *Orlando Sentinel*.

★ ★ ★

After losing the costliest fight of his career, Morrison and John Brown split acrimoniously. They would spend years entangled in legal knots. "My relationship with John Brown never was too stable," Morrison told Bill Haisten of the *Tulsa World*. "I wasn't pleased with the way he handled things. He's the hero of every story he's ever told. Everyone who works for him hates his guts. Anyone involved in Team Tommy has got to be 100 percent in my corner."

Morrison was certain that the outspoken Brown sometimes sounded as if he were in the corner of his opponent. "I heard a lot of bad things from John Brown," Morrison said. "He said I was overweight and had the body of a truck driver. Those sorts of things. A manager's job is to shield his fighter from negative comments. They shouldn't come from the manager. When things didn't go well, he tore me down. Bill Cayton along with myself will be managers."

According to Brown, his contract with Morrison had an option for a five-year extension that Morrison refused to honor. Brown took Morrison to court. "I sued him because I wanted to validate my contract extension," Brown says. "I spent a lot of time and money making a contract that would, you know, that would hold up because . . . I knew that it would take three to five years before you get to the top, and if you don't have some way of protecting yourself after that. . . . And so I had a five-year extension that I sued him over, and I won, except when the court was over, I said, 'okay, he owes me about $600,000, how do I get my money?' And the judge says, 'That's your problem.' So I hired a private detective to find his money; he couldn't find it. And I think, to this day, that he gave whatever money he had to Tony Holden, Tony Holden put it in his bank account, made it look like Tommy had no money. I ended up getting nothing on that."

Top Rank also severed its promotional ties with Morrison, well aware that a limited fighter who was also irresponsible and distracted could not justify further investment. After all, it was Top Rank that green-lighted Bentt, and promoters were not known to place their commodities in risky positions—especially with $7.5 million hanging in the balance. Boxing was not for the dilettante, and Morrison appeared unwilling (or incapable) of curbing his appetites and focusing on his hazardous trade. In the wake of the Tulsa disaster, Top Rank realized that no opponent was safe enough to draw interest from HBO or pay-per-view.

For the public, Team Morrison rarely strayed from message: "The Duke" was training harder than ever, he was ensconced in the Virginia Military Institute, where a monkish existence guaranteed peak physical condition, he was laser-focused on Michael Bentt. Only Bill Cayton would openly express measured pessimism to the press, but leaks to Michael Katz at the New York *Daily News* before the fight revealed that Morrison was, as usual, in disarray. His refusal to take his career seriously had now cost him more than $7.5 million. Later, his mother asked him: "I bet you feel like an asshole, don't you?"

★ ★ ★

After the second loss of his career, and the embarrassing arrest in Iowa that made the newswires, Morrison tries to lay low in Oklahoma. He buys a leopard and a cougar for his ranch in Jay, avoids the limelight, ruminates over his sudden change in fortune. "After the fight, every paper and magazine I picked up said what an idiot I was," Morrison tells the *Springfield News-Leader*. "That annoyed me quite a bit."

★ ★ ★

In place of Top Rank, Morrison turned to his advisor, Tony Holden, as his full-time promoter. A television producer based in Kansas City, Holden met Morrison in the late '80s, when he invited the rookie boxer to guest star in an episode of his syndicated fishing program. From there, Holden and Morrison, who were only a few years apart in age, became friends. As a favor to Morrison, who expressed misgivings about his early direction, Holden agreed to become his consultant during the developmental stage of his career. Holden was that rare figure in boxing: a reasonably honest man, one of the few Morrison would encounter in the last twenty-five years of his life. When Morrison was done as a fighter, Holden would go on to promote headliners as varied as Prince Naseem Hamed, Johnny Tapia, and Joe Mesi.

For now, however, his job went far beyond damage control—Holden would have to try to rebuild Morrison as a contender without the help of power brokers such as Top Rank or HBO. First, Morrison would have to take care of his legal issues. On January 25, 1994, he pleaded guilty to simple assault and public intoxication (via Alford plea) and was fined a total of $310 by Johnson County Magistrate Marsha Bergan. "I think it was blown out of proportion," Morrison said about his run-in with the law. "If the media tells the truth, no one cares. It happened at a restaurant, and the guy was obnoxious. I pushed him; I didn't hit him."

★ ★ ★

"With the Lucky Belle Club Card for frequent players, exciting entertainment, surprises, and fun for everyone. Especially you. It all happens aboard Biloxi Belle Casino, a replica of the graceful paddlewheeled steamboats that plied the Mississippi River at the turn of the century. We

treat you like a winner while you're ashore, too. With free parking. And admission. Plus valet parking whenever you choose. So party with a Southern Belle. Biloxi Belle Casino. It's everything you'd want in the 90s. The 1890s, that is."
—Advertisement, *Hattiesburg American*

★ ★ ★

With Bill Cayton slipping into the background, Holden, who believed Morrison was still young enough to earn a significant payday somewhere down the line, took "The Duke" back to the ESPN circuit. Morrison would not have to go far for his first knock over. His comeback fight would be against a former sparring partner, Tui Toia, on Sunday, February 20, 1994. Toia, who had been inactive for most of his career, was a Samoan club fighter based out of Independence, Missouri. If his management team had ever thought of Toia as someone who could build up a phantom record and then cash in on a headline fight in Europe or as a hapless challenger for some off-brand heavyweight title, then it must have given up long ago. Toia was already closing in on thirty years old, and his only distinction in a career had been a win over Tim Morrison in 1992. (This achievement, beating Tim, often seemed like a strange prerequisite for fighting "The Duke." Toia was one of five heavyweights who had beaten Tim and eventually wound up facing Tommy in the ring.)

At 238 pounds, Morrison was overweight, an indication of just how little he thought of Toia, "The Smokin' Samoan," a semiretired fighter who worked full-time in a potato factory. Toia had little interest in a boxing career, per se, but the $7,500 purse was enough for him to risk having his brains scrambled momentarily. As a late substitute for another lukewarm body (Jimmy Lee Smith), Toia did not even have the benefit of a training camp going into the Morrison fight.

For a reported $60,000, Morrison performed at the Biloxi Belle Casino, a docked riverboat in Mississippi. In a prefight interview with ESPN, Morrison explained, to an extent, why he was back on the cable TV circuit against another palooka. "I always train hard when I'm in the gym, extremely hard. In preparation for that bout (against Michael Bentt), I probably wasn't the most disciplined fighter out of the ring. You know, like I say, sue me, I love women. It's, uh, part of the package."

To the surprise of just about everybody, Toia, only five feet, ten inches, had a solid first round, landing the occasional lead right and a crackling uppercut in close. But Toia ran out of initiative at about the same time he ran out of gas—in the second round. By the third, Toia was gasping for air, and Morrison began hammering him around the ring. With about a minute to go in the round, Morrison tagged a weary Toia with an uppercut that floored him. Toia listened to the full count on his hands and knees. Although he looked sluggish and uncoordinated, Morrison was back. But did it matter?

★ ★ ★

A month after obliterating Toia, Morrison faces Brian Scott in a scheduled ten-rounder. It is a fight that highlights not only how far Morrison has drifted from center stage but how he seems at home in the carnivalesque atmosphere of the boxing substrata. They meet at the Expo Square Pavilion, where the Oklahoma City Cavalry (Continental Basketball Association) play, where the Shrine Circus performs, where the Cocker Spaniel Club sometimes holds events, where the Pinto Horse Association National Championships have taken place, where Royce Gracie wins UFC 4, in the days when MMA was considered human cockfighting, where the Gun and Knife Show is always a crowd favorite.

Like Morrison, Brian Scott is a graduate of the Toughman wars, and also like Morrison, he is from the Midwest, with a troublesome past, and, naturally, a troublesome future awaits him. Scott is a high school football star until he drops out to prowl the Kansas City streets at night. Without an amateur background, Scott turns to boxing for a living when he is twenty-two years old. He carries into the ring with him a scar from a switchblade attack when he was a teenager. Three weeks before meeting Morrison, he posts a first-round TKO against Andre Smiley, a fighter with a record of 0-17-1. One of the many pratfall artists used to manufacture phony records, Smiley never wins a fight in a career whose final tally is 0-26-1. Brian Scott has beaten Smiley twice.

Morrison has always feasted on perpetual losers and fringe professionals, but his latest ring resurrection emphasizes the fugazi nature of his career. His first two comeback bouts are against former sparring partners. First, there is Toia, then Scott. This pattern (one that John Brown initiated) has an insider-trading quality to it, a q.t. acknowledgment that Morrison needs more of an edge now than ever. Holden, Virgets, and Dragert know whether Morrison has handled a specific sparring partner with ease. They know that, at one point, Morrison was essentially an employer of each sparring partner, and that sparring partners often develop an overfamiliarity with their paymasters, one that prevents them from performing full-throttle under professional circumstances. It is as if Team Morrison, in the wake of the Bentt debacle, no longer considers "The Duke" anything more than a fighter whom they hope to cash in on one last time.

Scott enters the ring to "Hit Me with Your Best Shot" by Pat Benatar (even in 1994, she is considered archaic), Morrison counters with "Also sprach Zarathustra" by Richard Strauss as a prelude (most likely a nod to Ric Flair and not Stanley Kubrick), before making his ring entrance to Guns N' Roses ("Welcome to the Jungle").

With a jerry-built 14-0 record, which may encourage delusions, Scott is more ambitious than Toia and opens up early. He is tall, clumsy, and throws his punches without the benefit of technique, but he is willing. Morrison looks flat, his head movement is nil, and Scott, shockingly, connects with several right hands. When Morrison rips an uppercut home two minutes into the first round, Scott emerges from a clinch with a laceration above his left eye, which sends rivulets of blood pouring down his face. At the bell, he returns to his corner, where a man in a blazer and tie administers to his cut. In round two, Morrison backs Scott into the ropes and initiates an exchange. He takes a few punches, but Scott has limited power. A left hook shakes Scott and, halfway through the round, an uppercut drops him to the canvas. As the referee counts over Scott, his corner throws in the towel, sparking a torrent of boos from a crowd whose bloodlust has gone unsatiated by the brief action.

Now more than ever, it seems, Morrison and the boxing underbelly are intertwined like the characters in the final, bleak pages of *McTeague*, handcuffed to each other (one of them a corpse) in Death Valley, California, waiting for the blistering sun to render its impersonal judgment.

★ ★ ★

Eventually, the Kansas City fast lane, which would barely qualify as a pit stop compared to New York, Los Angeles, or Miami, sent Morrison packing. In late March, Morrison announced that he was returning to Oklahoma. "This takes away the temptation when he's not training," Tommy Virgets said. "When it's far enough away, it's harder to answer the call. Westport is always calling him. If you are twenty-three, twenty-four, or twenty-five, have a million dollars and girls all over the country calling you and have an entourage of twenty-five to thirty-five people always around, you might have to rededicate yourself a couple of times."

★ ★ ★

And so the barnstorming tour continued. For his third fight in three months, Morrison would face nondescript Sherman Griffin over a scheduled ten rounds. "My career at this point can't afford another stumbling block," a slimmed-down Morrison told the *Tulsa World*. "We're finally getting back to the threshold, the door we were at before. We can't afford any more screwups. I'm probably in better shape than I've been in a long time. I think the weight shows that. I've done a lot of extra work and run the extra mile."

Years of alcohol and drug abuse had left Griffin physically depleted, but it was his criminal past—and its dark consequences—that made him a desirable opponent for Morrison. The fact remains that Team Morrison worked, deliberately, to keep "The Duke" in the shadowy depths of boxing. They searched high and low (mostly low, naturally) for spoiled goods: fighters whose only skill was an ability to pass a CT scan, fighters who would not have to face the standards of boxing regulators outside of Oklahoma (where no commission existed), ex–drug users, ex-cons, ex-cruiserweights, fighters previously annihilated by Mike Tyson in the mid-1980s, ex–sparring partners, troubled movie costars or semiretirees, fighters with eleven or twelve outings under their belts, and professional losers, one step below journeymen and tomato cans.

Because Morrison had a fan base only slightly interested in boxing as an organized sport, this strategy was easier for him to undertake than it would have been for most heavyweights. It was as ugly and as cynical an approach as can be imagined, but Team Morrison was hesitant to deviate from it. The few times it had, after all, brought troubling results. It began with Yuri Vaulin, who had made Morrison look like a somnambulist in Atlantic City until he could no longer take the heat. Then it was Ray

Mercer, who nearly killed Morrison, also in overlit Atlantic City. Finally, while he may have trained on a reservation and while he shared a similar background of woebegone opposition with Morrison, Joe Hipp was in the mix at heavyweight, and he left Morrison with a broken jaw.

Only George Foreman had failed to keep Morrison where so many thought he belonged—with the bottom feeders—and Foreman was forty-four years old when Morrison gavotted around him for twelve rounds. For the B-team surrounding Morrison—a manager who had never managed a fighter before, an assistant trainer with no professional experience, and a head trainer who had been a boxing coach at the Virginia Military Institute and the United States Naval Academy—this subterranean route might have made sense. But Bill Cayton had guided clients to million-dollar purses (Wilfred Benitez) and unification bouts on HBO (Edwin Rosario); he had been part of the highest-grossing fight in history at the time (Tyson–Spinks); he had never been anywhere near Oklahoma or Kansas as a manager. All three of his previous fighters would eventually become Hall of Fame inductees. The fact that Morrison remained on the Bible Belt circuit after his rise to fame suggests Holden knew that this rebuilding process was a makeshift one. For Cayton, the ultimate target had been Mike Tyson, whose impending release from prison promised a potential payoff of millions if only Morrison could avoid another flogging. That meant Holden, who had the same end in mind, would have to navigate the flimflam world of boondock boxing. That meant finding disposable opponents such as Sherman Griffin.

In 1987, Griffin had been shot four times during a robbery attempt in Conroe, Texas. At the Regency Inn Motel, Griffin had tried battering through a door to attack a terrified couple barricaded inside. That was when a front desk clerk came out of his office, firing like Dirty Harry Callahan, but without the Smith & Wesson. Griffin underwent hours of surgery to remove the bullets, but one .25 caliber slug remained lodged in his back. Like so many boxers, for whom facts were merely jigsaw pieces to be sorted at random, Griffin downplayed the events that led to his pinholing via hot lead. "I had a disagreement with a guy, and he shot me in the back," Griffin told the *Tulsa World*. "It happened during my self-destruction period, when I was trying to be a wild child. I wasn't accepting life on life's terms. Everything's fine now. The bullet doesn't cause me problems; it's part of me now."

At the time Griffin was shot, he had been out on $20,000 bail for the armed robbery of a convenience store in Houston. Prison kept him out of the ring for years, and now, at thirty-one, he was in the middle of a return that promised nothing but hurt and the occasional $7,500 check . . . no matter how spin doctors tried to exalt his pedestrian 14-2 record as a part-time journeyman.

"I suffer a lot of criticism for picking guys like this," Morrison said, taking boxing hoopla to new extremes. "People think I'm crazy. People thought I was crazy for fighting Michael Bentt . . . but these are things I believe I have to do. I like fighting people that scare me a little bit. People that scare me seem to motivate me, and when you motivate me, you get the best performance out of me." According to this logic, Morrison was nervous about facing an ex–light heavyweight recently released from prison, with a documented history of drug and alcohol abuse, who had one fight over the span of six years—against the always-dependable Lorenzo Boyd—from 1987 to 1993, and whose last win was over an opponent with a 4-13 record.

The Brady Theatre in Tulsa was the latest whistle-stop for Morrison. This time, instead of ESPN, Morrison would take his drawing power back to the USA Network, home of the erratic, raucous, tacky weekly series *Tuesday Night Fights*.

With his weight down to 220 pounds (his lightest since 1990), Morrison once again resembled a fit heavyweight, but nowhere are appearances more deceiving than in boxing. A lively crowd roared when the opening bell rang in anticipation of the usual Morrison blowout.

Halfway through the first round, Griffin was on the canvas, courtesy of a scorching counter right that caught him on the temple and a follow-up flurry that sent him toppling like a precarious Ta-Ka-Radi structure. As an amateur, Griffin had shown potential; now, way past his best years, he still displayed the muscle memory necessary to finish the round and score with a few shots of his own.

Despite his consistent and insistent claims of newly found tranquility and a devotion to going the "extra mile," Morrison found himself weary as early as the fourth round. (Honesty had never been a part of his worldview, and these fibs about his dedication were noteworthy for the simple fact that they were undermined, instantly, by what happened in the ring. In the future, Morrison would ignore reality altogether, weave an impregnable fantasy world that would ultimately lead to his death.)

Griffin began to land slapping punches with a frequency that must have alarmed everyone on the Morrison Resurrection Train. If so, they hardly needed to worry about derailment, even with the bleak knowledge of how brittle Morrison was. A spindly light-heavyweight when he had turned pro in 1985, Griffin, nine years and fifty pounds later, did not have the firepower to hurt Morrison, a man who had frequently shown an erratic chin. In addition to uppercuts on the inside, Griffin repeatedly landed echoing left hooks to the rib cage. No one had ever attacked Morrison to the body consistently, and these blows, solid but not incapacitating, slowed him to a crawl.

By the eighth round, Griffin was also exhausted, barely able to move in the ring, and seemingly on the verge of collapse. He leaned on the ropes to remain upright but worked as hard as his cumbersome limbs would allow him. The infighting was sluggish but steady, and the two men mauled, clinched, and chopped at each other until the final bell.

"He had some good shots," Morrison would say after scoring a unanimous-decision win. "I wobbled around a little bit, but it wasn't because I was hurt. I was losing my balance because of fatigue." So arduous had the fight been for Griffin that he had to be carried back to his dressing room. In less than a month, however, he would be back in the ring, this time in Jasper, Tennessee, where he would score one of his last victories, a quick knockout of a fighter with an 0-7-1 record.

"I never got a second wind," Morrison said. "You just reach a point where you don't feel it anymore." What Morrison summarized with these words was not just an undistinguished win over another long shot, but, in fact, his career going forward. He had been hit—often and hard—by handpicked opponents from the back of the beyond, he seemed sluggish in each of his comeback fights, his lack of stamina was what you would expect from a white-collar boxer belaboring a heavy bag. If Morrison were to make a final push for an oversize paycheck, it would have to be soon. His peak was in the rearview mirror.

★ ★ ★

Less than three months after announcing that he was leaving Kansas City over "negative influences," Morrison was back on the police blotter, this time with nearly comic overtones. On June 19, Morrison was arrested on charges of non-aggravated assault stemming from a scrap that took place outside police headquarters. Morrison was at the station to post bond for a friend who had been arrested for an altercation when he ran into someone posting bond for the other half of that same altercation. "They got in a little argument, and Morrison punched the guy square in the face," said police spokesman Jim Dickerson. "The man who got hit fell down the stairs and twisted his ankle."

It was a Sunday morning, 4 a.m., and the incident that drew Morrison to police headquarters had taken place in Westport, where the bright lights of even a small-scale entertainment district had bewitched him so often in the past. "Tommy is very upset about this, strictly the fact that he shouldn't let this happen," Tony Holden told the Associated Press. "He has to learn when there is any trouble to get up and run the other direction. You can't babysit Tommy. There comes a point where Tommy has to take care of himself."

Morrison would never reach that point.

★ ★ ★

In keeping with their sly matchmaking scheme, Team Morrison chose a former football player for its next patsy. At 8-8, not only was Ross Puritty a .500 fighter (whose record was falsely listed by ESPN as 11-8 on its broadcast), but he was also a late substitute for another trial horse named William Morris. Top Rank matchmaker Ron Katz explained the last-minute switcheroo to the *Philadelphia Inquirer*. "Between the time I talked to Morrison's people and the time I presented the contract to Morris, the Morrison camp changed its mind. Morrison didn't feel he had enough time to prepare for someone like Morris." When he was scratched from a meeting with "The Duke," William Morris, five feet, eleven inches and usually around 219 pounds, boasted a ledger of twelve wins and ten losses.

Once a hulking defensive lineman for the University of Texas at El Paso, Puritty would challenge Morrison without the benefit of a single amateur fight. "I had a herniated disc in my back, and I needed to lose weight," he told the *El Paso Times*. "I used boxing to help me lose weight. I was training and sparring, and I took a fight on a whim." For two or three hundred dollars, Puritty turned pro and embarked on a painful learning process. He had already been stopped twice and was coming off of a unanimous decision loss to Kirk Johnson. He had never had a fight scheduled for more than six rounds. In the future, Puritty would become a fair journeyman, most famous for handing Wladimir Klitschko his first professional loss, in 1998.

Before the fight, which would lead to a match against WBO titleholder Herbie Hide, Morrison insisted, yet again, that his newfound Zen outlook, emphasizing God, fatherhood, and tranquility, would be a critical factor in his forthcoming victory over Puritty. "I've learned my lesson," he said. "I'm not partying anymore. I've gotten away from the people that got me in trouble. I have a new attitude." This, after having been arrested and charged with non-aggravated assault only a few weeks earlier. He also maintained that his focus on training had never been better. Once more, he referred to his calamity against Bentt. "I trained hard, but there was certainly a problem with my attitude," he told the *Philadelphia Inquirer*. "I was going through the motions in the gym. The priority was to get out of the gym as soon as possible and find out where the girls were. I paid the price against Michael Bentt."

On this low-rent ESPN card aired from the Convention Center in Atlantic City, Morrison shared top billing with his old tormentor, "Merciless" Ray Mercer, making a comeback of his own after being found not guilty of trying to bribe an opponent, Jesse Ferguson, during a 1993 decision loss. Mercer had spent most of the previous year under a legal black cloud or in court, where his unusual trial sparked headlines about the perpetual corruption of boxing.

Still, a crowd of nearly 3,000 attended, even if they spent most of the night booing. After Mercer and Marion Wilson fought to a disputed draw, Morrison followed Puritty into the ring for his fourth buildup fight in less than six months. It proved to be far more taxing than anyone had expected.

Plodding, cumbersome, and underprepared, Puritty nearly stopped Morrison in the sixth round, when he landed a series of clubbing blows punctuated by a final digging uppercut that left Morrison on the canvas. While Morrison had always been susceptible to right hands, his inability to defend uppercuts was almost comical. He beat the count and spent the rest of the round alternating between clutching and reeling as Puritty tried to land the finishing blow. But Puritty ran out of steam halfway through his assault and was merely pushing his punches by the time the bell rang to end the round. "After he got up, he was throwing one punch to my four," Puritty told the *Asbury Park Press*. "In the sixth, I thought I put him away. But he got up better than he has in the past, and I got a little careless."

For the next few rounds, the crowd was more active than the fighters. Boos filled the hall as Morrison and Puritty grappled. As ineffective as he was on this night, Morrison still worked the body well and landed the occasional hook, but his punch rate was stingy, and he found himself, as usual, exhausted going into the last rounds.

Puritty was surprisingly accurate with his jab but lacked the coordination to land clean combinations—until the tenth. Thirty seconds into the final round, Puritty opened up for the first time since the sixth and landed another right uppercut that dropped Morrison to his knees. Both men were spent, and Puritty, who had never gone more than six rounds in his career, who had taken the fight on short notice (ten days), who did not even have a winning record, was too weary to follow up. Morrison stumbled to the bell, his nose bleeding, a small bruise under his right eye. The official decision—a split draw—left the crowd perturbed, and they voiced their disgust with jeers.

After the fight was over, Morrison came up with an absurd reason for his struggles against an 8-8 fighter: He had injured his knee, he claimed, after a mishap in a dunking tank a month earlier, when he had been part of a charity event in Jay. Before he could get settled in the chair, a little girl had hit the target and sent him plunging awkwardly. "I hate to be the guy who makes excuses," he said, "but my mobility wasn't good enough to do what I wanted to do." Morrison had always been imaginative—he was the primary source for many of the bizarre stories surrounding him—but this tale was a doozy. In a few years, it would pale, of course, in comparison to the elaborate fictions and denials he would scatter hither and thither like some Johnny Appleseed of whoppers, but for the moment, the dunk-tank story was classic.

Because Morrison was already contractually locked into a title challenge against Herbie Hide in October, it seemed unlikely that he would risk a loss by entering the ring hobbled. Blowing another significant payday—as he had with Lennox Lewis—seemed inconceivable, even for Morrison. Despite his poor showing against Puritty, despite the pitiful quality of opposition he had been facing, Morrison was about to fight for the WBO title once again.

Next stop: Hong Kong. Maybe.

★ ★ ★

The crooked backroads Morrison had taken to the top (along with the occasional side trip on the interstates leading to Las Vegas or Atlantic City) had generated one strange pit stop after another, but his first international journey would surpass all of his previous prairie jaunts in one painful respect: He would not see a paycheck for his exertions.

His challenge of undefeated Herbie Hide for the spurious WBO championship, scheduled for October 22, would take place overseas. Although Top Rank was billed as the lead promoter, the driving force behind the entire disastrous event would be John Daly, the embattled head of the Hemdale Film Corporation. As a thorny producer with an eye for quality, Daly had won Oscars for *Platoon* and *The Last Emperor*, but he had also gained a small measure of notoriety in boxing (driven by his ceaseless rodomontade) for partially financing "The Rumble in the Jungle," one of the most chaotic headline promotions in history.

By the early 1990s, Hemdale had abandoned prestige cinema in favor of VHS distribution and shifty business practices that left the company perpetually dodging lawsuits from Los Angeles to London. (One producer, Tom Fox, who worked with Daly on a horror film, *Return of the Living Dead*, said this about the man who had been sued by, among others, Arnold Schwarzenegger and Gene Hackman: "If Daly was murdered, there would be 7,000 suspects.") This fact might explain why Daly, from seemingly out of nowhere, would try adding prizefight promotion to a gradually disintegrating portfolio. (Hemdale would eventually file for bankruptcy in 1995.) Twenty years after Ali–Foreman, Daly, whose father had been a journeyman pug in the 1920s, returned to boxing with a debacle that stunned even the stoic, phlegmatic, lethargic fight crowd. For his comeback, Daly chose the quixotic location of Hong Kong as his staging ground. Not only was Hong Kong generally indifferent to boxing, but this card would take place barely a year after Bob Arum had produced an appalling flop in Beijing, one that sparked litigation and accusations from nearly everyone involved and marked Asia as terra incognita for professional fisticuffs. That fiasco, which featured Mike Weaver–Bert Cooper as its nominal main event, should have been a warning to Daly, but Hollywood, like boxing, specializes in mulish personalities. Somehow Daly drew Arum and Barry Hearn (head of Matchroom in the United Kingdom and promoter of Hide) into this doomed affair with little more than a silver tongue known to occasionally fork. Kevin Mitchell, of *The Observer*, described, with some surprise, how cutthroat boxing big wheels momentarily forgot professional standards and wound up gullibly following Daly into the abyss: "Daly played a carrot-and-stick game with all of them in attracting them to Hong Kong . . . but failed to provide a letter of credit. Such a situation is unprecedented in modern times for a promotion at this scale."

Given the hokey title of "High Noon in Hong Kong," the card featured Frank Bruno facing Ray Mercer, Steve Collins defending his middleweight title against Lonnie Bradley, and Rafael Ruelas hoping to turn back Billy Schwer in a WBC lightweight fight. Top billing belonged to Hide and Morrison. When the fight was announced, Bob Arum explained, with the usual cockeyed boxing reasoning, the significance of the title. "The American fighters have always believed they are better than the British boxers; now they have a chance to prove it. Hong Kong is an exciting city that is the perfect location for this card because of the political and economic rivalry that exists between America and Britain."

In the lead-up to fight night, Daly riled everyone with his Tinseltown bullying, in the process proving that, despite his boasts over the years, he was only a bit player in The Rumble in the Jungle. If boxing habitués tolerated him (with a bloodshot eye on profit margins, naturally), the straight world—beyond Hollywood and certainly beyond the fight game—had little reason to indulge a power-mad film executive. Sky Sports, which had been set to air "High Noon in Hong Kong" in England, pulled the plug on it less than a month before the opening bell, stripping the promotion of revenue it could not afford to lose. With contractual deadlines looming, Daly now began a mad scramble for cash behind the scenes.

For his latest crack at the big time, Morrison left Oklahoma two weeks before the fight to fend off jet lag and acclimatize to the time change. It had been almost a year since Morrison had been smeared by Michael Bentt in Tulsa. He had been rebuilt via shortcut—one setup fight after another, mainly in the hinterlands—but his marquee value made his presence in Hong Kong essential, since the card was slated for pay-per-view in America. And if there was one thing Morrison could do without fear of flubbing or fumbling, it was sell pay-per-view units.

"I don't look at this fight as a must-win situation," Morrison told the *Philadelphia Daily News.* "But it is a golden opportunity. It's been a long climb, painful at times, but after I beat Hide, I will be right back where I was. That's a promise."

But was it a promise Morrison could keep? Although Hide was unknown to most U.S. fight fans, he had defeated the man who, a year earlier, had left Morrison with cartoon stars encircling his head. In his first title defense, Michael Bentt had been dropped twice and stopped by Hide in the seventh round. After the fight, whose ugly buildup included a melee at a press conference, Bentt slipped into a coma that lasted nearly four days. He retired without ever fighting again.

A relatively small big man who would eventually drop down to cruiserweight, Hide was a pesky boxer with fast hands and a clumsiness that offset his flashy style. He threw slapping punches, suffered from poor balance, held his jaw in the air, and had a tendency to clutch and clinch his opponents whenever they drew near. In time, his chin would prove as unreliable as that of Morrison. For now, October 1994, Hide was the latest British heavyweight hope (Lennox Lewis had been shockingly stopped by Oliver McCall a month earlier) to win an alphabet soup title after nearly a century of futility among heavyweights hailing from the Empire.

But Hide seemed far brasher than most British fighters of his era. In a 1995 interview with the *New York Times,* Hide recalled, with a certain amount of cockiness, his rambunctious beginnings. "I went away to boarding school; I must have been 10," he said. "I was getting into a bit of trouble as a kid, and my parents wanted to get me away from that. At the first boarding school, I was the only black kid. At the second one I went to, I was one of maybe four black kids. See, I was a big guy, and I could fight, so no one dared me. I'd throw punches, kick, everything. I'd be 11 or 12, and 15- or 16-year-old kids would be scared of me. I've always known I was going to the top because that was how I always looked at myself."

Against Hide, Morrison would have been facing an approach he had rarely seen before: a quicksilver mover who worked behind a flicking jab, darted in and out, and who threw combinations instead of the single, looping punches so common to heavyweights. The closest Morrison had come to such a fighter was Yuri Vaulin, who had given him fits in Atlantic City in 1991. Eventually, Morrison rallied to stop Vaulin, but he looked shaky from bell to bell. In more than forty professional starts, the overwhelming majority of Morrison opponents had been listless plodders in various stages of decay. As the matchup in Hong Kong approached, Hide was the slight favorite with oddsmakers, who undoubtedly had noted that the edge in recent form belonged entirely to the man who called himself "The Dancing Destroyer." In fact, Morrison had looked rotten in his post-Bentt fights, despite facing opposition selected with the sole purpose of making him look like a one-man gang.

Still, other than Bentt, Hide had, like Morrison, defeated a slew of trial horses and journeymen. There was a good chance Morrison would get stopped by Hide, whose flurries would overtax his limited defense; but there was also a good chance that Morrison would maul the smaller man in the trenches and connect flush with his shattering left hook, leaving Hide stretched on the canvas. "This is a very important fight for me," Morrison told the *South China Morning Post*. "I always fight at a good level when I know my opponents are good."

Ultimately, Morrison would never find out if Hide was as talented as his undefeated record suggested. On the night of the weigh-in, at the ballroom of the Regal Hotel, Barry Hearn officially cannonballed the entire card by withdrawing his clients Hide and Steve Collins. "There was a lot of hot air, a lot of good promises, a lot of warm words," Hearn declaimed, "but they don't pay the bills, and I'm not in Hong Kong for my health. We came here to see the fighters get paid."

Daly, who had failed to convince a bank to lend him the remaining balance to meet a contractual deadline, seemed shell-shocked. So did veteran manager Mickey Duff, who had two clients on the card (Frank Bruno and Billy Schwer). "I've never seen anything like it in forty years in boxing," Duff said. Then he began shouting at Arum. "You are in breach of contract! There are no grounds for postponing the fights. It is totally without reason. If you would let the fights go ahead, I guarantee the fighters would be paid." Both Duff and Daly assumed that the card would be an economic disaster for the producers and that the fighters would emerge from the fallout with their paychecks. Traditionally, a flop was a risk all promoters took, until the 1990s, when they had gotten so used to having events subsidized by casinos and television networks that the very notion of a financial setback was now anathema to them en masse. Now operating in the era of corporate underwriting, Hearn and Arum were unwilling to face what had once been a common hazard of their profession.

"It is terrible, disgusting, and shocking," Frank Bruno said. "The boxers were not consulted at all. When the announcement was made, we were left standing there like eight cabbages."

From the beginning, "Hong Kong in High Noon" augured disaster: There was an organizer who had dabbled only once in boxing, twenty years earlier; there was a host country without an affinity for prizefighting—fewer than 3,000 tickets had been sold to the 40,000-seat Hong Kong Arena before the show was canceled; British television rights had been lost; and the promoter of record, Bob Arum, had already produced a bomb on mainland China a year earlier.

For Morrison, "High Noon in High Kong" was just another outlandish situation in a career and life full of them. Later, he would openly rue the lost opportunity to fight Hide: "I would have killed Herbie Hide," he said.

A month after the card had been canceled, Morrison was no closer to challenging for the WBO title, despite Bob Arum having claimed that he would negotiate to stage the "postponed" bouts within sixty days. In fact, the only fight from "High Noon" that ever took place was Rafael Ruelas–Billy Schwer. Ruelas was the only fighter with a long-term contract binding him to Top Rank Promotions.

"I've heard rumours about Hide looking elsewhere for an opponent," Tony Holden told the *South China Morning Post*. "Obviously, that's his privilege. We don't have a problem with who he fights next. But we still have a valid contract with Top Rank. The Tommy Morrison camp have lost faith in Bob Arum and Top Rank. I don't see them as being serious about this. They're talking about staging the fight in February, but Tommy has already given up six months for this fight—should he give up another four? If the Hide fight never happens, we will be looking for payment plus damages for the time Tommy wasted getting ready for the fight. Since George Foreman won the world title, our phone has been ringing off the hook, and everybody wants to fight us."

The phone may have been ringing off the hook, but when Holden answered, it would just be another stumblebum on the other end of the line, looking for a modest payday in the Metro.

★ ★ ★

They must have known that Morrison was damaged goods. They must have known that even journeymen such as Ross Puritty and Sherman Griffin were too dangerous for him at this stage of his career. So they downgraded. The bodies who answered the bell against Morrison after the "High Noon in Hong Kong" washout suggested the days when odds-makers refused to post lines on fights involving "The Duke." From February 7, 1995, to May 1, 1995, Morrison annihilated three setups in a total of eleven rounds. These mismatches—including one against a journeyman that inspired the headline "Morrison KOs 7-foot psychology student"—were hot tickets in Oklahoma City, Muskogee, and Tulsa. While Morrison went through the motions in the ring, his team searched for a suitable springboard back into the title picture.

★ ★ ★

It would take place on an independently produced pay-per-view titled "Raw Power" and broadcast from the Municipal Auditorium in downtown Kansas City, Missouri, on June 10, 1995. Giving the event a circus atmosphere—seemingly a prerequisite for a Morrison affair—was the undercard, which featured a pudgy Roberto Duran (one week shy of his forty-fourth birthday) in a ten-rounder, and NFL running back Alonzo Highsmith in a preliminary. The main event, however, promised not just violence but a certain amount of intrigue as well.

From the very beginning, it seemed, Donovan "Razor" Ruddock and boxing were an explosive mix. Before he was ever a contender, before anyone in America had heard of him, Ruddock had already earned a reputation as a malcontent. Ex-heavyweight iron horse George Chuvalo, one of his early managers, found himself suing Ruddock in the late '80s. "The kid got too big in the head," Chuvalo told the *Ottawa Citizen* in 1989. "I got him a fight with Mike Weaver, he beats Weaver, who's a former world champ, and then he won't listen. He starts listening to his brother, who knows nothing, and his brother says, 'Razor, you don't need George; George can't get you what you want,' and then the big boys move in, and the kid's gone. I wish him well, he's got talent, but he's a pain in the ass."

In the span of a few short years, when he was a hot property, Ruddock would face an avalanche of lawsuits from trainers, managers, promoters, and paramours. It was enough to leave his head rattling like a speed bag. "There is no manual that tells you how to run your life, who to trust and who not to trust," Ruddock said. "I had to learn the hard way. I made some serious mistakes. My education was very expensive."

For a time in the late 1980s and early 1990s, however, Ruddock was considered a legitimate threat to his heavyweight peers. His destructive left hook, which sometimes resembled a modified uppercut and which he nicknamed "The Smash," and his surly demeanor gave him a mystique that separated him from so many late-stage "Lost Generation" heavyweights still plodding around rings in North America. At that time, it was Mike Tyson dominating listless retreads who had made their bones during the Reagan Revolution, what seemed like another lifetime: Larry Holmes, Carl Williams, Frank Bruno, and so on. When Tyson withdrew from a title defense against Ruddock scheduled for November 1989 in Edmonton, "Razor" saw his reputation skyrocket—via walkover.

Like Morrison, Ruddock had been a fresh new face with a pulverizing left, and, also like Morrison, there was some question as to whether he had the potential to be a world-class heavyweight. A former tennis player from Toronto, not exactly a boxing hotbed, Ruddock was physically imposing—six feet, three inches and 228 pounds—but his origins and buildup hardly diverged from Morrison's. Both men were solid athletes in another sport, both men came from provincial backgrounds when it came to boxing, both men had Mallomar chins, and both men led tumultuous lives outside the ring. They both also feasted on woebegone opponents during their careers.

Along the way to a top rating and, ultimately, riches (by fighting Tyson twice), Ruddock had defeated faded relics such as Mike Weaver, James Broad, and James "Bonecrusher" Smith, but his notoriety stemmed from his frightening KO of Michael "Dynamite" Dokes in 1990. In that fight, which took place in Madison Square Garden, Ruddock showed a nasty edge and a willingness to rumble in the trenches against a weatherworn but still dangerous Dokes, who had reigned as WBA heavyweight champion for less than a year in the early '80s. In the fourth round, Ruddock drove a groggy Dokes into a neutral corner with a series of shuddering blows before unleashing his dreaded "Smash" one last time, leaving Dokes flat on his face, unconscious, while physicians and cornermen crashed the ring like battlefield medics to aid him. It was the kind of chilling ending that would be seen in highlight reels on newscasts across the country, and that would mark Ruddock as a dangerous man in a dangerous sport.

In his heyday, Ruddock was a feared puncher who had staggered Mike Tyson in their first fight before being stopped and then willed his way to the final bell in the bruising rematch three months later. In one of the many disquieting paradoxes of boxing, where a solid performance in a slugfest can produce unintended consequences even for the winner, these highlights ultimately laid Ruddock low. The amount of punishment Ruddock suffered against Tyson over nearly nineteen rounds had a seemingly deleterious effect on him. Although he won his next two starts, Ruddock no longer looked like the same fighter. Then, in October 1992, came Lennox Lewis, whom Ruddock had defeated in the amateurs when they were both gangly teens fighting out of Ontario. Under professional auspices, however, Ruddock could not survive past the second round against the inexperienced Lewis, who dropped him three times en route to an effortless TKO in London. After that humiliating loss, Ruddock more or less vanished from the scene. "I never got tired of the boxing game," Ruddock said. "I just got tired of the people involved in the boxing game."

For Team Morrison, looking to detour back into the mix, Razor Ruddock was the perfect opponent. He still had name value from his battles with Tyson a few years earlier, and he was also long past his prime. Inactivity, promotional squabbles, legal hassles, and a lack of motivation ensured that Ruddock would be at just the right competitive disadvantage. His ties to the unscrupulous Don King and the unsavory Murad Muhammad (whom King once called "the stupidest man in boxing") left Ruddock entangled in a welter of legal wrangles so often, it came as no surprise that he spent more time in courtrooms than in gyms. Since his annihilation at the hands of Lewis, Ruddock had fought only once, in January 1994, a lackluster decision over an obese club fighter named Anthony Wade.

To make matters worse, Ruddock declared bankruptcy less than four months before his scheduled fight with Morrison. Just a few years after amassing nearly $10 million in purses, Ruddock was broke. Accepting a risky match against a crushing puncher such as Morrison after years of inactivity and turmoil reeked of desperation. Even Morrison understood the role Ruddock was meant to play. "I question his conditioning, and I question his motivation," Morrison told the *Miami Herald*. "If he took that much time off and was doing the right thing, it might not be hard for him to come back. I'm just not sure he has been doing the right thing."

Incredibly, only a few days before the fight, Ruddock was in a new legal dustup with Muhammad, whom Ruddock accused of forging contracts. Ruddock sued to void his promotional agreement with Muhammad, but U.S. District Court (New Jersey) Judge Alfred Wolin ruled against him. It was just another distraction for a fighter who could not possibly focus on the hazardous task at hand. A loss to Morrison would dash whatever hopes—real or half-imagined—Ruddock had of reestablishing himself in a sport that had passed him by when he was still in his twenties. But the air of distress that surrounded him practically guaranteed that he would fulfill the purpose for which he had been lured to Kansas City. "The only reason I would think about retiring," he said after the Morrison fight, "is because of the people who surround boxing. You can't train and fight outside of the ring twice as much as in the ring. By the time you're in the ring, you're mentally drained. The last two weeks were pure hell." Boxing had left Ruddock snakebitten for years, and now, perhaps, the effect of its venom would reveal itself under the hot lights. Although he was soft-spoken during the promotion, he was open about his bitterness. "I needed a break from boxing," Ruddock said. "I had too many people . . . too much baggage weighing me down. Everybody wanted a piece of me. I found myself boxing for everybody but myself. That wasn't right. The people around me were only out for themselves. For me, experience is a great teacher. I won't make the same mistakes twice."

In mid-1995, Mike Tyson walked out of the Indiana Youth Center after serving more than three and a half years for rape. His impending return to the ring galvanized heavyweights from London to Los Angeles, who understood that Tyson, the most controversial athlete of the last thirty-five years, would generate oversized purses that only a handful of fighters had earned since his absence from the scene. Like most big men, Morrison was open about his desire to face Tyson, and he now revised his career blueprint, with "Iron Mike" as its centerpiece. Tony Holden began tub-thumping within days of the Ruddock fight. "Tommy Morrison and

Mike Tyson would break pay-per-view records. How long will people shell out $49.95 to see Tyson fight people like Peter McNeeley? At some point, Tyson's got to step up to the plate."

As usual, Morrison offered the routine palaver of having changed his wanton ways to newspaper reporters. "There was a time where I went through a little bit of a metamorphosis where I wasn't the most dedicated athlete in the world," Morrison said. "But this is my last go-round, so to speak, and I'm looking forward to going out in good fashion." For once, at least, there were none of the open rumors about night crawling that had presaged so many of his other fights. "He just hasn't been able to bring himself into good condition," Bill Cayton said to the Associated Press. "He seems to be much more professional now. He has to be in shape to go twelve rounds."

No one, not even the principals, thought that "Raw Power" would go that far, if not for the combined KO percentage of both men, then because of the glaring flaw they had in common: an inability to take a solid punch to the jaw. A knockout was virtually guaranteed. "This is Tommy's hometown and his people are here," Ruddock said. "He'll be wanting to prove he has a lot of courage. I don't think he'll be moving. He'll come to fight. I'll come to fight."

For his part, Morrison predicted a slightly more strategic match. "I'm going to have to outsmart him," Morrison told the St. Louis Post-Dispatch. "This will be the toughest fight I've ever had. He is, and pretty much has been, a counterpuncher, a guy who never has been very effective going forward. I'm sure he's going to expect me to come right in after him. Which I'm sure I will do. But we'll try to throw the big reversal at him. Let him try and come at me and then try to counterpunch him. And when I do come forward, come hard and explode with bad intentions."

A raucous crowd of roughly 6,500 packed Municipal Auditorium to see if Morrison could enter his name in the Mike Tyson sweepstakes. The ring walks were pure overkill, featuring a colossal mirror ball, a flashing-light show, and a fireworks display that might have made the Grucci Brothers wince. When Morrison entered the ring, he looked like a different man, far older than twenty-six, despite the cropped leather jacket he wore (with the initials TCB embroidered on its back, a direct nod to his hero Elvis Presley). His hair was thinning, the mullet was gone, a goatee had been added (as if in compensation), the dye job was fading, his nose seemed rearranged by the rigors of his profession, and he had lost some of the definition that steroids had given him. But, at 228 pounds, he appeared reasonably fit.

The same could not be said for Ruddock, who disrobed to reveal a physique that seemingly betrayed his stated ambitions. He weighed 243 ¾ pounds, the heaviest of his career, and nearly fifteen pounds more than when he faced Tyson for the first time, in 1991. If Ruddock was looking for a fresh start, he underscored it with a new appearance, one that might have sent mixed signals about his readiness. By shaving his neat mustache and sporting a bald look—to go along with his flabby physique—Ruddock seemed more than just grizzled. Even so, when the opening bell rang, Ruddock pressured Morrison from the opening bell, eager to test what was known as one of the shakiest chins in the heavyweight division. No longer the spry boxer with nimble legs developed on tennis courts, Ruddock was now a man who relied solely on his paralyzing left, which he threw with maximum force as often as possible. There was a time when Ruddock mixed his hook with movement, feints, jabs, and the occasional right cross, but those days were already gone by the time he clashed against Mike Tyson. That Ruddock was uncoachable was clear from the number of trainers with whom he had fallen out over the years—Chuvalo, Art Miles, Howie Albert, Janks Morton, Floyd Patterson—so it was something of a surprise when he dropped Morrison in the opening round with a right uppercut.

Given that Morrison was on the lookout for a left, the right hand was completely unexpected. In close, Morrison had leaned forward, prepared to work the body or to fall into a harmless clinch, when Ruddock suddenly lashed out with an uppercut that left Morrison stunned, on his knees. Less than a minute into the fight, Morrison was already in straits. Was this a repeat of what had happened against Michael Bentt in 1993? Did the doubts about his belonging in the limelight—which had plagued him since turning pro—swirl as the referee tolled the mandatory eight?

As in his performance against Foreman—another clubbing puncher—Morrison employed a footloose style against Ruddock, flitting from side to side, flicking out a pesky jab, and consciously moving his head to make himself a hard target. It was this strategy that allowed him to recover his equilibrium and avoid a cautious Ruddock for the remainder of the round. At one point, he even wobbled Ruddock with a sharp uppercut of his own.

In the second round, Morrison returned the violent favor he had received in the first. Morrison showed his explosive hand speed and imaginative combinations when he landed a wide left-right to the body before exploding with a right uppercut that buckled Ruddock and sent him reeling around the ring, forcing referee Ron Lipton to issue a standing eight count. Because Ruddock had grabbed hold of the top rope to remain upright, Lipton ruled it a knockdown. Ruddock survived until the bell, but he now realized he was just as vulnerable to a knockout blow as Morrison was.

For the next two rounds, Ruddock and Morrison remained vertical despite trading leather throughout. To keep from being hit by a left hook, Morrison moved clockwise exclusively, but when Ruddock began landing his jab regularly, it seemed as if the fight would swing his way. But Ruddock was the personification of an in-and-outer, and his technical flaws were invariably exacerbated by mental lapses that often cost him terribly in the ring. Over the last fifteen seconds of the fourth, Morrison rallied with an extended flurry, and Ruddock reacted with a war cry, mouth wide open like Muhammad Ali after he had shocked Sonny Liston in 1964.

Then came the fifth, traditionally the point when Morrison would begin to decelerate. With the fight close on the cards, Ruddock began to reach Morrison with lead left hooks and even the occasional clubbing right. Once again, Morrison found himself flagging after only a handful of rounds. In the past, his conditioning had consistently been undermined by partying, by women, by 38 Special concerts, and now, despite his claims of having settled down, here he was, seemingly drained and on the way to another violent KO loss. As Ruddock chased him around the ring, Morrison looked both spent and discouraged. The bell rang to end the round, and Morrison, with a small cut above his left eye and a welt beneath it, wobbled back to his corner.

Ruddock took command early in the sixth, bombarding a retreating Morrison with lefts and rights. When Morrison visibly stumbled after taking a sweeping left, Ruddock charged him like a linebacker aiming at a tackling dummy, his eyes wide in anticipation. With Morrison reeling, Ruddock threw a wild right uppercut that not only missed but left him defensively vulnerable. In a split second, Morrison spotted the open target, set his feet, and launched the left hook that he had been honing since he was six or seven years old in Gravette, Arkansas. It landed point-blank.

If a shillelagh had struck him, Ruddock could not have plummeted any faster. When his skull hit the canvas, the secondary impact, with its whiplash effect, seemed to jar him back into consciousness. Flat on his back, arms outstretched, Ruddock raised his head and looked, cross-eyed, at Lipton, before shakily rising to his feet at the count of five. It was a remarkable show of resiliency, but Ruddock still had nearly a minute and a half to survive before the bell would offer a brief reprieve. With the crowd in an uproar, Morrison charged, windmilling both hands, in hopes of forcing a stoppage. What he got instead was another standing eight count, the second tallied against Ruddock during the fight.

When the action resumed, Morrison continued whipsawing his hands while Ruddock kept his guard high to block one flurry after another. But with less than ten seconds left in the round, Morrison pinned Ruddock against the ropes and crashed home a left that shook Ruddock anew. That was when referee Ron Lipton jumped in to halt the fight.

A weary but jubilant Morrison threw his arms up in victory and staggered to a corner, where his team mobbed him en masse. They all knew what Morrison knew: that there were still a few tomorrows left, in a sport where nothing is promised.

After the fight, Ruddock protested bitterly about the stoppage, maintaining that he was clearheaded throughout the bombardment and simply letting Morrison punch himself into exhaustion. Had there been a seventh round, the possibility that Morrison would have collapsed from fatigue was probably even money ("I was hoping to hell there wouldn't be another round," Morrison said in a post-fight interview), but there was no guarantee that Ruddock could have recovered from the beating he had taken before Lipton intervened.

Lipton, besieged by critics, explained his viewpoint to sportswriter Bill Haisten. "After the knockdown, Tommy comes back in, and Razor doesn't respond, and I gave him the standing eight," Lipton said. "I could still see the trembling in his body that was a result of the knockdown. When the final stoppage came, Ruddock had his back to the ropes and wasn't throwing a punch. Tommy hits him, snaps his head back, and I'm going to let Razor continue? No way. He's a good man. I didn't want to see him get hurt."

What hurt Ruddock most, perhaps, was the sudden obliteration of his future as a prizefighter. His hopes of returning to the spotlight were gone. Instead, it was Morrison who would advance to more opportunities.

Whether Morrison could take advantage of them was another question altogether. Since losing to Michael Bentt, he had looked listless in going the distance with Sherman Griffin, he had been dropped twice en route to a draw against Ross Puritty, and he had barely survived a crossroads shootout against a fighter—Ruddock—who was on his last legs. Whatever awaited Morrison, it would have to come soon; time was running out on him, in more ways than one.

★ ★ ★

Before his next move, however, Morrison underwent surgery to repair nagging, lingering tendinitis. "I had arthroscopic surgery done on my clavicle," he told *The Ring*. "There were two pieces of bone that came together, and there was no padding between them. I'm sure it had something to do with the football and boxing I've done over the years. It was always inflamed and sore, and there was a lot of pain. That's why a lot of people regarded me as a one-armed fighter. I always had a good right hand, it was just so painful to throw, subconsciously, I chose not to throw it a lot."

A surgically repaired Morrison was now ready for his next step. Reaction to the Ruddock destruction was precisely what Team Morrison had hoped it would be. Not only had Morrison scored a spectacular knockout, but he also proved that his drawing power was no fleeting thing. This pay-per-view, promoted by Tony Holden, reportedly sold 150,000 units, a solid figure for an independent production, and one that far outstripped some of the HBO/Top Rank TVKO events of the past, such as James Toney–Michael Nunn or any card featuring Jorge Páez or Tony Lopez.

Bob Arum gave Tom Wheatley of the *St. Louis Post-Dispatch* a solid example of the numbers Morrison could produce. "Every time Tommy fights on ESPN, the ratings double," Arum said. "Top Rank averages a 1.8 rating. When Tommy fights, the average is 3.4. This says something about Tommy's appeal."

The loss to Mercer, the Bentt debacle, the struggle against Ross Puritty, the frequent arrests—they could not crush the grassroots allure of "The Duke." He may not have been an elite heavyweight (in fact, he was unrated by the traditionally accommodating sanctioning bodies before the Ruddock fight), but his connection to his Midwestern devotees was seemingly unbreakable. That demographic, the blue-collar American heartland, more interested in football, rodeo, NASCAR, perhaps, would follow Morrison as far as he would go.

★ ★ ★

On July 12, Morrison was on a plane heading to New York City, where he and Tony Holden were expecting to attend a press conference to announce an October date against Riddick Bowe in Madison Square Garden. Once again, the target for Morrison was the WBO championship, the only title free from bewildering political turmoil unique to boxing in the early to mid-1990s, when the heavyweight title could still generate both commotion and cash. With Mike Tyson back on the scene—and only a month away from returning to the ring against the obnoxiously inept Peter McNeeley—the WBC and WBA titles were both conveniently under the control of Don King clients and earmarked for the fighter formerly known as "The Baddest Man on the Planet." As for the IBF championship, it was paralyzed in litigation and contractual boondoggles involving a handful of fighters off in a hermetic parallel universe of their own (George Foreman, Axel Schulz, Michael Moorer).

No one took the WBO title seriously, but Bowe (who had burned so many bridges during his brief reign as undisputed champion from 1992 to 1993 that he might have been taken for a pyromaniac) was forced by reduced circumstances to fight for the redheaded stepchild of sanctioning bodies. He won the WBO title on March 11, annihilating Herbie Hide in six rounds, scoring multiple knockdowns before Hide was finally counted out. (Hide had slipped out of "High Noon in Hong Kong" to have his jaw exposed in Las Vegas, the city of illusions, by an ex-champion on the comeback trail.) On June 17, Bowe defended his new title in a one-sided thrashing of the nearly talentless Cuban defector Jorge Luis Gonzalez, who absorbed a sustained pummeling until he wound up, semiconscious, flat on his face in the sixth round. Both of these fights took place on HBO, but now Bowe was searching for a pay-per-view bonanza, one that would fatten his bank account as well as catapult him back into the spotlight, which had dimmed considerably since he had lost his title to Evander Holyfield in November 1993.

Bowe had initially hoped to face Holyfield, now an ex-champion himself, in a rubber match, but Holyfield declined a third fight, believing that challenging for the WBO title would put his name on the same blacklist that had kept Bowe on the margins for the last year and a half. That was when Tommy Morrison stepped in. The buzz he had created against Razor Ruddock had made him a player in the corporate power struggle between HBO and Showtime (allied with Don King and Mike Tyson). And while that win merited more asterisks than exclamation points—Ruddock was semiretired, had lost three out of his last six fights by knockout, was at war with his promoter, and had entered the ring looking flabby—it was enough to make Morrison a commodity for the first time in nearly two years.

But instead of a press conference to announce a fight against Bowe, Morrison found himself frozen out. At the eleventh hour, Evander Holyfield had decided that a third fight with Bowe (who had vacated his WBO title to entice Holyfield) was suitable, and when he verbally accepted terms, representatives of TVKO (the pay-per-view subsidiary of HBO) reportedly crashed a meeting between Bowe and Morrison to exercise its contractual rights.

As a consolation prize of sorts, HBO expressed interest in a matchup between Morrison and Lennox Lewis. It was Lewis, of course, who had been the walking, talking $7.5 million jackpot that Morrison had infamously sabotaged in 1993, and now he was back, albeit at a discount rate. "When they offered me Lewis, I said, 'Sure, but only if I got the same money I would have gotten for Bowe,'" Morrison told the *Philadelphia Daily News*. "Those guys all had heart attacks. They said there was no way they could do that. But they ended up doing it, anyway. In fact, I'm getting a little more for this fight."

Further proof of how marketable Morrison was came when he and Holden detoured from New York City and flew down to Florida to meet with Don King, who had under his control the biggest moneymaker in all of sports: Mike Tyson, a few months removed from a prison stint and scheduled to make an obscene $30 million for his first fight in years. A matchup between Tyson and Morrison would have been one of the most profitable fights in boxing history, grossing more than $100 million. King, whose masterful manipulation of the sanctioning bodies had allowed him to annex the WBA and WBC titles with his seemingly endless collection of middling heavyweights, had always drooled over the Great White Hope concept. In 1980, his first "White Hope" foray had been a miscalculation when he staged a racially charged fight between then-heavyweight-champion Larry Holmes and Minnesota truck driver Scott LeDoux. A working journeyman, LeDoux had never been "built up," and his pedestrian record reflected the actual vicissitudes of professional prizefighting. And while a 21-8 ledger was unremarkable, it was also not fabricated. There was nothing illusory about LeDoux, and observers saw his challenge of Holmes as more than just a one-in-a-million proposition: It was a suicide mission. In front of a smaller-than-expected home crowd, LeDoux took a beating en route to losing via TKO, and the promotion failed to turn a profit.

But King hit pay dirt in 1982, when he succeeded in signing "Irish" Gerry Cooney for a title fight against Holmes, in one of the bitterest matchups imaginable. Cooney was the epitome of the Great White Hope, a power-punching brawler from a blue-collar enclave (Huntington, Long Island) who had knocked over a slew of aged veterans and no-hopers, in the process raising delirious hopes that he would defeat Holmes. After a little over four years of scoring knockouts in the tri-state area, Cooney parlayed a manufactured 26-0 record into a $10 million fortune and a blockbuster closed-circuit extravaganza. King made a fortune from Holmes–Cooney, and his eye was now forever peeled in search of the next Great White Hope candidate.

In Tommy Morrison, King saw a fighter who fulfilled more than just race requirements. The veteran promoter recognized all the lucrative angles in a potential Tyson–Morrison matchup: two bad boys constantly flirting with disaster, the sheer power of each fighter, the sour Bill Cayton–Tyson connection, and, yes, the racial overtones. Both men were also, in their own ways, glib enough to trash talk each other into headlines during the promotional buildup.

According to Michael Katz of the New York *Daily News*, King offered Morrison $1 million for a tune-up fight, with the promise of a showdown against Tyson in the future. A cash signing bonus may also have been part of the package. The big payoff, of course, would come against Tyson, where a potential $8 to $10 million windfall awaited Morrison. It was a tempting offer. But the threat of legal action from Time Warner (which, at the time, owned HBO) and Main Events (which promoted Lewis) was enough to keep Morrison from defecting to King.

In retrospect, of course, Morrison would never have been able to keep that date with Tyson. Fate would make sure of that. And Don King? Years later, after Morrison became a wholesale conspiracy theorist, one who also believed he had mastered the arcane power of teleportation, King would be at the center of a particularly lunatic hypothesis.

To face Lewis, on the comeback himself, Morrison would reportedly receive $2.1 million, roughly $750,000 more than he would have gotten against Bowe. "It was a long day, but a good day," Morrison said after news of the Lewis fight broke. "Things are finally going my way."

In a sense, they were. Just a few months earlier, Morrison had been on the cracker-barrel circuit, far from the limelight, even if his bouts were invariably aired by ESPN or the USA Network. Now he would be back in Atlantic City and on HBO, where the biggest payday of his career awaited. In addition, Morrison believed he had benefited from seeing Bowe replaced by Lewis, whom he considered less dangerous. "Lennox is not a guy who likes to mix it up," he told *The Ring*. "He's a pretty boy. He doesn't like to get in there in the trenches. He's made a lot of money. This is not a guy who is going to take a beating. I don't think he has a whole lot of balls. You get him in a corner and start to hurt him, he's going to fold his tent and go home."

It was true that Bowe had faced better competition than Lewis, it was true that Bowe had never been knocked out (as Lewis had), and it was true that Bowe was a far more aggressive fighter than Lewis, but Bowe had also shown a lack of dedication that had ultimately led to a brief— and undistinguished—title reign. Bowe was, after all, a man who had a kitchen built in his bedroom, a sign of both conflicting priorities and bad taste.

A reluctant puncher, Lewis was given to longueurs in the ring, and his overly cautious approach made him a target of the professional critics in America. Across the Atlantic, Lewis fared much better as the "first" Englishman to win the heavyweight title in a hundred years. In December 1992, Bowe, who had just beaten Evander Holyfield for the undisputed championship, tossed the WBC title into a prop trash can at a London press conference after failing to come to terms with Lewis for a mandatory title defense. Within hours of his stunt, the WBC named Lewis its champion, and for the first time since 1987, when Mike Tyson had finally unified the division after years of chaos, the heavyweight title was fragmented. That he was a paper champion hardly mattered to the 25,000-plus who attended National Stadium in Cardiff to see Lewis stop the beloved Frank Bruno in an all-UK championship showdown, which was rarer than a sighting of the transit of Venus. Lewis, who had stopped Bowe in the 1988 Olympics en route to winning a gold medal, went on to make three desultory title defenses against unexceptional opposition before losing via TKO to a middling journeyman named Oliver McCall on September 24, 1994, at Wembley Arena. Overnight, Lewis became just another heavyweight reclamation project. "The loser of this fight has nowhere to go," said his manager, Frank Maloney, about Lewis–Morrison. "He might as well go out on the beach and walk into the sea."

In an effort to revitalize his career, Lewis had fired his trainer—the obnoxious Pepe Correa, whom Lewis referred to as a Muppet—and hired Kronk guru Emanuel Steward. Lewis had beaten a pair of mediocrities in return fights, and now the talented cosmopolitan (he was raised in Canada and was proud of his Jamaican heritage) was ready for a marquee fight. Despite his second-round TKO loss to McCall, Lewis retained an arrogance that might have left many nonplussed. This egotism served Lewis well, it seemed; in a few years, he would establish himself as the best heavyweight of the late 1990s and early 2000s. Morrison was just an afterthought to Lewis, hardly worth his air of hauteur. "I don't see anyone out there who scares me," he told the *Asbury Park Press*. "I look at a boxer like Morrison, and I see someone who will look good on my resume, nothing more."

As expected, the opening odds favored Lewis, who was an all-around professional, in contrast to Morrison, who spent most of his career shuttling between the darkness of low-level boxing in Oklahoma and Missouri and the spotlight of Las Vegas and HBO. On his way to becoming a contender, Lewis had pounded some of the usual suspects (including a few Morrison victims: Dan Murphy and Mike Acey), but he had also stopped undefeated Gary Mason (35-0 at the time) and had won the European, British, and Commonwealth titles before solidifying himself as a contender. (So stage-managed was Morrison that he had never fought for one of the numerous regional championships available to fighters in the early 1990s. His only gewgaws were the WBO strap he had wrested from George Foreman and the absurd IBC heavyweight championship, a title that no longer exists.) Then Lewis obliterated Donovan Ruddock in two rounds, years before Morrison struggled with a war-torn version of "Razor." A handful of title defenses on HBO against journeymen (the moderately talented pros Morrison spent years avoiding) gave Lewis a surfeit of experience.

But it was his teaming with Steward that likely put this fight out of reach for Morrison in a way that might not have been true had they fought in 1993. Under the tutelage of Steward, Lewis was less herky-jerky, more flat-footed, and now worked exclusively behind his powerful jab, without the skittishness he had shown in the past. The thunderous right hand Lewis possessed became even more dangerous combined with a jab that not only set up the cross but was a stinging blow in its own right. Except for the proverbial lucky punch, Morrison seemed outclassed entering the ring against Lewis. Still, that left hook, the one that had sent Razor Ruddock crashing and had bailed him out in fights against Joe Hipp and Carl Williams, was all the equalizer Morrison needed.

★ ★ ★

October 7, 1995. Atlantic City, New Jersey. More than 8,000 spectators gather at the Convention Center to see what promises to be a heavyweight apocalypse. What they witness instead is a tedious dismantling. Lewis enters the ring first, his head poking through a white towel with a hole cut in its center, a homespun poncho that symbolizes his focus and gravitas. But Lewis looks loose and ready in his corner; his team also exudes confidence. The same cannot be said for Tommy Morrison. His ring walk seems funereal, and the strange music that accompanies it (Vangelis, "Conquest of Paradise") underscores the air of gloom surrounding him. Waiting in the crowded ring, Tony Holden looks glum and ashen. Tommy Virgets tries halfheartedly to psych up Morrison and ceases after a second attempt. In his cutoff leather jacket, Morrison seems almost out of place, a man who now wears glasses and claims to study scripture, a man who appears far older than twenty-six, trying to exude an energy he no longer possesses.

When the opening bell rings, the contrast between the two fighters is stark: Lewis is the much bigger man, with a far more fluid style and a ranginess that will be hard to bridge; Morrison is smaller and far less athletic. He lacks the verve to mount a full-scale attack, and that leaves him at a distance where Lewis can hit and not get hit in return. In the second round, Morrison accelerates for the first time in the fight, drives Lewis to the ropes, and takes a counter left that sends him to the canvas.

It is only a flash knockdown—but Morrison ends the round with a small cut at the corner of his right eye. Boos from the restless crowd arise in the third round because of a lack of action. By nature tentative, Lewis chooses his shots carefully, and Morrison, already bleeding and behind on the scorecards, is hesitant to lead. To the frustration of all—especially Morrison—Lewis stays behind his jab and uses his right cross sparingly. But the jab Lewis throws is both thumping and accurate. Now, Morrison begins to bruise, his right eye begins to swell, and his left cheek has a puffiness that resembles the beginnings of anaphylactic shock. With his right eye closing, Morrison is soon to be at a serious disadvantage but rarely does his corner apply an Enswell to his discolored face. By the fifth, Morrison is visually compromised, and paws at his right eye repeatedly. Late in the round, Lewis lands a right to the rib cage and a right uppercut—a combination straight out of the Tommy Morrison manual—that floors Morrison for the second time in the fight. Two more knockdowns in the sixth and referee Mills Lane, seeing a dispirited Morrison peering at him through one bloodshot eye, stops the mismatch.

"He was tough, very tough," Morrison says after the fight. "Trying to fight guys like that with that reach is tough, especially with one eye. I'm not used to fighting with one eye. He's definitely got some of the longest arms, I'll tell you that. After the second round, my eyes started swelling. I faced just about every kind of adversity there is in the ring: broken hands, broken jaws, hurt legs, hurt back, cut eyes. But never a swollen eye. That was an adversity I wasn't used to. When you're fighting with one eye, it makes for a depth perception problem."

This is the third stoppage defeat of his career. It will also be his last. Tommy Morrison has finally reached the end of the road.

★ ★ ★

"How about never? Is never good enough for you?"
—*New Yorker* cartoon

★ ★ ★

There was no shortage of epitaphs for the career of Tommy Morrison after his catastrophic showing against Lewis. The national press, which had long considered him something of a joke, pounced, offering one punch line after another. Local reporters and columnists, who had covered Morrison from the beginning, doubted his ability to bounce back and urged him to retire. "He has gone as far as he can go in the heavyweight ranks, and it just isn't far enough to beat a contender in his prime," wrote Jonathan Rand of the *Tulsa World*. "Lennox Lewis didn't just beat Morrison when he knocked him down for the fourth time and stopped him midway in the sixth round Saturday night, Lewis also exposed him as a semi-skilled worker."

And yet Morrison was only twenty-six, just a few years removed from the legal drinking age, and a physical marvel, even if his impressive traps and wide lats were by-products of the periodic table of elements. At a press conference before facing Lewis, Morrison responded harshly to hearing what Frank Maloney had said about the loser of Lewis–Morrison being finished. "That's bull. In the heavyweight ranks, you're always one punch from redemption. If I lose this fight, people will say I should pack it in; I don't believe it. People are so quick to write you off. I wish I had a dollar for every time that's been said. I'd be a rich man. Uh . . . I am a rich man."

He was also young enough to rationalize his woeful performance against Lewis. This was something Morrison began to do almost immediately, in the ring, during the post-fight interview with Larry Merchant, when he blamed the loss on his swollen eye and a poor strategy. Because egotism is a prerequisite for every successful boxer, doubt, even a hint of doubt, is taboo, but Morrison seemed more than just obstinate about his limited prospects as a fighter; he seemed almost delusional. That Morrison had been humiliated by Lewis was not a factor in his assessment, nor was his poor recent form. All that mattered was what he wanted to believe. In a year or so, he would become a categorical fantasist.

It was not just the beating he took from Lewis that raised flags about Morrison. Since stopping the sadly overmatched Tim Tomashek in August 1993, Morrison had been thrashed by Michael Bentt, struggled to a draw against Ross Puritty, needed a miracle left hook to keep Razor Ruddock from coldcocking him, and resembled a sparring partner against Lewis. He had also taken flush shots from opponents who were little more than setups: semiretirees, ex–bar fighters, and recently paroled felons. Over the span of two years, from October 1993 to October 1995, Morrison had been knocked down ten times, a sign of diminished resiliency.

All fighters reach a peak, a point at which the rigors of training and the punishment received in the ring combine to break them down. For some fighters, particularly aggressive ones such as Morrison, short peaks are the rule; for others, defensive wizards such as Pernell Whitaker or Floyd Mayweather Jr., longevity is feasible if not guaranteed. No sport takes a toll on its athletes the way boxing does. Between training, fighting, and aging, a boxer is in a perpetual state of deterioration. This process, which is inevitable, ultimately presages tragedy. The "shot" fighter, the man whose balance is haywire, the man whose coordination is off, the man whose chin short-circuits with every flush punch that lands on it, is a preview of a potential future with CTE. Little by little, or seemingly overnight, most boxers deteriorate long before they retire. Often their last years in the ring are marked by beatings and losing skids. The purses dwindle, the crowds dwindle, the marquee fights dwindle—everything in the world of the prizefighter is subject to diminution, with blood and pain as a backdrop. Was that the future for Tommy Morrison?

It was clear that Morrison was beyond his best days. His defense, never particularly good, suffered as his reaction time slowed, and this shortcoming exacerbated his fragile chin. The question of his durability, which was once considered suspect, was now settled. A broken jaw, a torn rotator cuff, two surgeries for compartment syndrome, fractured hands—Morrison had been injury-prone to a rare degree for someone who had been a professional for only seven years, most of that time spent pummeling weak opposition. Now Morrison began to cut, bruise, and bleed with regularity, and the repeated knockdowns he suffered confirmed his brittleness. Of course, for most of his career, Morrison compounded these issues with a torrid nightlife, a lax attitude toward training, and a dependency on steroids that likely had an adverse physical effect on him.

★ ★ ★

More disturbing, perhaps, than his professional outlook was yet another extracurricular fracas that put Morrison in the crosshairs of the law. In the early hours of Sunday, October 15, a little over a week after the Lewis fight, Morrison and Tammy Witt, mother of his five-year-old son, McKenzie, clashed at a party in Grove, Oklahoma. According to Witt, Morrison had crashed her party, and when he was asked to leave he became violent, punching Witt in the face and biting the finger of another guest, Kim Dunham. Both women sought medical attention, and Witt filed charges against Morrison. A few days later, the Delaware County District Court hit Morrison with two misdemeanor counts of assault and battery. Team Morrison, including his lawyer, Stuart Campbell, immediately accused Witt of gold digging. "I don't care for his money," Witt told KOTV in response to questions about her motives. "I want him out of my life and my son's life."

Among the witnesses to the altercation were a few Morrison friends, eager to publicly absolve the former heavyweight contender. "Tammy slapped Tom, and Tammy had Tom's finger, bending it," Tony Rutherford told the Associated Press. "He pushed her out of the way, and she fell down. He said, 'All right, let's go, let's leave right now.' And that's when Kim Dunham came up and started going stupid on him, cussing and carrying on and telling him she was going to whip his ass. She grabbed him, and he pushed her back, and that's when she went to screaming and carrying on. That's all that happened. That's it."

This version of events was contradicted by a telling paragraph from the *Tulsa World*: "Stuart Campbell . . . acknowledged that photos show Witt with a black eye, but he contends Witt sustained the injury after Morrison and his friends left the party."

On October 25, Morrison, through his lawyers, pleaded innocent and posted $1,000 bail in absentia.

★ ★ ★

With his career seemingly in pieces and an assault charge now looming over him, Morrison found some relief on soundstages for the first time since *Rocky V*. In early December, Morrison flew to Los Angeles to shoot an episode of the CBS sitcom *Cybill* (starring Cybill Shepherd), where he played a dimwitted boxer named Leo, in a minor subplot that jarred with the usual *Cybill* shenanigans. Leo has part of his contract purchased by the character of Maryann, a frisky lush (played by Christine Baranski) whose attraction to prizefighting goes beyond a mere sporting interest.

On screen for only a handful of minutes, Morrison threatened no future Emmy Award nominees, but while he seemed physically uncomfortable at times, he had a comic air befitting the zany story line. There is a restaurant scene where Leo is depicted as a dullard, a gym scene where Leo works the speed bag and kisses Maryann while still wearing his mouthpiece, and a brief fight scene, with Maryann and Cybill at ringside.

Ironically, the romance between Maryann and Leo ends when Maryann learns that boxers often go through long periods of celibacy before a fight, a rule Morrison certainly never followed in real life.

On the set, Morrison bonded, to an extent, with Shepherd by revealing a common interest: Elvis Presley. In the early 1970s, Shepherd, a Tennessee native, had dated Presley; that was enough for Morrison to bare his strategically placed tattoo of The King: "Of course I had to show her my butt," he told the *Kansas City Star*. "She got a kick out of it."

For Morrison, hearing the sound of a clapperboard again was part of a potential exit strategy. "Boxing is not a sport to stay in for a long run," he told the Associated Press. "Acting has a lot to offer, and if I dedicate myself to acting like I have to fighting, I should do it well. Anything makes more sense than being punched in the head."

When the episode aired, on January 14, 1996, Morrison was already in the midst of training for his umpteenth comeback fight. He was also less than a month away from seeing his future vanish.

★ ★ ★

The $2 million he had earned against Lewis, while far short of what he would have made just a few years earlier, was enough for Morrison to continue his up-and-down career. Tony Holden, who had guided Morrison back to HBO following the Bentt loss without Top Rank, decided that he would need help for the latest rehabilitation program. To that end, he turned to Don King, the electro-haired promoter who had been interested in Morrison as far back as 1989. "King has always been after Tommy," Holden told the *Kansas City Star* in December. "If we decided to go that route, it will probably be a partnership between King and myself. It will probably be a three-fight deal. Right now, King is the most attractive avenue. He holds all the titles."

The bombastic, indefatigable master of malapropisms, King, a twenty-year veteran of the sport, was back in the high life again after a fallow period without Mike Tyson. When Tyson returned from his prison stint to shatter pay-per-view records in his first comeback fight, in August 1995, it was King who had him under control once more. That made King the top power broker in a fractious sport filled with cutthroats (not only from the streets but from corporate boardrooms as well) constantly on the lookout for a treacherous laissez-faire edge. With Tyson, King had the biggest edge of all. (King had also maneuvered his heavyweight stable into title shots, resulting in his control of the WBC, WBA, and IBF championships.) His connection to Tyson brought King not only a contract with the MGM Grand in Las Vegas but also an exclusive output deal with the premium cable network Showtime. It was this Showtime deal that would serve as a springboard for the latest resurrection of Tommy Morrison. For years, King had eyed Morrison as a possible rival for Tyson, aware of how marketable such a fight would have been. In July 1995, King would make overtures to Morrison (including a $1 million offer for a tune-up) when Morrison had already verbally committed to facing Lennox Lewis. If Morrison had been able to command a $7.5 million check for his eventually aborted challenge of Lennox Lewis, then he might have earned $10 million for a Tyson fight in late 1995 or early 1996. Instead of waiting for a potential bout with Tyson to materialize, however, Morrison accepted a long-shot opportunity against Lewis. The reasoning behind this painful decision was clear: Morrison could not be trusted to keep a winning streak alive, not with his recent shoddy form.

One of the most recognizable faces in boxing (even as a nonparticipant), King had built a reputation for malfeasance shocking even for an industry known colloquially as the "red-light district of sports." Indeed, the villainous promoter of *Rocky V*, George Washington Duke (played with cartoonish verve by Robert Gant), is a transparent imitation of King, who inspired more than just one fictional portrait. In a 1984 made-for-television movie, *The Vegas Strip War*, James Earl Jones hammed it up gleefully as a Don King clone (replete with skyscraper afro), and Frank Diamond, the duplicitous dealmaker of *Casino Moon*, a novel by Peter Blauner, was also modeled on King.

Although John Gotti received the lyrical nickname "The Teflon Don" from New York City tabloids, King might have been considered the perfect alternate for it. By late 1995, King had twice walked out of federal court unscathed—once by acquittal, once by mistrial—he had been sued more often than Cindy Crawford had been photographed, he had been the target of an aborted undercover sting operation by the FBI, he had invoked the Fifth Amendment during Senate hearings when pressed about his association with the mafia. Meanwhile, Gotti, finally brought down by the RICO Act, was languishing in the United States Penitentiary in Marion, Illinois.

If Morrison and Holden had been suspicious of King in the past, it was more than just his public record that had spooked them. In the late 1980s, King—using every ounce of his street-hustler flair, or what an old-time manager named Jimmy Johnston might have called "the sweat of his imagination"—had pried Tyson away from Bill Cayton, reducing both his role and his percentage as manager. To the press, King vilified Cayton every chance he got, in equal measure malicious and mellifluous: "I said publicly that Bill Cayton was a liar, a hypocrite in the worst form, Satan in disguise, an egregious, self-centered, egotistical maniac who felt he had control of the universe."

Not surprisingly, Cayton had warned Team Morrison about associating with King. Whatever Cayton had said to Morrison and Holden about King, they had refused his offers until Morrison had nowhere else to go and Holden had run out of choices. A few years earlier, in an interview with *KO* magazine, Morrison had made several comments on the subject of Don King and Mike Tyson. "Inside, he knows he screwed up," Morrison said about Tyson. "In *The National*, there was a chart showing what Tyson would have made had he stuck with Cayton, and what he's made since he's been with Don King. Tyson knows he screwed up, but he knows that going back to Bill Cayton would be admitting to the world that he was a dumb dick. I don't think Tyson has the balls to do that."

Except for a possible high-risk, low-reward matchup with Andrew Golota, HBO showed little interest in Morrison after the Lewis rout, and the ESPN road would take too long to reestablish Morrison as a viable contender. It would also be risky, considering how poor Morrison had looked in many of his post-Bentt fights. An upset loss to an ex–football player (like Ross Puritty) or a tattered veteran (like Razor Ruddock) at the Brady Theater in Tulsa or the Civic Assembly Center in Muskogee would put an end to his career once and for all.

By teaming with King, Holden ensured that he had a vested partner working on behalf of Morrison. As a promoter, self-interest would compel King to protect Morrison long enough to make a smashing match against Tyson a reality. The buildup process would take place on his own network, Showtime, which acted as a de facto marketing department for pay-per-view bouts involving Tyson, and King would be on hand for every Morrison appearance, hyping a future Tyson fight with his outlandish rat-a-tat-tat soliloquies and sales pitches.

How did Morrison characterize his new business relationship with Don King? "I don't mind being in a room full of snakes if the lights are on," he told the Associated Press, and to the *Kansas City Star*, he philosophized, "In order to get a shot, you have to dance with the devil sometimes."

★ ★ ★

"Everything you hear in boxing is a lie."
—Don King

★ ★ ★

When Bill Cayton signed on to co-manage Morrison in 1989, it was with an eventual Tyson blockbuster in mind. Cayton envisioned an explosive matchup whose box-office appeal would be further enhanced by various subplots, including his own fraying relationship with Tyson. In fact, Morrison commented on the Tyson–Cayton rift in the media, as if laying the groundwork for future discord. "What it amounts to is allowing himself to get sucked in and be manipulated by Don King," Morrison said in 1991 about Tyson splitting with Cayton. "Don King is a master of black rap. You know, 'Us blacks, we gotta stick together.' It's Tyson's fault that he ended up with King, and I think he deserves everything that happens to him."

Building Morrison as his personal avenger was only part of what Cayton had in mind. As bizarre as it seems in retrospect, Cayton also hoped to contrast personalities, in the kind of hokey morality tale that had formed the basis of so many boxing promotions of the past. To Cayton, Morrison–Tyson would be another chapterlet in the never-ending saga of Good vs. Evil, never mind the fact that Morrison was no more a saint than GG Allin or Sid Vicious was.

In 1986, Cayton was marketing Tyson as a virtuous athlete who had overcome a hardscrabble childhood prowling an inner-city hellscape, and this branding strategy, which sounds absurd today, ultimately led to lucrative endorsements from corporate superpowers such as Pepsi and Toyota. This PR scheme meant coaching Tyson on checking his unruly impulses and, more important perhaps, burying his transgressions from public scrutiny, often via buyout—cash settlements to victims and potential litigants. But Tyson bristled at the phony "nice guy" act, regardless of the money generated from advertisements and commercials. As his curbside Mr. Hyde persona began to reveal itself more often, Tyson started losing one deal after another, morals clauses repeatedly triggered, like a run of bullseye targets in a pinball machine.

With his bleached pretty-boy look, his genuine charm, and his heartland roots, Morrison was billed as a wholesome All-American type, despite an unsavory background that included any number of misdeeds, if not misdemeanors. Like Tyson, Morrison could not restrain his tumultuous nature—not for long, anyway. For ESPN, John Brown recalled how Morrison and alcohol were an explosive mix from the beginning, sparking a local reputation for debauchery that clashed with the upstanding image Cayton tried developing for commercial purposes. "We had friends at the bars in Westport, and they'd call us up at midnight, one o'clock, and say, 'Hey, you'd better come and get your boy, he's laying passed out on the floor. You might want to come and get him before the media gets here.' So we'd drive down and pick him up and throw him in the back of a pickup truck and carry him home."

Two years after Cayton began his makeover program, Morrison was arrested for driving under the influence in Grove, Oklahoma. That would be the first public accounting of the less-than-upstanding Morrison, but it would certainly not be the last. If the story line Cayton had concocted for Morrison was ersatz, the possibility of a Tyson fight had always been in the realm of possibility.

What would have happened if Morrison had faced Tyson?

During his prime, the savage years between 1986 and 1990, Tyson would have annihilated Morrison, whose only chance at winning was landing a fortunate left hook. Even such a blow might not have made a difference. Tyson, after all, had been thumped by James "Bonecrusher" Smith, Tony Tucker, and Frank Bruno—flawed heavyweights, certainly, but all avowed punchers—without ever having hit the canvas. One of the hardest punchers of his era, Razor Ruddock could not topple Tyson over eighteen rounds despite repeatedly landing his crushing left hook on the mark. And the Tyson of the '80s was an elusive target; his bobbing-and-weaving style, combined with accurate counterpunching, reduced his opponents to landing isolated blows from time to time.

Even the post-Douglas Tyson, the fighter who eschewed rapid-fire combinations and defense in favor of a power game that relied on a new, primitive one-punch-at-a-time philosophy, would have been too powerful and aggressive for Morrison. While Tyson no longer put his punches together in blurring sequences, while he had lost the ferocious craftsmanship that had made him such a devastating force, he still applied full-bore pressure from round to round, something for which few heavyweights were prepared, carried power in both fists, and wielded a titanium chin.

If there had ever been a chance, however unlikely, for Morrison to capsize Tyson, it was in late 1995, when Tyson was in the middle of his comeback. Following his ludicrous knockout of Peter McNeely, a fight that lasted all of eighty-nine seconds, Tyson was no less rusty than he had been before returning to the ring after a layoff of more than four years. The fact that Tyson also received a $30 million payday for the McNeely farce might have made it easier for him to view training as a distraction from lavish extracurricular activities.

On December 16, 1995, Tyson squared off against a feather-fisted roly-poly named Buster Mathis Jr. (whose father had been trained by Cus D'Amato) and looked uncertain at times before scoring a knockout in the third round. That was the Mike Tyson—version 3.0—Morrison might have been able to surprise, as far-fetched as oddsmakers might have considered such a result. With less than two minutes of action under his belt since 1991, Tyson might also have had stamina issues that even Morrison, with his iffy conditioning, might have exploited. Against George Foreman, Morrison had proven that he could effectively flit around the ring for five or six rounds or long enough, possibly, to exhaust a Tyson in hot pursuit. Whether Morrison could have capitalized on a weary Tyson is debatable, but the unpredictability of boxing meant that his chances were at least zero.

Later, when Morrison had severed ties with reality—when the whole world seemed to be one vast plot against him, when he made one mad declaration after another, including a bizarre claim of possessing powers of teleportation—he would blame a labyrinthine conspiracy theory for the Tyson fight never materializing.

Like so much else in the Tommy Morrison universe, this was nothing more than a lie.

★ ★ ★

"He came walking through the casino at the MGM Grand in Las Vegas with a woman on each arm the other night, which makes this night like so many others."
—Mike Lupica

★ ★ ★

Four months after his poor showing in Atlantic City, Morrison is scheduled to fight again on February 10, 1996. As if to prove his good intentions, King immediately pairs Morrison with a fighter who poses no threat to anyone with even a modicum of talent. Arthur "Stormy" Weathers is thirty-three years old and has been kicking around the fringes of boxing since 1984. It is almost certain that Weathers has never made more than $10,000 for a fight. A cruiserweight with little punch resistance, Weathers also shreds as easily as a Noguchi lamp. "I bleed when I watch fights on TV," he jokes. Weathers is so undistinguished, so obviously a soldier of misfortune, that oddsmakers once again refuse to post a line. In his first outing since being stopped by Lewis, Morrison is back to his sideshow roots. Except this time, the sideshow will take place not at a state fair but in the sparkling MGM Grand Arena in Las Vegas. It will air on Showtime, a premium cable network, a Viacom subsidiary, and will open a telecast headlined by a future Hall of Famer, Felix Trinidad. As usual, Morrison plays up his role as a fighter in a legitimate contest: "When that bell rings, I am on this guy's chest," he says. "I am just going to go in there and maul this guy. That is the most effective Tommy Morrison." A few days before the fight, Morrison is asked to take an HIV test by a member of the Nevada State Athletic Commission. He refuses.

PART II

First of all, I'd like to thank everybody for being here today. I'm sorry that I couldn't be here in person on Monday, when Tony informed you of what the present situation was. At that time I felt it was more important to be with my family, somehow help them through the initial shock of what we'd learned.

Since that time I've taken the action to have more extensive tests run. I was informed just a little while ago that those tests do in fact confirm that I have tested positive for the HIV virus.

I spent the last three days contacting the people that I have come in contact with over the last three or four years. There was a number of sparring partners out there that I've worked with over the years, but more importantly, the young ladies I've been intimately involved with over the past three or four years. Those people who I have not been able to contact have contacted me. My prayers go out to them nightly, and their families, in hopes that everything somehow will be okay. If there's anyone out there that feels they have come in contact with me either directly or indirectly, I would truly encourage them to get themselves tested for their own sake and certainly for their own peace of mind.

The big question for me, and I guess for my family as well, is where do I go from here? I haven't had a whole lot of time to reflect on that. Uh, but one thing is for certain: It's that I want to do what's right. I spent the last few nights on the phone with Magic Johnson and some of his representatives, talking in depth about what we can do as a team, and what we can do as individuals, to truly promote awareness to every single person out there, particularly those of my generation.

Speaking of myself, for a moment, there was a certain point and time in my life that I lived a very permissive, fast, reckless lifestyle. I knew that the HIV virus is something that anyone could get, but I also believed the chances were very, very slim. I thought that the real danger of contracting this rests in the arms of those who subject themselves to certain types of lifestyles, addicts who share needles, people who practice a homosexual lifestyle. I honestly believed that I had a better chance of winning the lottery than contracting this disease. I have never been so wrong in my life.

The only sure prevention of this disease is abstinence. This is a disease that does not discriminate. And, as you know, that is very, very clear to me now. It doesn't matter if you live in the drug-infested ghettos of New York City or if you live on a ranch in Jay, Oklahoma. This is something *that can jump up and bite you no matter where you're at. And I'll tell you something else: It doesn't matter what color you are, it doesn't have a favorite color. I realize that there's a whole generation of kids out there like me that have totally disregarded our moral values that were taught to us by our parents. We've somehow seemed to treat sex as some kind of social activity, rather than a monogamous expression of love. I hope that I can serve as a warning that living this lifestyle can only lead to one thing, and that's misery. I've made a lot of mistakes in my life; however, if getting up here today, confronting this problem out in the open, can get just one person out there to take a more responsible attitude toward sex then I feel I would've scored my biggest knockout ever.*

On a personal level, I'm going to spend as much time as possible educating myself and doing everything I can to educate others about how serious this is. I would like to ask everyone out there not to say a prayer for me but to say a prayer for the true victims of this disease, these being the HIV-infected children of this world. I had a choice, but they didn't.

To all my young fans out there, I'd ask that you no longer see me as a role model, but see me as an individual who had an opportunity to be a role model and blew it. Blew it with irresponsible, irrational, immature decisions, decisions that one day could cost me my life. Think about that.

To my family, and my friends, I wish that there was somehow a way that I could go through this by myself. I'm sorry that I had to drag you guys through this with me. Many times in my life I've had to pick myself off the floor. This has certainly been one of those times. I was raised in a sport—over the last eight years, most of my life—that being weak just wasn't allowed. And now I know why. Mom, dad, I love you.

—Tommy Morrison, February 15, 1996, the Southern Hills Marriott in Tulsa, Oklahoma

★ ★ ★

On the afternoon of February 10, 1996, only a few hours before broadcast time, Nevada State Athletic Commission executive director Marc Ratner announced that Tommy Morrison had been scratched from the card at the MGM Grand for medical reasons. When Ratner declined to specify what ailed Morrison, rumors began circulating within the boxing community. "All we know is we were told Tommy failed his medical," Tony Holden said, in response to the stories that were raging. "Give him a couple of days before you make any judgments."

A couple of days were too much—even then, during the nascent internet era—before the blitzkrieg social media strikes of Facebook and Twitter. Within hours, the word had spread that Tommy Morrison had tested positive for HIV, the virus that causes AIDS.

★ ★ ★

Later, the fact that Morrison initially refused to take his blood test would draw a certain amount of skepticism, but at the time, it fell by the wayside in the wake of larger cultural overtones. HIV, and by extension, AIDS, was the disease of the millennium, an affliction whose fatal consequences and sexual transmission gave rise to metaphorical interpretations that obscured other concerns. "After two decades of sexual spending, of sexual speculation, of sexual inflation, we are in the early stages of a sexual depression," wrote Susan Sontag, in 1987. "Looking back on the sexual culture of the 1970s has been compared to looking back on the jazz age from the wrong side of the 1929 crash."

Still, the fact remains that Tommy Morrison rejected a test that he would eventually fail. It took Dr. James Nave, the Nevada State Athletic Commission Chairman, to intervene before Morrison finally yielded. "I was called and told he did not want to take the test, citing religious beliefs," Nave told the Associated Press. "I said it was my order as chairman to take the test or he would not fight."

Because of privacy laws and the threat of litigation (past, present, and future), the steps for the testing protocol from February 8 to February 10 are nearly impossible to reconstruct. This is just another aspect of the

Tommy Morrison story that, by necessity, remained shrouded, shrouded enough to become another example of skulduggery for the conspiracy theorists who would later emerge like so many maggots on a rotting corpse.

Marc Ratner received the results of the HIV tests on Saturday afternoon, around 12:30 (PST), and announced the cancellation of Morrison–Weathers at 1:00. For an hour or so, Ratner tried unsuccessfully to locate Morrison, who had left his hotel room (where Dawn Gilbert, his companion in Las Vegas, remained) for lunch. Eventually, Ratner reached Tony Holden and told him that Tommy Morrison had tested positive for HIV. There is some question about whether Ratner had the right, legal or ethical, to inform someone other than Morrison about a serious medical condition. Although Ratner remained tight-lipped with the press about the specifics concerning Morrison, even citing the advice of Attorney General Frankie Sue Del Papa, he gave several read-between-the-lines answers that all but confirmed an HIV diagnosis. He made certain of this by asserting the strange clause of a "worldwide" suspension, an inflated mandate with little standing beyond the borders of Nevada, and by adding that Morrison had not been tested for steroids or drugs.

Now, it was Tony Holden who had to break the news to Morrison. He left a message with Dawn Gilbert, who told Morrison that Holden needed to see him. That was when Morrison knocked on a door at the MGM Grand, where he learned about the first of his last days. "The hardest thing I've ever done in my life is to tell Tommy the news," Holden said.

Of the more than 1,500 fighters tested for HIV since Nevada began mandatory screening in 1988, only one had ever tested positive, an inept Los Angeles featherweight named Eduardo Castro, who retired in 1993 with a record of 0-7.

★ ★ ★

As awful as this development was, it may not have come as a surprise to those closest to Morrison. Years later, Diana Morrison would hint, shockingly, that her son had already had an ominous inkling of his condition before the canceled Arthur Weathers fight. In 2016, Diana Morrison spoke to the producers of ESPN *30 for 30* for their documentary, *Tommy*. She recalled the night that she tuned in to see her son face Arthur Weathers on Showtime.

Diana Morrison: I was in the living room in Jay, waiting for him to fight and then they announced that he could not pass his physical and I knew what it was. We had talked about this before.

Producer: Talked about what?

Diana Morrison: The HIV.

Producer: He knew before?

Diana Morrison: He suspicioned. He did not know for sure.

★ ★ ★

Shell-shocked, Morrison returned to his hotel, packed his bags, and, along with Dawn Gilbert, bolted to McCarran International Airport and flew back to Oklahoma, where he sequestered himself in Jay, under the care of his mother. A small trailer on Cherokee Street now harbored one of the most famous athletes in America. In the meantime, Holden, who joined Morrison the next day, worked out a short-term plan that included a second test in Tulsa followed by a press conference when the results came through. The follow-up test confirmed what the Nevada State Athletic Commission had discovered—that Tommy Morrison was HIV-positive—and that the original diagnosis was correct. No one, not even Morrison, denied this basic fact, not until a decade had passed and he was plotting a farcical return to the ring. Indeed, after a short preamble, Morrison opened his press conference at the Southern Hills Marriott, which was aired live on ESPN, and was rebroadcast on local and network affiliates, with this stark fact: "I was informed just a little while ago that those tests do in fact confirm that I have tested positive for the HIV virus."

Future conspiracy theorists and HIV deniers, including Morrison himself, of course, would later conveniently pretend that this second positive test, which Morrison openly acknowledged at the time, did not exist. For them, it is incontrovertible evidence that Morrison was HIV-positive, and it had to be scrubbed if not from the record (an impossibility because of its prominence at the time) then at least from their shared mania.

Moreover, HIV patients do not merely show up at a clinic to have their blood pressure taken and have prescriptions signed over to them. Nearly every time an HIV patient sees a physician, he or she has tests to determine T-count levels, viral load, the presence of opportunistic infections.

And Morrison would go on to see several doctors in the aftermath of his diagnosis, including leading experts in the field, such as Dr. David Ho, famous for treating Magic Johnson. "Tony Holden had immediately begun to seek medical help for Tom," Dawn Gilbert wrote in her memoir. "He first obtained an appointment with Tulsa AIDS specialist Dr. James Hutton. After a full examination, Dr. Hutton told Tom that the HIV was rampant in his system. According to him, the numbers were off the charts."

When Morrison made a shambolic comeback in 2007, he would claim that he had been the victim of a false positive test administered under the auspices of the Nevada State Athletic Commission in 1996. And the subsequent tests? The tests taken in various settings for the rest of his life? The results of some of these tests were publicly exposed during the discovery phase of a 2016 lawsuit.

That 2016 lawsuit brought to light dozens of documents revealing medical records that repeat, over and over, the fact that Tommy Morrison had HIV. These records include prescriptions, credit card statements, test results, memos from physicians, expert testimony, even psychiatric intake notes. The evidence that Morrison had been living with HIV for years is overwhelming. Over and over, he admitted, publicly, to taking HIV medication. To ESPN, to *Sports Illustrated*, to the *Tennessean*, to the *Kansas City Star*. His mother, who had come off in several interviews as a straightforward, no-nonsense woman, confirmed that Morrison was on antiretrovirals. "By 1998 Tommy was looking pretty bad," she told *Details* in 2007. "I took him to a doctor in Kansas City. He sat him down and convinced him, and Tommy took the lightest possible cocktail until a couple of years ago—just three little pills a day."

Everywhere one looked there was corroboration. In 2007, when Morrison had launched his quixotic comeback, Tony Holden did not hesitate to tell the truth. "I took him to several doctors after the Nevada test confirmed that he was HIV-positive and we got the same result," Holden told the AP. "Without a doubt he was HIV-positive. He was diagnosed by several doctors with HIV."

Under oath for their court depositions, his two ex-wives described aiding Morrison with his pill regimen, and, in 2003, he underwent a sperm-washing technique to conceive a child with Dawn Gilbert. That procedure was intended to ensure that his baby would be HIV-free.

Morrison spent years denying that HIV caused AIDS, not denying that he had contracted the virus. Until one day, roughly a decade after his emotional press conference, he decided that he had been misdiagnosed. Even for someone as erratic as Morrison, the idea of being misdiagnosed for something that he believed to be harmless was bizarre.

★ ★ ★

"Although State boxing officials declined to comment on Morrison's case, the commission's chief physician, Dr. Flip Homansky, said that if a boxer were to test positive for HIV, the test would be repeated. If it still comes up positive, a more sophisticated test is administered. That analysis takes 24 hours. 'So in essence we would check it three times,' Homansky said." —Associated Press, February 11, 1996

★ ★ ★

Nothing, not his role in *Rocky V*, not his win over George Foreman, not his appearances on HBO, would bring Morrison the kind of notoriety he had achieved by being the most prominent athlete since Magic Johnson to contract HIV. Not since N.W.A rapper Eazy-E died in 1995 had AIDS made national headlines, and before that, it had been Olympic swimmer Greg Louganis and actor Ray Sharkey, whose grim last years, leading up to his death in 1993, became tabloid fodder.

In the weeks following his diagnosis, Morrison made several media appearances on the talk-show circuit. He popped up on *Dateline NBC* with Maria Shriver, *The Maury Povich Show*, *Larry King Live*, and ESPN. At every stop, Morrison spoke eloquently about his failures, his hopes, his uncertain future, his desire to become a spokesman for AIDS charities. To King and Povich, he reiterated, plainly, that the second test—administered by a physician of his own choosing in Oklahoma—had left no doubt about his HIV status.

A few hours after Morrison gave his press conference, he was on the air with Larry King on CNN. "The first thing I wanted to do, obviously, was to get somewhere where I could get more blood drawn," Morrison said. "Uh, I know that, uh, there is a possibility of, uh, there being a mix-up. My hopes, uh, hinged on that. Once we got back here, then we obviously had the test done, and we just found out earlier today that, uh, the results of those tests did confirm that I have tested positive for that virus."

Morrison told Povich something similar. "You always hang your hat on the possibility that there was a screwup," he said, "but when we got the other test back, and I found out for sure, we had to—I had to—make a statement, had to have that press conference."

By 1996, AIDS had slipped from the public consciousness since the days when it was viewed as a potential extinction-event plague. Combination therapy had removed guaranteed mortality from the AIDS equation, and the fact that the disease had not spread widely beyond its initial targets—gay men, IV drug users, prostitutes, and hemophiliacs—gave most of the country, particularly straight men, a sense of complacency. Magic Johnson and Tommy Morrison were exceptions to the notion of a low-risk group, of course, but as heterosexuals, their HIV status was a reminder that the general population was also in jeopardy.

In the case of Morrison, however, there was another X factor involved. For years he had been using steroids to bulk up to compete in a division where it was common to see fighters who weighed over 230 pounds in the ring. As a small heavyweight who began his career at a pudgy 199 pounds, Morrison injected steroids repeatedly; that he contracted HIV from sharing a dirty needle with a training partner is a possibility, one that Morrison, in the days when he was still acknowledging his medical condition, certainly believed to be true.

In an interview with ESPN for *30 for 30*, Tim Morrison Jr. suggested that his brother had contracted HIV through some of his sexual quirks. "He was sleeping with everything in the country," Tim Morrison said. "He had run across some medicine that you shoot right into the side of your shaft, and you do it about ten minutes before you have sex, and it makes you good for four hours. You know, if you're poking a brand-new wound in the side of your penis ten minutes before you have sex, you know, to me, that's how he got it."

One of the potential side effects of heavy steroid usage is erectile dysfunction. Was it possible that Morrison, the macho, muscle-bound heavyweight contender who seemed to exemplify satyriasis, suffered from ED and used vasoactive drugs? (It should be noted that erectile dysfunction is also a side effect of HIV.)

To questions about how he contracted the disease, however, Morrison remained largely noncommittal. "That's not important," he said at the Marriott press conference. "Very few people give a crap how I got it. It's what I do now. I've had thousands of sparring partners, forty-nine fights, a promiscuous lifestyle. Go fish."

But he was more ambiguous a few weeks later during a televised interview with Karen Kornacki, a reporter for KMBC in Kansas City. When Kornacki asked Morrison if he knew who had infected him with HIV, he answered: "I have a basic idea, yeah."

★ ★ ★

At the peak of his stardom, between the premiere of *Rocky V* and his upset loss to Michael Bentt on HBO, Morrison lived out an adolescent fantasy that might have been the rudimentary plot of a teen sexploitation film from the 1980s—*Hardbodies, Screwballs, Porky's*. While training (nonchalantly) for his disaster against Bentt, Morrison infamously tacked up a map of Tulsa, divided into quadrants, in his hotel room, each quadrant representing the location of a specific woman, imported for his time away from the gym, geographically separated to avoid conflict. "In the boxing community this week there was sympathy for Morrison," wrote Graham Houston after Morrison had been diagnosed, "but his wild ways were such common knowledge that as soon as his worldwide medical suspension was announced in Las Vegas last Saturday, hours before he had been due to box at the MGM Grand Casino Hotel, the immediate assumption around ringside was 'HIV Positive.'"

★ ★ ★

"Careful? What for? Last one out closes the coffin door!"
—Bobby "Blitz" Ellsworth

★ ★ ★

Wherever Morrison went, he trailed yearning women behind him. They shadowed him at personal appearances, before fights, after fights, in lobbies, restaurants, bars, and clubs. "They used to be all over him, everywhere he went, and I guess you can only beat them off with a baseball bat for so long," Bill Cayton told the *Vancouver Sun*. "His attraction to women was more than anything you can imagine, including some of the most gorgeous women around. Of course, he's a good-looking guy, and starring in one of the *Rocky* movies helped. But he was a womanizer beyond anything I've ever known."

Few celebrities, even minor ones, spend their nights partying in Kansas City or Jay or Iowa, but Morrison had little interest in the bright lights of New York City or Los Angeles. The local whirlwind he created in small towns was more than enough for him. This big-fish-small-pond quality in which Morrison reveled seemed almost deliberate. It was as if he knew how hungry some of these women were; it was as if he knew that there would be no competition in trying to satiate them. Or was it Morrison who needed satiating? "It was unbelievable," Morrison told *Sports Illustrated*. "It was all right there. You could feed yourself as fast and as much as you wanted."

When Magic Johnson announced that he had contracted HIV, it sparked a series of feature stories about sports groupies in the AIDS era. (Groupies themselves, just a few years after Pamela Des Barres published her behind-the-scenes tell-all *I'm with the Band*, became the subject of pop psychology theories. "Some are looking for a good time; others are desperately seeking attention, love, self-esteem, feelings of desirability. It all plays to American fantasies—male and female," wrote Linda Yglesias in a syndicated column.) Libidinous athletes, on the road for weeks at a time, entrenched in a subculture of "freaks," "puck bunnies," "fatal attractions," and "desperadoes," began reassessing the risks of reckless hookups in light of what befell Magic Johnson and, to a lesser extent, NASCAR driver Tim Richmond.

But Tommy Morrison was beyond change, regardless of the inherent danger of sleeping indiscriminately with hundreds, possibly thousands, of women, whose names he never bothered to learn. To Morrison, women were little more than props. "If I met a girl, I'd tell her straight up, 'I might run into someone else I want to go out with, don't be offended.' Was that acceptable to them? It had to be. There were enough girls. They were expendable."

"What you've got to realize is that the people Tommy was picking were, well, I don't think there were any virgins in the crop," Tommy Virgets told the Associated Press. The fact that Virgets passes a moral judgment on the women looking to bed Morrison (for pleasure, for distinction, for debasement) and not to Morrison himself is, to an extent, a sign of the times, but it also reflects a hypocrisy about Morrison and his own depraved activities. "I could tell a classy chick from a trashy chick," Morrison said to Larry King. "But, obviously, I'm here to tell you that's not enough." And all those women? Could they tell a classy jock from a trashy jock?

If Morrison felt that fucking in bathrooms, limousines, and motels (that doubled as drug spots), sometimes drunk, sometimes sober, if participating in trains, orgies, and trios with strangers and near-strangers, gave him some sort of moral high ground, then it was obvious, in retrospect, to understand how he contracted HIV and it would become apparent later how he could manufacture elaborate conspiracy theories that would expunge HIV from his existence. The distance between his actions—how he construed them—and reality was unbridgeable.

★ ★ ★

"Q: Did Mr. Morrison ever test positive for HIV before 1996?

A: He said he had.

Q: Okay. I want you to tell me what Mr. Morrison told you about testing positive for HIV before 19—before February 1996.

A: He didn't tell me till about 2000—I mean it wasn't after '96. It wasn't until about 2000/2001, he said he found out back in 1989 that he had it.

Q: And tell me how that conversation arose.

A: I don't remember how it arose. He just—it was almost like a—he—like he was bragging about it, in a way. And to be honest, I didn't believe him because, you know, I told him, 'I saw your face when you walked back into the room, you were white as a ghost,' you know. And I said, 'I just can't believe that.' And he said that he—he had tested negative. I mean, positive. Tested positive, I'm sorry. And that was in '89 before I ever knew him . . . I didn't believe him because of what I saw in Vegas and then reading that he had told other people, you know, I started thinking, well, maybe—maybe he was positive. I don't know that I ever told him that—that I believed that he had it in '89. I did one time, he was doing an ESPN interview at our house, and he was talking to the reporter there and kind of like bragging that he knew about it since '89, and he was kind of laughing about it. And I kept telling him to shut his mouth and he just kept on, and so I went into the other room and called Stuart Campbell. And I'm like, 'he's giving—he's telling this guy off the record that he's known since 1989,' I said, 'you need to shut him up from saying stuff like that.' And so, Stuart got on the phone and said, you know, 'you're opening yourself up to a lot of lawsuits by telling people that you knew in '89, you know, all the women you slept

with, you could open yourself up to a lot of lawsuits.' When Tom heard that, he—he quit saying it, at least to that reporter, but he kept telling other people."
—Dawn Gilbert, court testimony, 2016

★ ★ ★

No longer was Morrison limited to industry coverage in *The Ring* and *Boxing Illustrated* or the sports sections of newspapers. For a little while, at least, Morrison transcended sidebars, agate type, the inverted pyramids of wire reports. Now, he was the subject of major dailies—front page, bold-face—talk shows, nightly news broadcasts, and mainstream magazines. Even peripheral events related to Morrison became significant stories.

His old costar, Sylvester Stallone, the man who made it possible for Morrison to live out some of his libertine dreams, released a statement to the press that ran from coast to coast. "This truly tragic situation," he said, "brings to light that no one, including some of the strongest men in the world, are (sic) immune from this insidious disease. Meeting and working with Tommy Morrison was one of my fondest memories, and nothing will ever change that."

In an interview with ESPN, Magic Johnson offered his thoughts on "The Duke." "Tommy's done a wonderful job in boxing," he said, "and now he can do a wonderful job in helping people educate themselves about HIV and AIDS. I hope he joins into that fight. What he has to understand is to continue to be himself, continue to keep a smile on his face and just learn what he has to do to beat it."

Referee Mills Lane, the third man in the ring during the Lewis–Morrison butchering in October, announced that he would undergo an HIV test. "I had blood all over me," Lane told the Associated Press about his gory experience. "He bled all over me and everyone else. I've got a family. I've got a wife and two children. I'm not really worried, but it will make me feel better to know for sure."

Similarly, Christine Baranski, the actress who shared a protracted kiss with Morrison during his cameo on *Cybill*, publicly announced that she would seek an HIV test. "I will get a test because everybody is talking to me about it," she said. "I'm not scared. There's a one-in-a-million chance of getting the virus from a kiss."

If Baranski was unperturbed about her limited physical contact with Morrison, the same could not be said about many other women who had been intimate with him. In the days following the blockbuster news that Morrison had tested positive for HIV, Kansas City spiraled into a local panic. "I had three women call me this morning," Peyton Sher told the *Kansas City Star* a day after giving his thoughts to local media. "They were all scared because they'd been with Tommy Morrison. 'Is it true? Is it true?' That's what one of them shouted in my ear at 7:30. She saw me on TV and wanted to know if it was true that Tommy had HIV."

The Kansas City Free Health Clinic saw a significant spike in appointments for HIV tests. "Our phones have just rung continually," said Sheri Wood, executive director of the clinic. "They want appointments to be tested. They want to know if it can be anonymous. They want results quickly."

Brian Schmidt, a phone operator for an AIDS hotline run by the Health Department, spoke to the *Kansas City Star* about an uptick in calls. "We've had around 20 people call, women who said, 'Hey, I slept with this guy,' and believe it or not, calls from men whose girlfriends had previously seen him," he said.

To the public, Morrison was more than just another athlete whose downfall functioned as a celebrity reckoning. He was a symbol not only of excess but of the potential vulnerability of a demographic—straight white males from the heartland—that had disregarded AIDS in recent years. Even Alison Gertz, the teenager who contracted HIV after a one-night stand with a bartender from Studio 54—and earned a bitter fame thereafter—had been an iffy emblem for Middle America. She lived in New York City, after all, and came from an affluent family from the ritzy Upper East Side. When she died, in 1992, at the age of twenty-six, her tragic story promptly faded into the past. With his blue-collar background and minor celebrity that preceded his HIV status, Morrison had a better chance at reaching the Bible-and-Rust-Belt set. But Morrison would never be comfortable with the role he had tragically inherited.

If nothing else, Morrison shined a brief light on the potential dangers of HIV and sports. His misfortune led to a broad discussion about mandatory testing in boxing, an industry with limited oversight, a lack of uniform standards, and an ethos of grift/graft that frequently taints the regulators themselves, who are often little more than political appointees and beneficiaries of cronyism. Some of the busiest boxing states in America did not require HIV testing, including Texas, California, New Jersey, and New York. Indeed, in the early 1990s, several states did not have boxing commissions at all. Of these, one of them—Oklahoma—was where Morrison lived and fought most often during the last year of his career.

That a sport whose participants regularly bled and competed with open cuts could exist without precautions against a disease that only a few years earlier had evoked images of an apocalyptic outbreak seemed, on its surface, absurd. "It's a sorry situation," Bob Arum told the Associated Press. "It's preposterous that in a sport like boxing that testing isn't mandatory. You should think of the other fighter first." (Eventually, the debate about HIV in boxing, unlike so much else in a shadowy industry where reform is perpetually improbable, led to several states adopting mandatory testing.)

In March 1996, ESPN aired an episode of *Outside the Lines*, a special on AIDS in sports, focusing on Magic Johnson, Greg Louganis, and Tommy Morrison. Among the boxers who insisted that HIV posed little threat to contestants in the ring was George Foreman, who even floated the possibility of a rematch with Morrison, less out of a need for revenge than out of a sense of righteousness. "I would box him tomorrow," Foreman quipped.

One of the most fervent voices in favor of barring HIV-positive boxers from competing came, surprisingly, from Tommy Morrison. "I certainly believe that it can be passed in the ring," Morrison said. "I mean, I've dealt with cuts and bleeding and nosebleeds and mouth—you know, everything in the ring, and I believe it could, one hundred percent, I believe it could happen."

★ ★ ★

"Now, where does a champion go when he takes off his gloves?"
—*Rocky V* poster

★ ★ ★

Like Magic Johnson before him, Morrison was now thrust, suddenly, into a limelight of a different sort: He was a serious—even tragic—figure, not just an erratic athlete whose exploits merited the occasional clip on *SportsCenter*.

This put the impulsive Morrison in a situation where he may have felt bound to adhere to a heroic story line imposed on him by the vagaries of chance. Morrison had always been an embellisher, sometimes to further his career, but now he began lying publicly, obviously, repeatedly, to serve a far broader audience as a spokesman, as a role model, as a cautionary tale.

Across his media tour, Morrison alternated between raw confessions and the occasional untruth. He lied to Maria Shriver on *Dateline* about having returned to Oklahoma by himself after learning of his HIV status. He had, in fact, been accompanied by Dawn Gilbert, who was not, it should be noted, the woman whom Morrison would repeatedly reference in the weeks following his diagnosis.

It was an innocuous lie, perhaps, but it was one that hinted at what was to come. Morrison also lied repeatedly about being in a monogamous relationship with a woman named Dawn Freeman. Even while Morrison spoke wistfully of his quiet days spent mainly on a ranch in Jay and his devotion to Freeman, he was leading a double life. Although it was Freeman who accompanied Morrison to his press conference in Tulsa, and it was Freeman who was part of the melodramatic story lines on *The Maury Povich Show* and *Outside the Lines*, there was also Dawn Gilbert, whom Morrison saw regularly. In fact, Morrison had split his life between these two women, weekdays in Tulsa (under the pretext of training) with Dawn Gilbert and weekends on his ranch in Jay with Dawn Freeman. This triangle, which had been taking place since late 1994, was further complicated not only by the fact that Morrison now had an incurable, contagious disease, but by his inability to curb his sexual gluttony, to restrain the impulses that had initially led to his downfall. His talk of Bible-inspired morality never stopped him from drinking, womanizing, and siring children out of wedlock. Nor would scripture prevent a future of drug use, bigamy, divorce, domestic violence, racism, drunkenness, and prison. "He would always say he was changing, but he had a hard time with it," Tony Holden told the *Los Angeles Times*. "He was trying to get his life in order. He was going to church more. But he figured, those times when the discipline was off, when he was off the wagon, he might as well go all the way."

And his insistence that he was in a monogamous relationship with Freeman was nothing more than a doozy. Fidelity was as alien a concept to Tommy Morrison as quantum mechanics.

★ ★ ★

Nearly fifteen years after its discovery, HIV (and its often-tragic conclusion, AIDS) still carried a stigma that reflected a certain amount of intolerance. That this disease arrived during the evangelical revolution of the Reagan Era only made it that much easier to demonize. The marginal groups afflicted by AIDS during its early, relentless circulation—gay men, IV drug users, prostitutes, hemophiliacs—combined with its spread in urban capitals such as New York City and San Francisco, which had already been deemed modern-day Sodoms by conservative mouthpieces, galvanized Bible Belt bigots, who conflated their prejudices with Christian values. Moral Majority founder, PTL host, and committed segregationist Jerry Falwell made clear the outlook of most born-agains when he said: "AIDS is not just God's punishment for homosexuals; It is God's punishment for the society that tolerates homosexuals."

In 1986, William F. Buckley, editor of the *National Review*, wrote: "Everyone detected with AIDS should be tattooed on the upper forearm, to protect common-needle users, and on the buttocks, to prevent the victimization of other homosexuals."

For a few weeks in the early 1990s, right-wing blowhard Rush Limbaugh aired a segment on his syndicated radio show that mocked people with AIDS and sometimes tolled their deaths to the sounds of double-entendre pop songs such as "Back in the Saddle Again" and "Looking for Love in All the Wrong Places."

Even Billy Graham, addressing a crowd of more than 40,000 in Columbus, Ohio, said: "Is AIDS a judgment of God? I could not say for sure, but I think so."

Against this background of loathing and hostility, AIDS patients often viewed themselves as pariahs. Of the most famous early AIDS victims, only a few—most often heterosexuals who had contracted HIV through blood transfusions, such as Arthur Ashe—publicly acknowledged their condition. The rest of them feared being professionally blacklisted or feared public ridicule or feared being "outed" via inference at a time when homophobia was far more virulent than it is today.

During the last year of his life, 1985, Rock Hudson, whose death brought AIDS to the attention of millions, alternated between denying his HIV status to his friends and resigning himself to an agonizing death before sixty. While on his deathbed in Los Angeles, his publicity team released a statement, one Hudson had no part in composing, that would set the blueprint for belated celebrity disclosures. A few years later, Freddie Mercury and Anthony Perkins both released statements when they were drawing their last breaths, acknowledging that it was AIDS that would end their lives. (In his final public message, Perkins seemed to address the dehumanizing viewpoints of Falwell and his ilk. "There are many who believe that this disease is God's vengeance, but I believe it was sent to teach people how to love and understand and have compassion for each other. I have learned more about love, selflessness and human understanding from the people I have met in this great adventure in the world of AIDS than I ever did in the cutthroat, competitive world in which I spent my life.")

Then there were the celebrities who denied having AIDS until the bleak and bitter end and whose deaths were attributed to the opportunistic diseases that afflicted them as a by-product of unchecked HIV. These included Liberace, Roy Cohn, Michel Foucault, Robert Reed (of *The Brady Bunch* fame), Isaac Asimov, and designer Perry Ellis.

Although Morrison had achieved a level of fame most Oklahomans would never dream about, he was not exempt from discrimination. Not long after being diagnosed with HIV, Morrison found himself being ostracized. "People wouldn't shake his hand, wouldn't come close to him, wouldn't let babies next to him," Tony Holden told ESPN. "And I saw that, and you took a kid from this height of stardom, being in movies, to the point where everyone wanted to be Morrison's friend to the point where, man, nobody wanted to be in the same room with him. I witnessed it. And it was heartbreaking."

"Nobody wanted to touch him; nobody wanted to be around him," Diana Morrison recalled, for *30 for 30*. "It just really, really hurt him. It hurt him inside, it really did."

Gone were the entourage, gone were the parties, gone were good times, at last. "HIV," Morrison said, "is considered a loser's virus."

★ ★ ★

Less than a month after Morrison had confirmed his HIV status by a second test, he was at ringside for the Mike Tyson–Frank Bruno title fight, doing commentary for Showtime on its pay-per-view telecast. Morrison showed potential as an on-camera analyst, and his professional future, at least, offered a glimmer of hope. That glimmer would ultimately turn out to be a mirage.

On March 19, Morrison pleaded no contest to two misdemeanor counts of assault and battery stemming from his October altercation at a party thrown by Tammy Witt, the mother of his son Trey. Special Judge Martha Sue Thompson gave Morrison a suspended sentence (for each charge) and fines that totaled $600. In addition, Morrison was ordered to perform thirty hours of community service.

On July 17, Morrison suffered a seizure and lost consciousness while at the wheel of his pickup truck after overdosing on what most reports called "medication." He was transported to Grove General Hospital before being airlifted by helicopter to St. John Medical Center in Tulsa. Local newspaper accounts stressed that Morrison had suffered a reaction to "legally prescribed" drugs, which seemed an odd way of phrasing it, almost as if they were trying to link his collapse with HIV. A month later, Morrison would blame his blackout on amino-acid supplements. "I was in a hurry," he told the *Kansas City Star*, "didn't want to measure it out and took three times as much as I should've. Fortunately, it happened in town, and I wasn't going down the highway seventy miles an hour."

How could Morrison have suffered an adverse reaction to HIV medication, anyway? After all, he had decided to bypass HIV drugs altogether.

★ ★ ★

Not until 1987 would the FDA approve the first effective medication to treat HIV: a forsaken antiretroviral drug originally developed to fight leukemia in the 1960s. Before the arrival of AZT (manufactured under the brand name Retrovir and produced by Burroughs Wellcome), treatment for HIV was scattershot and ineffective. Desperate victims often turned to charlatans for help in managing a novel disease without a cure, without treatment, without apparent hope. Once the inexorable spread of HIV led to AIDS, only palliative care remained. But AZT, which was controversially fast-tracked by the FDA in less than two years, had limitations. Its drawbacks included toxic side effects (nausea, fever, vomiting, and insomnia) and, worst of all perhaps, viral resistance. The longer a patient used

AZT, the likelier the virus would adapt or mutate in response, developing an immunity that would eventually destroy its efficacy. For as long as patients avoided viral resistance, AZT functioned as a life extender, but its toxicity and its history of diminishing returns meant that valid long-term treatment remained in the future.

In a few years, scientists developed dual-combination therapy (blending AZT with lamivudine, brand name 3TC) followed by the triple "cocktail" treatment, a mixture of antiretroviral drugs (which included AZT) and newly developed protease inhibitors such as saquinavir, ritonavir, and indinavir. Given the acronym HAART (Highly Active Antiretroviral Therapy), this new treatment lowered viral loads to undetectable levels, limited the opportunistic diseases that emerged as HIV progressed, and extended life far beyond what AZT managed in the late 1980s. Far more effective than anything that had come before it, HAART arrived at around the time that Tommy Morrison contracted HIV.

★ ★ ★

By August, only seven months after his diagnosis, Morrison went public with his decision to turn his back on science. "I'm not taking any medications up to this point—why try to fix it if it ain't broke?" Morrison told the *Kansas City Star*. "There may be a time I have to reconsider, but now I'm perfectly fine. From day one, they wanted me to get on medication, and I chose to approach things in a more natural way, with vitamins, workouts, and diet."

Dr. David Ho, who treated Magic Johnson and was named Man of the Year in 1996 by *Time* magazine, stopped seeing Morrison after Morrison declined a regimen of pills. Later, Morrison would reveal a characteristic common to all conspiracy theorists and delusional personalities: In his mind, he knew more about any given subject than trained professionals and renowned scientists. "All Dr. Ho did was do my blood work," Morrison told *POZ* magazine. "And then he tried to give me the damn medication. The top guy in the field doesn't even understand that HIV isn't a germ, it's a virus. It's not alive, so you can't kill it—which is why, thirteen years later, we're no closer to a so-called cure."

This sort of certainty goes hand in hand with magical thinking. Morrison, like so many other fanatics, ignored facts and substituted intuition or a "gut feeling" for verifiable science. "I don't have a lot of confidence in all this medication," Morrison told the *Desert Sun*. "I've chosen not to take it. See, I don't think that HIV causes AIDS. Some of the research I've read and some of the doctors I've talked to—there are still a lot of unanswered questions. It hasn't been proven scientifically to my satisfaction that HIV leads to AIDS. They've been saying for two years that HIV may not be the sole cause of AIDS. It's not the cause at all. I believe that in my heart. I'm not a doctor, but it's never been proven."

★ ★ ★

For Morrison, indeed for anyone looking for alternative viewpoints (or a way to subvert reality), educating himself could only mean one thing: He had found himself under the spell of Peter Duesberg, a professor of molecular biology at the University of California, Berkeley, who single-handedly kick-started the HIV denialist movement in 1987.

In *The Epidemic: A Global History of AIDS*, Jonathan Engel describes how Duesberg explained away the shocking AIDS body count. "Virtually all were dying of other infections, of overdoses of drugs and of ancillary contagions, and HIV simply happened to be found in their blood in low levels. Duesberg particularly emphasized the dangers of recreational drug use and conjectured that the sexual revolution had greatly increased incidences of syphilis, gonorrhea, and various other STDs. . . . That HIV existed, he did not deny. That it caused AIDS was, for Duesberg, a myth constructed in the interest of 'careerism, job security, grant money, financial benefits, and prestige.'"

Although Duesberg was a pioneer on retroviruses, he never researched HIV or AIDS, basing his theories instead on social-data trends and his knowledge of other retroviruses, but that fact did not disqualify such an eminent name from the denialist movement. He remained (and remains) the single most accomplished figure to dissent from the established science, and HIV denialists quote him, directly or indirectly, as often as true believers quoted Big Brother in 1984.

By insisting that the cause of AIDS in America was drug use, Duesberg not only perpetuated the prejudicial "lifestyle-as-disease" argument but conveniently ignored the thousands upon thousands of people with AIDS who had never taken illicit drugs of any kind. He had ignored other risk groups, namely infants of HIV-positive mothers and hemophiliacs, whose HIV status had nothing to do with amyl nitrates, heroin, or cocaine.

Even more fantastic (and irresponsible), Duesberg, along with his zealous followers, insisted that the AIDS plague in Africa, where millions had died, never occurred. To Duesberg, those millions of dead Africans—stretching from Cape Town to Algiers—were the inevitable by-product of malnutrition, poor sanitation, and contaminated water.

Finally, Duesberg promoted the outlandish theory that AIDS is also caused by the medication taken to prevent its emergence. The idea that a disease—one that had already existed without remedy for several years—could be caused by the drugs subsequently developed to treat it is fantastical, but it was only part of the Duesberg package. Seth Kalichman, professor of social psychology at the University of Connecticut, summed up just how ludicrous these theories are in his book, *Denying AIDS: Conspiracy Theories, Pseudoscience, and Human Tragedy*: "For Duesberg, HIV infection may or may not occur at all in people who have AIDS. HIV is inconsequential and is only sometimes present in people who develop AIDS. Which cause of AIDS we are talking about depends on where you live as well as your lifestyle. For gay men, drug use causes AIDS. For gay men who do not use drugs, HIV medications cause AIDS. In Africa, malnutrition causes AIDS. If you are a wealthy African, AZT causes AIDS. If you are a hemophiliac, treatments for hemophilia cause AIDS. No research has ever suggested the Duesbergian view of AIDS is true."

Why would anyone subscribe to such absurdities? In 1984, when Duesberg rejected his own cancer theories, which had been advanced by other scientists in the years since his discoveries, he began to earn the label of "crank." An accomplished microbiologist who had done groundbreaking work on retroviruses (he had discovered and mapped the cancer gene), Duesberg managed to lose the support of the scientific community in the span of four or five years. But because of his previous accomplishments—his lauded work on oncogenes, his tenured position at the University of California, Berkeley, his membership in the National Academy of Sciences—Duesberg flaunted a credibility that almost guaranteed his word would be considered an imprimatur, of sorts, to skeptics and hucksters now free to misconstrue science as they saw fit.

This argumentum ad verecundiam had done untold damage to thousands, particularly when Duesberg played a part in the health policy of

South African president Thabo Mbeki in the early 2000s. Authority, without professional consensus, is hardly infallible—morally, ethically, scientifically. Think of the infamous Nazi doctors who performed atrocities in the name of the Reich, the medical professionals involved in the Tuskegee experiments, the scientists behind covert CIA operations such as Project MK-Ultra. (Vis-à-vis HIV, Kary B. Mullis, a Nobel Laureate who wrote the introduction to *Inventing the AIDS Virus*, claimed to have been abducted by aliens; and Henry H. Bauer, former professor of chemistry and social sciences at Virginia Tech, was once a devotee of the Loch Ness Monster.) For his own twisted reasons, Duesberg perverted the scientific method when it came to HIV, lost the standing he had developed over the years, and became an outcast from his peers.

To understand how Morrison might have fallen into the world of tinfoil hats, one also has to consider the cultural zeitgeist. When Duesberg published his book *Inventing the AIDS Virus* in 1996, the Satanic Ritual Abuse phenomena had just wound down, only to be overtaken by a new generation of conspiracy theories and panics. The mid to late 1990s was ground zero for conspiracy theories, ignited a few years earlier by Oliver Stone (*JFK*) and the premiere of *The X-Files*. Black helicopters, Area 51, Waco, Princess Di, UFOs, Whitewater—the decade was overrun by far-out hypotheses. ("Alien Beings Abduct Pop Culture" read a 1996 *New York Times* headline.) Of course, the key generator of mid-1990s paranoia was the World Wide Web, which enabled disinformation to spread at dial-up speed and allowed far-flung true believers to coalesce in cyberspace, where they built echo chambers designed to codify their outlandish fantasies. Before the internet, having alternative beliefs meant subscribing to an underground newsletter, haunting the occult sections of dusty bookstores for vanity press titles, or pamphleteering in the streets. The dot-com universe changed all that, and the idealistic notion of an Information Superhighway soon morphed into a Misinformation Superhighway.

Unlike today, when quackery and conspiracy theories are often disseminated by anonymous internet accounts on fringe chat rooms or by obvious crackpots raving on podcasts or YouTube, the Satanic Ritual Abuse panic (and its predecessor, the Recovered-Memory Movement, in which hundreds of subjects suddenly found themselves afflicted with dozens of personalities) was sparked by clinical psychologists, social workers, and psychiatrists. What Duesberg offered—distortions, suspicion, circular logic, and irrationality—was in the air.

All HIV denialists and conspiratorialists over the last thirty years owe their oddball theories to Duesberg, including Tommy Morrison, who routinely parroted Duesberg talking points whenever the subject of HIV popped up.

★ ★ ★

In a 2001 article, "The AIDS Deniers," GQ profiled the raucous and ultimately tragic leaders of San Francisco ACT UP, a bizarre splinter group of the original, confrontational ACT UP, founded by Larry Kramer. Where ACT UP in the 1980s and 1990s advocated—through civil disobedience and political action—for treatment, legislation, and research on behalf of people with AIDS, San Francisco ACT UP, incredibly, were HIV deniers.

Two of these perverse activists—David Pasquarelli and Michael Bellefountaine, both HIV-positive—would infiltrate marches or events and spit on their ideological enemies. A third member, Ronnie Burke, once dumped a bag of used cat litter over Pat Christen, executive director of the San Francisco AIDS Foundation, at a conference. Their collective outlook on HIV/AIDS was straight out of Peter Duesberg and *Inventing the AIDS Virus*. "Well, yeah, gay men were getting sick in the early '80s," Pasquarelli said, "and there were gay men that were dying in large numbers. The reasons are related to recreational and pharmaceutical drug abuse."

All three members of San Francisco ACT UP profiled in "The AIDS Deniers" were dead a few years after the article appeared. Ronnie Burke, forty-seven, died in March 2003. David Pasquarelli, thirty-six, died in March 2004. Michael Bellefountaine, forty-one, died in June 2007.

In fact, the most notable characteristic of committed denialists who also happen to be HIV-positive is that they die. They die young, and they die of uncommon ailments often categorized as AIDS-defining illnesses. That dismal, dispiriting list includes Casper J. Schmidt, a psychiatrist who claimed AIDS was not a disease but the manifestation of collective hysteria; Karri Stokely, who died four years after abandoning antiretrovirals when she saw a denialist video; Tony Tompsett, publisher of "Continuum," a pseudoscience newsletter focusing on denialism, and a publication whose entire editorial board died, one by one, of AIDS; Christine Maggiore, a woman so caught up in the fantasia of denial, that her own daughter, only three years old, died of untreated HIV.

For a feature printed in the July 1997 issue of *POZ* magazine, Tommy Morrison visited Aaron Todd Shriver in Chelsea, Oklahoma. A young man struggling with his own HIV diagnosis, Shriver was at a vulnerable tipping point when he reached out to Morrison for a pep talk of sorts. Morrison, by then already hitched to the rickety Duesberg bandwagon, encouraged Shriver to reject his treatment. "This kid was perfectly healthy before he started taking the medication," Morrison said. "He knew something wasn't going right. All he needed was me to put him over the edge."

Ten years later, Shriver, not yet forty, was dead.

★ ★ ★

There had never been anything wholesome about Tommy Morrison—who often claimed he had lost his virginity before he was a teenager—and his performance as a contrite sinner, newly reformed, who had been in the midst of a committed (as well as monogamous) relationship when HIV had struck him down did not convince everyone.

In her overview of sex and morality in the 1990s, *Last Night in Paradise*, cultural critic Katie Roiphe took aim at Morrison from the comfort of her Manhattan living room. "There was something unlikable about Tommy Morrison—some of the violence and the trailer park, the self-interest and the appetite—that showed in his face."

It took only a few months for his straitlaced image to unravel, both publicly and privately. In public, Morrison pleaded no contest to his assault charge, faced possible indictment for carrying a concealed weapon, and undermined his activist efforts by refusing to take HIV medication.

Nor had that earlier promise to become a spokesman for AIDS gained much momentum. His connection with Magic Johnson had dissolved before they could team for a public awareness campaign, and, although Morrison made several charitable appearances throughout the first half of 1996 (some of them stemming from his plea-bargain deal in March), he found it harder and harder to address the topic of HIV. That was because he had already begun to doubt the lethality of the virus and the merits of pharmaceutical treatment. He had already made his bizarre views on medication clear to the *Kansas City Star*, and he would double down on his rapidly developing rebellion against reality in the July 1996 issue of *The Ring*. "As far as medication, I've heard a lot of negative things about AZT and how it kills you faster than the virus," Morrison told Steve Farhood. "I have mixed emotions about it. You know, since all this came about, through the mail I've received about forty different cures for AIDS. All kinds of stuff."

★ ★ ★

"I broke a thousand hearts
Before I met you;
I'll break a thousand more, baby,
Before I am through."
—George Thorogood

★ ★ ★

In private, Morrison had married Dawn Freeman in Las Vegas on May 18, 1996, but he continued his affair with Dawn Gilbert, nullifying his family-values posture and, in the process, potentially endangering two women he claimed to love. But adultery was not enough for Morrison. Nothing was ever enough for him. Married for less than four months to Freeman, Morrison decided that matrimony was worth doing all over again.

So he married Dawn Gilbert down in Mexico.

According to Gilbert, who documented her unromantic lead-up to matrimony in her memoir, she had accompanied Morrison to San Diego and Tijuana, where Morrison was getting alternative HIV treatment. While they were in their hotel room one morning, Morrison had injected himself with what Gilbert called an "HIV inoculation." When he was done with the syringe, he surprised Gilbert with an act that bordered on madness. "I was standing there in great sympathy when he removed the needle and plunged it into my hip, saying, 'Ooooh. There, now you have AIDS, too,' Gilbert wrote. "He thought it was funny and continued to laugh for the next few minutes. This time I was scared to death knowing the virus is most easily transmitted by needles. I shrieked, and he just shrugged. No apologies, no nothing. I was speechless and horrified. Finally, when I recovered from the shock, I asked, 'Are you insane?'"

That, in essence, was what bound Gilbert to Morrison, bound her enough to agree to marry him. "Then after our return, he persisted without letup," she wrote. "'We need to do this—go back to Tijuana and get married.' You could say that he simply wore me down. I believe that I was in the [HIV] window. But I further thought he had plunged the needle into my thigh [sic] on purpose to be sure I had the virus, in which case I would finally accept his wishes and marry him. With all of these thoughts in my head, I accepted and accompanied him on a flight to San Diego two months later."

They were married in a Tijuana courthouse, with their cab driver, Raul, as their sole witness.

★ ★ ★

Among his many other foibles, Tommy Morrison was, in fact, a premeditated bigamist. Even in the mid-1990s, bigamy seemed quaint, a strange holdover from sensational Victorian romances. The occasional real-life scandal involving double families—take Charles Kuralt, for example—and the polygamous sects scattered across the Mountain West carried with it a hint of the surreal, an atmosphere Morrison would master in the coming years. But perhaps nothing about his carnal lifestyle—reckless, aimless, remorseless, seemingly bottomless—is as shocking as the willingness of dozens of women to risk a potential death sentence by sleeping with the most famous carrier of HIV outside of Magic Johnson. Those scenarios would play out in the future—the limited future that remained for Morrison, but that two women would marry "The Duke" and accept not only a dubious triangle but his crackpot theories on HIV and AIDS is shocking. (In her memoir, Gilbert also wrote that Morrison had once physically assaulted and threatened to kill her before they were married.) And his behavior, now growing increasingly erratic, left Morrison in a state of confusion that would send him searching for something that would give him a measure of stability.

★ ★ ★

Under normal circumstances, which are few and far between in boxing, Nevada State Athletic Commission executive director Marc Ratner would have issued a medical suspension, placed Morrison on an ineligible list, and would hope that other states would honor the sanction. But Ratner sat down with blow-by-blow announcer Steve Albert during the opening moments of the notorious February 10, 1996, Showtime broadcast and declared that Tommy Morrison had been suspended "worldwide," a statement that surprised Albert enough for him to push for confirmation.

The phrase "worldwide suspension" rippled throughout media coverage, despite its flimsy grounding in reality. In October 1996, the Professional Boxing Safety Act, spearheaded by Senator John McCain, became law. One of its provisions was that each commission would abide by and acknowledge suspensions of fighters imposed by other commissions. Before the Professional Boxing Safety Act, commissions often recognized suspensions across the board informally, as an act of bureaucratic decorum. Only an unofficial policy of reciprocity between states kept fighters from circumventing disciplinary action. Over the years, boxers had avoided suspensions merely by fighting in other states or adopting fake names and identities. These cloak-and-dagger maneuvers on the part of desperate or unprincipled fighters required the aid of amoral managers, vulturous promoters, and incompetent if not corrupt commission members. And while most of these shenanigans took place in backwater states with little oversight (or no oversight at all) and featuring C-level talents, there were a few high-profile cases of negligence or corruption that highlighted just how haywire boxing could be.

Early in his career, Roy Jones Jr., who would become one of the most recognizable and dynamic talents of the 1990s, knocked out an imposter in Pensacola, Florida. Jones was scheduled to fight a journeyman named Derwin Richards on July 14, 1990, but wound up flattening a car washer named Tony Waddles instead. Florida officials arrested Waddles, Elvis Belt, a manager, and Gerome Peete, a matchmaker, on charges of grand theft by fraud. (It should be noted that Waddles and Elvis Belt, who was eventually acquitted, both hailed from Oklahoma.)

In 1999, Stephan Johnson, a competent junior middleweight who had recently hit the skids, died after suffering a TKO at the hands of a former world titleholder named Paul Vaden. Unfortunately, Johnson did not belong in the ring against Vaden, not because of a talent gap—par for the course in boxing, which specializes in mismatches—but because he was under medical suspension by the Ontario Athletic Commission, following a savage KO loss to Fitz Vanderpool in Toronto a few months earlier. Johnson, knocked cold, had to be taken from the ring on a stretcher for immediate medical attention. But Johnson somehow slipped through the regulatory cracks and went on to fight in the laissez-faire states of Georgia and South Carolina before his tragic date with Vaden in New Jersey, which somehow failed to notice that Johnson was on a suspension list.

Because boxing in the mid-1990s suffered from fractured and even fractious regulatory oversight, there was nothing legally binding about the procedure that barred Morrison from fighting. At the time it suspended Tommy Morrison, just before the passing of the Professional Boxing Safety Act, the Nevada State Athletic Commission had no jurisdiction or authority over any state (especially those without athletic commissions), much less over international bodies. This fact would become preposterously clear before the year was even over, when Morrison would seek and obtain a license to fight in Japan. For Ratner to make such a statement, overblown and technically inaccurate, he must have assumed that no regulatory body with any standing would sanction a bout involving an HIV-positive participant. He was wrong.

★ ★ ★

September 19, 1996. The Southern Hills Marriott in Tulsa, Oklahoma. This time, Tommy Morrison stands at the dais, head shaved, slightly bloated, wearing a white band-collar shirt and a 90s-patterned vest, to declare what had previously seemed impossible: that he will return to the ring for one last fight. It is a vague future that Morrison suggests. There is no date set, there is no opponent, there is no venue, there is no plan beyond the ever-present now. In that sense, it is a typical Tommy Morrison action—only the moment seems to matter.

In contrast to his last press conference, when Morrison appeared regretful and tortured about his yesterdays as much as he was about his tomorrows, there is an air of defiance to his new announcement. "I know there's a lot of people out there who probably are not going to like what I'm doing," Morrison says. "But they will have to listen to what I have to say."

A few months earlier, when Morrison had first announced his HIV diagnosis, the gloom at the Marriott had been palpable. Among the television cameras, microphones, tape recorders, and popping flashbulbs, Morrison, his voice cracking repeatedly, had excoriated himself for his personal failings. That was a mass media auto-da-fé, broadcast live across the country. Behind him stood his glum team; in the audience, sitting with his parents, was his "fiancé," Dawn Freeman; and somewhere in the crowd was Dawn Gilbert, his shadow fiancé, proof, in retrospect, that Morrison had never meant for his solemn words to be taken seriously.

"When all this happened," he says, "I thought I would change my lifestyle and become a role model and spokesperson for these kids. But the bottom line is I'm not now nor have I ever been a good role model." (Here, Morrison echoes NBA lightning rod Charles Barkley, whose "I am not a role model" commercial for Nike was both edgy and obnoxious, and Magic Johnson himself, eventually to express his own doubts about public duty: "I never wanted to be a hero.")

Morrison insists that his return to a blood sport is driven by a desire to raise money for his charitable organization, the KnockOut AIDS Foundation, specifically for children with AIDS. "The last six months I have been with children a number of times, children with AIDS," Morrison says, "and I have seen them rejected and shunned in their communities, at schools. The rejection is probably more harmful than having the actual virus itself."

Despite his apparent sincerity, Morrison triggers backlash for his plans. The day after the news conference, Jason Whitlock of the *Kansas City Star* lambastes "The Duke" in a column. "What Morrison has been good at is manipulation. Morrison perfected the art of holding Bibles at news conferences and holding down boilermakers in Westport."

Even Magic Johnson, who had made his own controversial return to the NBA just before Morrison announced his HIV diagnosis, reproves Morrison. "After talking to my doctors, which is where I get my information from, I feel that he shouldn't be doing it because it's a blood sport," Johnson tells the Associated Press. "If something were to happen, it would set the fight against HIV and AIDS back five to ten years. All the good work we've done for the last five years—I'm talking about educating people and tearing down some of those barriers of discrimination and getting TV time to get our message across—that could be lost. The fight has been going good, maybe not as good as we want, but still pretty good. Now, if something happens, oh my, the fear just jumps right back up again."

Notably absent from the press conference is Tony Holden, at war with himself over what Morrison proposes. "I was in a lose-lose situation," he says. "If I go to the news conference, it shows that I support HIV and boxing. If I stay home, it looks like I'm abandoning Tommy."

★ ★ ★

In the two years since he had shocked the sporting world by winning the heavyweight title—twenty years after he last held it—George Foreman had come close to exhausting the goodwill he had generated since he returned to the ring in 1987. So allergic was Foreman to the possibility of legitimate competition that he wound up being stripped of his titles rather than face opponents he could not personally handpick. Instead of defending his established WBA and WBC belts, he took on the mantle of another fly-by-night sanctioning body—the UK-based WBU—and absorbed the taunts of sportswriters who recognized his championship reign as a money-grab cynical even for boxing.

The ring proved just as inhospitable to him. A controversial decision over an unheralded heavyweight named Axel Schulz in April 1985 left Foreman not only battered but also delegitimized, to an extent, as a fighter. After an absence of a year and a half, Foreman, now forty-eight, decided to take his act on the road, returning to Japan for the first time since 1973. His opponent, Crawford "The Terminator" Grimsley, was an ex-kickboxer with a record so bogus that it might have qualified him for a matchup against Tommy Morrison. Indeed, Grimsley himself joked about his standing as an undefeated heavyweight. "Seven or eight guys were real stiffs," he said about his dubious 20-0 record. "Then the rest of them aren't anything to write home about either."

After HBO declined to air a fight with all the makings of a farce, promoter Ron Weathers switched gears and offered the matchup as a pay-per-view broadcast, scheduled for November 2. When it became clear that Foreman–Grimsley was a financial disaster in the making, Weathers began brainstorming. Although the card already had a gimmick scheduled—two NFL players, Alonzo Highsmith and Mark Gastineau, squaring off for the benefit of an as-yet-undetermined demographic—Weathers decided to add another, one whose hot-button topicality guaranteed feverish publicity. That was how George Foreman invited Tommy Morrison to be the co-feature of an event dubbed "Real Fights." It was Tony Holden, perhaps, who had his finger on the pulse regarding the maneuverings to export Morrison to Japan. "Controversy sells," he said. "Controversy is a moneymaker."

Despite the short notice, Morrison agreed to fight, citing his desire to raise money for the KnockOut AIDS Foundation. He would, he said, donate his reported $350,000 purse to his charity. Not everyone was warmed by the prospect of Morrison boxing again. "Anybody who gives him a license to fight ought to have his head examined," Bob Arum said. "All the medical evidence indicates there is a risk. The concern is justified."

Japan, where the Nevada State Athletic Commission had no jurisdiction, where a "worldwide suspension" was nothing more than rhetoric, simply shrugged its approval.

★ ★ ★

A date, a site, a broadcast outlet. Only one thing remained: an opponent. Regarding that final piece of the comeback puzzle, newspapers and insiders asked a simple if salient question: who would want to fight Tommy Morrison? "I have fifty fighters who want to fight Tommy Morrison," Ron Weathers told the Los Angeles Times. "He's a credible fighter. If they knock him out, it's instant money. With the business they are in, these fighters are not concerned with HIV. In this sport, they put themselves on the line every day." That may have been true, but Weathers would have to strike anyone with a real chance of winning from his extensive list of willing fighters.

With Tony Holden back on board (despite his misgivings), it was business as usual for Team Morrison. That meant casting a dragnet for an appropriate stiff. Eventually, Team Morrison settled on an Oklahoma felon named Anthony Cooks. Just as a burnt-out Mike Williams refused to submit to a drug test, and Toi Toia was semiretired and working in a potato factory, barely fit to go three rounds, and Sherman Griffin had recently spent more time in prison than in a gym, Cooks was a risky proposition—but to the event itself, not to anyone answering the bell against him.

When matchmakers and promoters scrounge the grimiest corners of Podunk gyms for opponents, they do so with the full knowledge that the fight might fall through due to the very reasons they find such opponents appealing: They are borderline personalities as well as borderline professionals. This strategy was particularly true of Team Morrison, which specialized in dredging opponents from the boxing underbelly, where booking agents might trawl halfway houses or YMCAs for live bodies.

To his (dis)credit, Cooks, with a record of 8-5, lived up to expectations. A few days before the bout, a warrant was issued for his arrest on charges that he had raped a fifteen-year-old girl in Oklahoma. A criminal multitasker, Cooks was also on the run for failing to appear before a jury on charges of intent to distribute cocaine and marijuana. For Team Morrison, Cooks had precisely the kind of experience necessary to qualify for the co-feature in Japan. He had spent a total of at least ten years in prison on a variety of charges: armed robbery in Oklahoma County, attempted robbery with a dangerous weapon in Tulsa, and larceny of merchandise in Okmulgee County. In a career stretching back to 1983, Cooks had only thirteen professional fights between prison stints, and he had been knocked out in the first round in his last start, three months earlier. Finally, he had never weighed more than 200 pounds in his career, and a vague air of desperation surrounded him. "A lot of people have been saying I'm crazy to fight, but I need the fight," he said about his only chance at significant cash. "I need the money." He was, in fact, the perfect opponent and the latest in a long line of patsies that Morrison had been cuffing around since he had been a teenager.

"I'm making sure [Morrison] won't face Joe Killer or this being treated like a circus act," Tony Holden had said about his involvement in what was, essentially, a circus act. "I know I'm going to get beat up for what I'm doing. But I have to do what's right." As a promoter, Holden had always been honest—one of the rarest traits in boxing—but, like so many others in a sport that seemingly took its cues from Dada or the Marx Brothers, he was susceptible to delusion. Of course, when it came to delusion, Morrison surpassed Holden with ease. Without a hint of irony, Morrison weighed in on the Cooks fiasco. "We don't want the fight tainted in any way with something negative," he announced. "I said, 'Let's get someone else.' That's what happened."

"Someone else" turned out to be Marcus Rhode, an ex-lineman at Missouri Western State College, who had fought three weeks earlier (a knockout of a body named Jim Davis, record 1-1). Another wobbly circuit fighter from the Midwest, Rhode was barely acceptable as a replacement for Cooks. His reported 15-1 ledger was as fraudulent as a junk bond offering from Charles Keating. Because a circuit fighter is a quasi-professional whose only purpose is to build up a statistically impressive record against local push-overs, in hopes of receiving a substantial payday somewhere down the line, Rhode instantly jumped on the short-notice opportunity. The $25,000 he earned to face Morrison is exactly the kind of payoff a circuit fighter, along with his crew, coveted; it is exactly the kind of payoff that justifies all the scheming that leads to four- and six-rounders at the Argosy Riverboat, the Capitol Plaza Hotel, the Beaumont Club, and the State Park Fair.

With only a few days until fight time, Rhode was still scrambling in St. Louis, preparing for a flight to Los Angeles, where he hoped an expe-dited passport process would allow him to cross the Pacific. "It's been a pretty rough morning. It's never a done deal until you get in the ring," Rhode told the *St. Joseph News-Press*. Even Tim "Doughboy" Tomashek had a better chance at preparing for Morrison than Rhode did. After all, Tomashek did not have to make an international flight, sixteen to eighteen hours long, or suffer jet lag from a time-zone differential.

The only rider added to the usual rules of fisticuffs was simple: If Mor-rison suffered a cut at any point in the fight, his cornermen would have one minute to stanch the bleeding. If they failed, Morrison would forfeit and lose via TKO. The chances of Morrison suffering any damage to Rhode were negligible, however, and the Tokyo Bay NK Hall would be spared any chilling bloodshed.

For his first fight in over a year, Morrison entered the ring wearing a cropped gold jacket with bell sleeves and "TCB" stitched on its back. He had weighed in at 228 pounds, and although he looked a bit chunky, he seemed almost lean compared to his press conference appearance in September. In the opposite corner stood Rhode, a flabby 250 pounds, wearing generic white trunks (red stripe) and a blank look on his face.

Japanese crowds are notoriously reserved (the eerie silence that accom-panied the James "Buster" Douglas–Mike Tyson fight, the biggest upset in boxing history, seemed almost perverse), and when the opening bell rang, the hush seemed to underscore the dreamlike quality of the entire card.

The two men met at ring center, where Rhode flicked out his jab double-time while Morrison stalked. It took only forty-five seconds for Rhode to take his first tumble. Morrison countered a lazy jab with a straight right that sent him somersaulting to the canvas. Two knockdowns later, it was all over. Tommy Morrison, the first openly HIV-positive boxer in history, had scored his first victory in his shocking comeback. All it took was ninety-eight seconds.

★ ★ ★

Not long after losing to Morrison, Rhode would become an expert in his specialized field—which involved a gift for drama and choreography—building a record of 35-55 over twenty years. He was knocked out forty-four times, usually in the first or second round, and was so inept he sometimes lost to the setups intended to pad his win column. Of these setbacks, none could be more embarrassing than losing a decision to Lorenzo Boyd, who had dropped twenty-two out of his previous twenty-three fights.

★ ★ ★

When his predictable if controversial comeback was over, talk of a potential rematch against George Foreman (who had scored a monotonous decision over Grimsley in Tokyo) began making the rounds. After the fight, Foreman spoke glowingly about Morrison and about his accomplishment in Japan, which, while negligible as a sporting affair, certainly merited some sort of milestone distinction. No one, after all, had ever competed in an event while openly being HIV-positive. (Greg Louganis competed in the 1988 Summer Olympics after being diagnosed with HIV, but he had kept his illness a secret until 1995.) "Tommy Morrison did something very important today," Foreman said during the post-fight press conference. "He's back in the ring and executed his profession. No one can ever say now, 'what if?' or 'maybe' or 'he should' or 'he shouldn't.' It's done now. Now it's time for someone else to come and do it again, but he's already stepped in, the water's fine, and nobody can take that away from boxing."

If Morrison was looking for the quickest possible way to raise money for his KnockOut AIDS Foundation, then another fight with Foreman would have guaranteed instant funding. "If the opportunity presents itself, I would be stupid not to fight him," Morrison said. "Foreman portrays a good guy, and this could prove to everybody that there is no risk. It's strictly up to him."

Although Foreman had expressed interest in facing Morrison again—for revenge, for money, for altruism—the fight never happened. In fact, it would take more than a decade for Morrison to step into the ring again. "People ask me all the time, 'Are you going to fight again?' The answer's no because I don't have the desire to fight again," Morrison said. "I'd tell you why—but I don't really know why. The competing I do miss. But the training I don't miss at all because my style of fighting, the training was very hard. I wasn't a boxer; I was a banger. And that means you get beat up a lot in training and you're always sore. I don't miss that part of it at all."

★ ★ ★

In 1997, the new life Morrison had tried to stitch together began to unravel. At the same time, little by little, he started losing his grip on reality. The year started on a high note for Morrison, who had signed a contract with Fox Sports Network to provide color commentary for a boxing series staged by Dan Goossen and America Presents. On January 17, 1997, Morrison was at ringside in Reseda, California, where he worked a card headlined by Michael Nunn and Rudy Nix. Paired with veteran Barry Tompkins, who had made his name in the 1980s as blow-by-blow announcer for HBO, Morrison seemed awkward and hesitant behind the microphone.

While his fledgling broadcast career promised professional stability, his personal life mainly offered chaos. He was still married to the two Dawns, alternating between them in Oklahoma, and adding other women to the mix as time allowed, along with a new dependency on marijuana. Dawn Gilbert described Morrison during this dreary period: "Because Tom was no longer training, he seemingly had no real purpose in his life," she wrote in her memoir. "His longtime friends of the past were mostly in Fayetteville. Because he seldom saw them, Tom began to acquire new friends, most of whom were druggies who lived in Tulsa. He also brought many of his girls from the past back into his life. His drugs became a priority, and he began to make many trips to Tulsa, sometimes stopping by to see me, but more often than not, hanging with his newfound friends, most of whom I despised. At the start of the year, we talked almost daily, but by the end of the year, our visits were seldom. When we did see each other, Tom was nearly always out of it on pot. Essentially, he spent '97 as a huge 'pothead,' and in doing so, he pushed me further and further away, to the point that I moved, left no forwarding address, and changed my phone number."

As usual, what Morrison told the public seemed to clash—at times violently—with reality. Since his HIV diagnosis in early 1996, Morrison had painted an idyllic portrait of his relationship (and then marriage) to Freeman, but it was a tortured romance that might have inspired a chapter of *Codependent No More*. "I plan on being with her forever, anyway," Morrison told the *Kansas City Star* about marriage to Freeman. "I said, especially after she got tested and was negative, 'I totally understand if you want to go. I'd be silly not to understand that.' She looked at me and said, 'I love you, and I don't care.'"

★ ★ ★

On March 20, 1997, Morrison once again became hot copy; it would be years before he ceased being so. At 3 a.m. on a Thursday morning, Morrison was arrested in Fort Scott, Kansas, and charged with driving under the influence. His blood alcohol level was .016, twice the legal limit of .08. Morrison had been on his way back from a speaking engagement at Appleton City High School in Missouri, where he addressed first-year students about the hazards of excess. "Here I am teaching about responsibility and then I pull something stupid like that. It kind of makes me feel uncomfortable." Worse, Morrison had violated the terms of his suspended sentence from his last arrest.

★ ★ ★

"Morrison told the rapt audience there were three things he tried to do every day, things he felt they should do: 'Every day I look in the mirror and ask if I am being true to myself. I set goals. Ask, *Is this responsible?* Make a change in your life,' Morrison said. 'Start living your life to make people proud.'"
—Travis Millsaps, *Daily News Journal*, Murfreesboro, Tennessee

★ ★ ★

In April Morrison pleaded innocent to all charges and waited for a trial date. The arrest had more than just legal ramifications for Morrison—as a result of the negative publicity he received, Fox Sports Network fired him. He filled some of his spare time by training Brenda Rouse, a flyweight from Bartlesville, Oklahoma, whom Morrison began coaching in late 1996. An ex-kickboxer looking to ride the Christy Martin wave, Rouse, undefeated at 6-0-1, was preparing to face Yvonne Trevino in Las Vegas on a card televised by ABC. "If she were eighteen or nineteen, I probably wouldn't work with her," Morrison said about training Rouse. "She's very career-oriented. When I was nineteen, my heart wasn't in it. I hated training. On a skill level, it blows my mind how quickly she made the transition from kickboxing to boxing. She's very hungry to learn, so that makes it a joy in the gym."

The joy was short-lived, however, when Trevino bombed out Rouse in the first round.

★ ★ ★

"For five frustrating years I managed and trained Tommy Morrison and spent an inordinate amount of time trying to teach him the fundamentals of the sport and of life. I failed in both areas but one can only lead a horse to water; you cannot make them drink. I recently watched Tommy Morrison's female boxer on ABC and saw her get annihilated in the first round because of a lack of boxing fundamentals. She got knocked out with an uppercut, the same punch that always penetrated Morrison's defense because he refused to keep his elbows in proper defensive position. That probably cost Morrison the heavyweight championship and worldwide fame and will probably end the career of his female boxer. It is ironic that, in spite of everything Tommy has been through, he still continues to get arrested for DUI and is handing down a philosophy of boxing that doesn't work. Some people never learn."
—John Brown, Fan Mail, *Kansas City Star*, May 4, 1997

★ ★ ★

Without his boxing career, without his Fox Sports Network job, Morrison was adrift. He held occasional charitable events for his KnockOut

AIDS Foundation, such as a June celebrity golf tournament in Springfield, Tennessee, and thumbed through the occasional film scripts sent to him, but he began losing himself in a fog of liquor and marijuana. On July 17, 1997, Morrison withdrew his guilty plea on his drunk driving charge in Fort Scott and accepted a one-year diversionary agreement. That arrangement kept Morrison from a trial and a potential prison sentence, but it also meant that he would have to avoid trouble for the duration of the agreement. For Morrison, that would be a Herculean task. Since his knockout loss to Michael Bentt in October 1993, Morrison had never gone more than thirteen months without some legal misadventure.

It would take a little more than a month for Morrison to violate the terms of his diversionary agreement. On August 19, 1997, Morrison precipitated a traffic smashup in Jay that injured three people, including a twelve-year-old girl. Morrison, intoxicated behind the wheel, rammed into the rear of a car on U.S. Highway 59 and Ninth Street, triggering a chain reaction. Police found a half-empty bottle of Crown Royal in his vehicle, along with two loaded pistols and several whiskey miniatures, still unopened. After failing a field sobriety test and refusing a Breathalyzer, Morrison was taken into custody. He was charged with four misdemeanors: driving under the influence of intoxicants, carrying a loaded firearm while under the influence of intoxicants, transporting an open container of alcohol, and following a vehicle too closely. Witnesses would later testify that Morrison had been seen at a Walmart before the accident, unsteady on his feet, reeking of liquor. That might have been a description of his life now, of his life for the next few years.

In his previous entanglements with the law, Morrison seemed more than just lucky when it came to avoiding prison. This time, he could not parlay his local celebrity into another lenient verdict. On December 20, 1997, a jury found Morrison guilty on three of the four charges (he was found innocent of following a vehicle too closely, and the DUI count was lessened to driving while impaired), and Special District Judge Alicia Littlefield sentenced Morrison to six months in Delaware County Jail. While Judge Littlefield made her announcement, Morrison munched nonchalantly on sunflower seeds at the defense table. His lawyer, in a final attempt to avoid incarceration for his client, urged the court to consider the fact that Morrison had a serious medical condition—he had HIV.

★ ★ ★

Then came the fire. In mid-January 1998, Morrison, out on bond and appealing his sentence, decided to take a ski trip to Colorado. He returned to Tulsa the night before his ranch house in Jay suddenly burned to the ground on January 26. The stone and cedar house, valued at $500,000, went up in flames at around 4 a.m. By the time the fire department showed up, there was no salvaging it. "The house itself had already collapsed," said Mark Goeller, fire chief, "and all that remained was an attached garage."

Ultimately, the cause of the fire, which was unusual because no one was home at the time it broke out, was labeled "undetermined." "There's nothing suspicious about the fire," said Fire Marshal spokeswoman Shannon Rowland, "but they can't find a source, an actual cause." Later, Morrison would say that arson had been the cause and that he had been targeted because of his HIV status.

Morrison and Freeman stayed in his Tulsa apartment, waiting for his insurance payout to come through.

★ ★ ★

"Pray for Tommy Morrison, but please, please do not listen to him."
—The *Kansas City Star* editorial board, May 9, 1998

★ ★ ★

The next time Tommy Morrison crashed center stage, only a few weeks later, he set a tone for his public image that would last the rest of his life: He looked and sounded like a man who belonged in a straitjacket.

In the premiere issue of *ESPN The Magazine*, which hit newsstands on March 11, 1998, a feature written by Tad Friend depicted Morrison as a basket case whose bleak and baroque childhood had led to a series of irresponsible decisions that had culminated in his contracting HIV. Friend described Morrison as a physical wreck, suggesting that untreated HIV had progressed to the point that Morrison had begun to suffer cognitive decline.

Although Morrison had already made several dubious statements about HIV and its treatment, he had done so without a manic edge to the *Kansas City Star* in 1996. A year later, a profile in *POZ* magazine revealed him to be a Duesberg acolyte bordering on conspiracy-theory mania, but *POZ* had limited pop visibility, and the feature barely resonated outside of the HIV/AIDS community. The launching of *ESPN The Magazine*, however, was a media event, and now, for the first time, a widespread audience would witness his crack-up in flashy '90s graphic design, a fashionable black-and-white font, and a price tag of $3.95.

What readers would now realize was that Tommy Morrison believed that HIV was a hoax and, in true *X-Files* style, that the drugs developed to fight it were, in fact, designed to kill you. "You unravel the little piece of paper in the bottle," Morrison said, "and you read about the side effects and they match identical with the symptoms of AIDS. So it's the medication that's killing people. HIV's never been proven to cause AIDS. HIV ain't never killed anybody."

It was a wide-ranging profile, one that depicted the Morrison family to be as stable as the atavistic desert tribe of *The Hills Have Eyes*. For the first time, the Morrison saga appeared in its squalid entirety: the abusive father; the mother charged with murder; the brother in prison for rape; alcoholism, sex, and violence scattered throughout the narrative. At the center of it all, however, was Tommy Morrison, a version of "The Duke" that few had ever seen before. Here he was, surveying his incinerated ranch in Jay, Oklahoma, his pet monkey perched on his shoulder, rambling about sinister plots and End Times. Morrison, it seems, was a Y2K fanatic. He bought an acre of land in Flippin, Arkansas, primarily for its most pragmatic feature—a cave—and became a doomsday prepper, stockpiling food, water, and guns. "Am I gonna be around in five years?" he asked. "I'll be in heaven in five years. The world won't be here in five years."

Other quips from Morrison included his theory on Magic Johnson lying about taking antiretrovirals—"I don't think he's taking the medication"—and Dr. Ho being a pawn of a conspiratorial government—"There are a lot of things he can't say or they'll shut down his business."

★ ★ ★

"Just because of who he is, because of his celebrity status, he could have an effect on others when he opens his mouth about this subject. That's the most irresponsible thing of all in my mind. And what he doesn't realize is with the advancement of treatments and with the drugs that are available

today, people with this disease can survive to live what we'd consider a normal lifespan. A lot of progress has been made."
—Dr. Patrick Nemechek

★ ★ ★

If the quotes Morrison gave to *ESPN The Magazine* hinted at a mind in disarray, his subsequent behavior confirmed it. On Thursday, July 16, 1998, at 3:42 a.m., Morrison was again arrested for driving under the influence. This time there was an almost zany edge to the circumstances: For nearly five miles, Morrison weaved through Broken Arrow, Oklahoma, with a gasoline nozzle and hose attached to the tank of his Jeep Cherokee. He was charged with suspicion of drunk driving, destruction of private property, running a red light, and driving with a revoked license. "He ought to be treated just like anybody else," said Ray Hollingshead, member of the State Board of Mothers Against Drunk Driving. "He ought not be allowed to get away with it just because he's a sports figure, a boxer." A month later, Morrison, now a man who appeared in court dockets nearly as often as he had in the pages of *Boxing Illustrated* or *The Ring*, pleaded not guilty to each count.

By November of that year, Morrison and Dawn Freeman had moved to Fayetteville, Arkansas, where he began visibly deteriorating. "He says he's doing OK," Tony Holden told the *Kansas City Star*. "But he's sick, I'll tell you that. He's got the virus." He was pale and thin, and his hair had been falling out in clumps. Morrison also seemed scattershot—unable to concentrate, twitchy, forgetful. (His plural or parallel marriage to Gilbert had also collapsed; a few months earlier she had her Mexican vows annulled and moved to Michigan.)

In Fayetteville, Morrison began running with bad company—tweakers and backsliders. To his drinking and marijuana habits, he now added methamphetamine and Adderall, which he took intravenously. "I understood that he was actually taking the Adderall and somehow liquidating it and using it in a syringe to put it in his arm," Dawn Freeman said in a court deposition. "He would spend a lot of time in the bathroom, and I would find the spoon that he used and just—I think, if I recall correctly, someone else had told me that you could—that that was something that people did with that medication and I just figured it out, basically."

According to Freeman, Morrison was taking his HIV medication regularly, as specified by Dr. Stephen Hennigan in Fayetteville. Freeman would pick up the HIV pills from a Collier pharmacy (along with Adderall prescribed by another doctor in Kansas City). This suggests that Morrison began physically declining because of his newfound addiction to methamphetamine and not from a progression of HIV. Crank, as it is commonly known, is not only highly addictive because of its euphoric qualities, but it is also deleterious, both physically and psychologically.

Methamphetamine affects the central nervous system and wreaks neurological havoc, causing several potential psychotic reactions, from paranoia to hallucinations and delusions, with decreased cognitive functioning a certainty. The recent weight loss that had startled many—and that drove speculation of AIDS into overdrive—was also partly due to methamphetamine use. While Morrison preached healthy living as a holistic cure for HIV, he was ingesting more street drugs than vitamins and chasing them with Crown Royal instead of MET-Rx or orange juice. Morrison was sick, all right, in more ways than one. And as he grew more and more addicted to drugs, his lifestyle would counteract the benefit of his HIV medication.

For the rest of the year, Morrison laid low in Fayetteville. He took his meds, took his Adderall, took his meth. On January 14, 1999, Morrison received some good news about his growing legal troubles. The Oklahoma Court of Criminal Appeals overturned one of the charges stemming from his 1997 conviction (for driving while impaired) and reduced his sentence from six months in prison to thirty days. "The court said a 9mm pistol found in a leather briefcase on the backseat of his car did not fit the legal definition of 'carrying' a firearm," reported the *Joplin Globe* about the charge that had been dismissed.

★ ★ ★

Whatever relief Morrison must have felt from avoiding an extended prison stay was short-lived, however. Two months later, he missed a court date for his recent arrest in Broken Arrow because he was in a rehab center in Missouri. Morrison had been sent there as a result of his winning appeal in January. Instead of thirty days in jail, Morrison had received a suspended sentence and was ordered into a drug treatment program, the latest pandy for a repeat offender incapable of straightening himself out. With overlapping legal entanglements dogging him, Morrison faced the real possibility of disaster, especially since he was unable to slow his downward spiral. "My life was spinning out of control," Morrison would tell the Associated Press. "People thought I was crazy." He proved just how powerless he was against his demons when he failed to complete his rehabilitation stint, forcing Special Judge Bill Culver to sentence Morrison to finish out the remaining eighteen days left on his original suspended sentence from his 1997 Fort Scott conviction.

Tommy Morrison, who had fought in Toughman contests as a teenager, who had claimed to be an enforcer for an organized crime ring, who had battled some of the most famous heavyweights of his era, could not last two weeks in Delaware County Jail. Shockingly, his health had declined to such an extent that officials released him outright, crediting him with "good time" and negating the rest of his sentence. The reported cause of his deterioration was HIV. "When the medical complications developed while he was in jail," said District Judge Robert Haney, "the sheriff contacted Morrison's doctor, who said he should be transferred immediately to a hospital. At that point, the county had two options. The sheriff could have released him on furlough, which would have meant the county would have to maintain his supervision while hospitalized and also bear the cost of his treatment. We would have faced additional complications if he were returned to the jail, and we were aware he was having complications from the HIV, which is what his doctor advised us. You have people working in the jail and deputies who would have to be in close contact with him if problems arose, and that would pose a potential medical liability."

As sick as Morrison was, he was back in court a few days later, this time in Tulsa, where he pleaded guilty to a slew of counts hanging over him from his Broken Arrow mishap. These new charges carried a maximum penalty of two years in prison. No one thought Morrison would ever see a day behind bars.

★ ★ ★

With his looks rapidly deteriorating, Morrison turned to plastic surgery as a solution. The first time he underwent the knife for a major cosmetic upgrade, he would have been better off undergoing surgery at a Lee Myles. The butchery that left Morrison with raw wounds in his chest and arms was performed by an unscrupulous Tulsa ear, nose, and throat practitioner dabbling in body sculpting as a sideline. Underground quackery was only the latest netherworld for Morrison, whose preference for the subterranean was a lifelong habit. Topside seemed to mean nothing to him, and Dr. Scott E. Gilbert joined a crowded field of crooked associates who would eventually include a psychologist who dispensed Adderall prescriptions like they were Chiclets, a sleazy lawyer who practiced "law" without a license, a shady promoter destined for prison, and a handful of women who would link themselves to Morrison (and enable his HIV delusions) for a chance at washed-up celebrity distinction and ersatz social media stardom.

In June 1999, Morrison underwent a series of surgeries for chest and biceps implants (as well as liposuction) in Tulsa with nightmarish results. When the last procedure was over, Morrison and his chauffeur/wingman (named Landon) checked into a motel for a brief recovery period. That was where Dawn Gilbert found Morrison, looking like the creation of a Hollywood-style mad scientist. According to Landon, Dr. Gilbert used calf implants for the biceps rebuild. "They appeared to have been from a sporting goods store," wrote Dawn Gilbert in her memoir, "as his biceps appeared as if the doctor had inserted the type of shin guards used by soccer players, protective lumps and all. As disturbing as his new implants were, the most shocking part of his appearance was the multiple tubes that now protruded from his body, each attached to one of the four bags surrounding him. Tubes came from each armpit and each bicep, and the bags contained a yellowish gunk and blood. Landon told me these had been positioned to collect the drainage that would continue to flow from Tom's body—for how long, he didn't know. If there was ever a need for in-hospital surgery, this had been it. Because this doctor was not licensed to practice such surgery, Tom had been an outpatient procedure."

The next day, Morrison, with the help of Landon, pulled the tubes out of his body so they could go out and shoot pool at a local bar. A bloody Morrison stanched his wounds with towels and hit the road for revelry. Like so much else in his life, his healthy-living regimen—the natural cure for HIV—was a sham. The physique for which he yearned would not be the result of exercise or a lean diet but from the trembling scalpel of an incompetent surgeon. At least, that was what Morrison hoped, but his poor decision-making, warped by cocaine, Adderall, and metham-phetamine, once again led to a fiasco. "Tom later told me that after he and Landon returned to Fayetteville," Dawn Gilbert wrote, "he discov-ered that his left arm implant was protruding from a hole the size of a silver dollar. As the evening progressed, his drainage increased, as did his drug-induced high. Finally, in a desperate move to curtail the drain-age, he went to the garage, got some pliers, and pulled out the implant. Then looking at himself in the mirror, he noticed how lopsided he was. He proceeded to pull out his right arm implant in order to balance his appearance."

Not long after mutilating Morrison, Dr. Scott E. Gilbert had his med-ical license revoked when one of his patients died. Dr. Gilbert collected negligence lawsuits the same way Morrison collected bail receipts. The *Tulsa World* listed a sample of his misdeeds: "Gilbert was accused of using wood screws and Super Glue on patients, coercing sedated patients into approving additional surgeries, allowing unlicensed personnel to per-form procedures and stealing narcotics to support a longtime drug habit."

★ ★ ★

"He claims that he was first told he was HIV positive in 1989. He hid this from nearly everyone until 1996 when it was discovered and made public. At that time, he was forced to stop his professional boxing career. He believes he got his HIV from injecting steroids."
—Valley Hope admissions interview, February 1999

★ ★ ★

At a court hearing on July 2, 1999, Tulsa County Special Judge Kyle Haskins ordered Morrison, "wearing shorts and carrying a small book," to undergo a competency evaluation. In September, Haskins gave Morri-son a two-year suspended sentence, and Morrison was free to stagger off into the shadows of Fayetteville once again. There, out in the real if neb-ulous world, Morrison seemed almost helpless, incapable of functioning for more than a few hours at a time, if at all. Barely a week after avoid-ing prison in Tulsa, Morrison was arrested again and charged with drug possession. On Thursday, September 16, Morrison was stopped by police after driving erratically in Fayetteville. When the police searched his car, they found marijuana, more than a gram of cocaine, and the inevitable firearm. Another night in jail, another bond paid, another set of charges: possession with intent to distribute cocaine, possession of marijuana, driving under the influence of drugs, simultaneous possession of drugs and a gun, careless driving, refusing to submit to a drug test, and driving without liability insurance.

From the late 1990s to the early 2000s, Arkansas was the meth capital of America (its staunchest competition for that distinction came from two other Morrison strongholds, Oklahoma and Missouri), and the pervasive drug subculture in the Ozarks enshrouded Morrison in its gloom. Like his father, who had covered every window in the house with aluminum foil all those years ago, Morrison shunned light. "Tom started hanging out with people who are into crank, and he let it get out of control," Dawn Freeman told ESPN The Magazine. "I could see the residue on the bathroom counter, and I was finding gutted-out ink pens everywhere. I saw the person I was in love with slowly dying in front of my eyes."

Essentially, this drug underworld was an extension of what Morrison had known all his life: the hard times growing up in a dysfunctional environment, the squalid Toughman circuit (which included bars and roadhouses), the supposed ties to organized crime, the peculiar fringe realm of boxing. Now it was the treacherous demimonde of tweakers, spinners, and thwackers. Morrison would disappear, often for days, on binges with his new friends, sometimes supplementing his meth use with Adderall, cocaine, marijuana, and liquor. All the fame that Morrison had, now gone, replaced by a twitchy permanent midnight, where sleeping and eating were distant memories.

★ ★ ★

"Tom has been in the care of Dr. Pat Nemechek who is a leading expert in the treatment of AIDS. Tom was initially reluctant to receive treatment and would only allow for correction of his malnutrition, treatment of his endocrine abnormalities, and severe sinus infection. He has subsequently allowed for treatment of his AIDS with specific medication to target this."
—Dr. Paul Richard Epp

★ ★ ★

For a few weeks, Morrison managed to stay out of trouble; his only appearances in the local newspapers were for pleading not guilty to his most recent arrest and for paying a settlement of $21,500 to the family of the twelve-year-old girl who had been injured in his Jay smashup of 1996.

Then came the final catastrophe before the darkness closed in on him. On Thanksgiving Day, November 26, 1999, Morrison fled the scene of a crash a few miles west of Huntsville. He was the passenger in a Corvette driven by one of his hot-rolling cronies, a man with the cartoonish name of Bart Bumpass. When Bumpass lost control of the Corvette, he swerved off the road and into a thicket of trees. Morrison, awaiting trial on a slew of charges from his September bust, and mindful of the fact that his freedom was at stake, emerged from the wreck and bolted into the woods, like Pretty Boy Floyd fleeing the FBI. A few hours later, police found Morrison less than a mile away from the crash site, where he initially gave officers a false name. (If Morrison had failed to dupe the police, he did a thorough job of hoodwinking the *Madison County Record*, whose lede must have triggered an ulcer in the editor: "Tommy David, 30, a former World Boxing Organization heavyweight champion, was arrested in Madison County Thursday following an automobile accident. David apparently gave a fictitious name, Tommy Morrison, when arrested.")

Even worse than abandoning the scene of an accident was what authorities found in the car: a mini-stockpile of firearms, including a .45, two .22s, two .40s, and a riot gun. "I don't know what so many guns were doing in that car," said Sheriff Philip Morgan. "We're going to have to investigate that further."

If Morrison thought his Thanksgiving was ruined, his Christmas was even worse. With his bail revoked, Morrison spent the holidays at Washington County Jail, where he survived the apocalyptic threat of Y2K, even while his health forced his lawyer, John "Rusty" Hudson, to request medical examinations on his behalf. Morrison underwent tests at Washington Regional Medical Center. "I requested it in order to determine if he merely has HIV or has full-blown AIDS," Hudson said, "as well as to determine if he's stable, in general, and well enough to be in jail."

★ ★ ★

"I said, I don't know whether I'm the boxer or the bag."
—Pearl Jam

★ ★ ★

On January 14, 2000, Morrison pleaded guilty to an assortment of charges stemming from his September arrest and was sentenced to ten years in prison, with eight years suspended. Judge William Storey considered Morrison a flight risk and denied him bond. What had started as the pursuit of a dream had now turned into a nightmare. Tommy Morrison, whose unlikely ascension to fame and riches in a sport already on the verge of marginalization in the United States, was now at bedrock.

★ ★ ★

Judge William Storey: "Your situation is terribly sad, Mr. Morrison. In many respects, you had it made financially and squandered it all with your involvement with drugs. I hope you have learned your lesson."

Tommy Morrison: "God put me in jail to wake up."

Judge William Storey: "I hope you got the call."

Tommy Morrison: "I made a promise to my wife and to God that if I ever, ever put another drug in my body that wasn't prescribed by a doctor, that God would take me out of this world."

★ ★ ★

Prison would be his crucible for the next fourteen months. From the Washington County Jail, Morrison was transferred to the Southwest Arkansas Community Correction Center in Texarkana, most famous, perhaps, as the home of the Phantom Killer. There Morrison was treated with antiretrovirals for his HIV, despite his future public protestations and denials. "I think he refused at first, when he first got to Texarkana, but me and his mom just kept on him and kept on him, and he said he did it to shut us up," Dawn Gilbert said in a court deposition. "But he started taking them and he, I mean, he looked good. He was—he was big and healthy-looking—and so yes, he took them when he was incarcerated."

Being forced to take medication was only part of the ignominy Morrison would suffer while imprisoned. "I feel like I'm being paid back for every bad thing I ever did by being here," he told the Associated Press. "They bring you in here and try to tear you down to a piece of dirt on the floor, and when you have a problem with that, they don't know how to handle that. If you have any pride at all, they try to strip you of it."

His wife, Dawn Freeman, decided that her chaotic life with Morrison had finally run its zigzagging course. She saw his incarceration as an opportunity to pursue her own freedom. "Tom going to jail was my way out of a horrible situation," she told writer Tad Friend. Dejected, Morrison beat Freeman to the trigger and filed for divorce from behind bars. During an interview with ESPN aired from Texarkana, Morrison gave his side of the story. "Well, what happened to the marriage is me coming here. You know, I can't expect any woman to not get lonely, you know. I mean, I, uh, was very apprehensive about coming here. I was thinking about catching the next plane to Cancun or something. She promised me she would be here when I got out, and it wasn't but a month or two later, once I got here, she told me that she wanted to file for divorce. This is a woman I've been in love with for fourteen years. I met her when she was a freshman in high school. And we were off and on for a lot of years, and it was, uh, come as a big shock to me and saddened me a great deal. I'll never get over her."

As had been the case since 1994, Dawn Gilbert materialized whenever Freeman allowed daylight. Gilbert visited Morrison every week, driving from Oklahoma to Texarkana, a distance of more than 500 miles round trip, and fell in love, once again, with a man whose last two years suggested the nightmare quality of a William Burroughs or Hubert Selby Jr. novel. With a history of drugs, adultery, promiscuity, HIV, domestic abuse, alcoholism, bigamy, and a lawless streak that had landed him in prison, Morrison seemed to have few prospects, but Gilbert remained smitten nonetheless. He was a broken man, and his tearful pleas, his neediness, his reduced circumstances, stirred the savior complex in Gilbert, a characteristic that would eventually lead her to marry him for a second time. "I have been asked countless times why I would go back to him, much less marry him again," Gilbert wrote. "I guess the primary reasons were he was now sober and he was studying his Bible. In doing so, he gave the appearance of becoming closer to God. He was humble, remorseful, and he had begun to own up to many of his wrongdoings of the past. Furthermore, he was so sad, just like a crying little boy. So again I came to his rescue." They planned a future together, one that, given the circumstances, could only have seemed frail and far-fetched.

Even in prison, with its lack of stimulus, Morrison could not keep his delusions from flourishing. Now Morrison was the center of his own rebel drama, like Paul Newman in *Cool Hand Luke*. Among the sensational tales about his new environment were a sadistic floor supervisor (a woman he nicknamed "The Hitler Bitch") who tormented him, targeted harassment from other officials because of his potential to spark an uprising, and months spent languishing in solitary confinement. Given how Morrison twisted everything into a fantasy, the concept of solitary confinement morphed into a metal box with round-the-clock floodlights provided for sleep deprivation. "They put me in the hole to break me," he told *ESPN The Magazine* in a 2003 interview. "You're talking a metal box, in the middle of summer. I was convinced they were never going to let me out."

According to Gilbert, they let him out much sooner than he claimed. "In reality," she wrote, "Tom was put in solitary confinement on two occasions, once for one week, and once for thirty days. This meant they locked him in a cell where he was kept by himself."

What was true was that Morrison had enough disciplinary problems to undermine the good-behavior provisions of his original sentence. In December 2000, his defiance led to a transfer from Texarkana to the Central Arkansas Community Punishment Center in Little Rock and delayed his release by two weeks.

Inmate 64281 finally walked out of prison on February 28, 2001. He was met at the gate by Dawn Gilbert, and they drove off to Fayetteville to begin a fairy-tale romance that would eventually transform into a Grand Guignol. Within weeks of being set free, Morrison began shooting up Adderall again. Throughout his life, Morrison would associate with numberless people who traveled under morally cloudy skies, and this knack extended to professional contacts as well. To meet his voracious demands for Adderall, Morrison connected with a Dr. Feelgood in Kansas City who prescribed the drug virtually on demand. Every month Morrison would receive a box of pills that would last him only for a week or two. Eventually, he returned to using meth, despite his scorn for the rehab programs offered to him in prison, despite his repeatedly denying that he was an addict.

The contrite Morrison, the one who read his Bible regularly in prison and had apologized for a devilish past, dissolved with every shot of Adderall. His erratic behavior included an episode of physical abuse after he and Gilbert returned from church one day. An argument culminated with Morrison throwing Gilbert headlong into a wall.

Then old cellmates began visiting him in Fayetteville and encouraging him to misbehave. To eliminate this noxious influence, Dawn Gilbert gave Morrison an ultimatum: Move out of Fayetteville and leave those associations behind or lose her (as well as her son from a previous relationship). Soon, Gilbert and Morrison were living in Sparta, Tennessee, with Morrison still injecting Adderall but otherwise free of methamphetamine. By September 2001, Gilbert and Morrison were married again.

★ ★ ★

When Morrison was released from prison in 2001, he had few options for making a living. His primary source of income in the early 2000s was memorabilia signings. As his savings dwindled, it became harder and harder to afford his HIV medication. At the suggestion of his doctor, Morrison contacted the Ryan White Foundation, which paid for a limited amount of treatment. Then Morrison, who was part Native American, turned to the Indian Health Service, a federal agency, which covered his costs for an undetermined length of time. Finally, Morrison applied for disability and eventually received monthly Social Security benefits.

According to Dawn Gilbert, Morrison took his HIV pills religiously while they were married. "He had a beeper set for 8:00 a.m. and 8 p.m., and he would take a shot glass and put it on his side of the bed and that's where he'd put—the night before he went to bed—he'd put his morning pills there," Gilbert said in a 2016 deposition. "So when the 8:00 a.m. beeper went off, he'd just take his pills. If we were going out at night, if we went out to dinner or something, and we weren't going to be home at 8:00, he was faithful to get those pills, so he'd have them when the beeper went off. I filled up his tray—he had like a weeklong tray—and I'd fill that up and he would take it from there."

Despite the rotting foundation on which she based her dreams, Dawn Gilbert never gave up on the idea of having an "All-American" family. That meant church services, a monogamous marriage, a house, and another child. An episode of the *Montel Williams Show* led Gilbert into researching the possibility of conceiving an HIV-free child through a specialized in vitro fertilization process. She contacted Dr. Ann Kiessling, who had founded the Special Program of Assisted Reproduction (SPAR) in Boston a few years earlier. Kiessling pioneered the process of safe IVF procedures in America for men with HIV. "It's something that seemed so out of reach when we first started this process," Morrison told the *Tennessean* in early 2003. "But we're getting a lot of encouragement from the doctors, so we're excited."

It was both an acknowledgment of his HIV-positive status and a grudging nod to reality, in general (after all, who would suffer through a testicular biopsy if his HIV diagnosis had been a false positive?) that Morrison underwent several procedures to ensure the safety of his future child. There was also the irony of Morrison cooperating with a fairly new, experimental treatment when his open distrust of science had led him to the depths of quackery and denialism.

His third son, Tristan Duke Morrison, was born in September 2003.

Even as Morrison descended into denialism post-HIV, he did not have a support system that enabled his delusions about his disease. He had codependents who facilitated, to an extent, his alcohol and drug abuse, but no one close to him—not his mother, not his father, not his Dawns, not his friend Tony Holden—encouraged him, no one spurred him to pursue his dark fantasies about HIV all the way to the grave.

That would come later, after Morrison lost his family, his house, his illusions.

★ ★ ★

January 2003. For the first time since his infamous 1998 interview, Morrison returns to the oversized pages of *ESPN The Magazine*. The photo layout remains kitschy, but overall, the air of madness is diminished. Morrison is beefier; the grayish pallor is replaced by a healthy tan; the monkey is a distant memory. He has added devil horns to an image of Dawn Free-man tattooed on his back. Instead of the louche bed shot of five years earlier, with Freeman and Morrison both naked under the covers, there is a photo of Morrison tenderly resting his head on Gilbert, her stomach exposed. And then there is a close-up of Morrison, across the spread, propped on his elbow, in bed again, the eyeliner that once earned him the nickname "Maybelline" conspicuous enough, but more striking, perhaps, is the prop held in his hand: a weekly pill organizer, fourteen small com-partments, two rows of seven, alternately labeled A.M. or P.M., in orchid and cerulean, respectively.

★ ★ ★

Fatherhood and improved health (from taking his HIV medication) were not enough to keep Morrison from giving into his self-destructive impulses. In the years that followed his release from prison, Morrison maintained his Adderall habit, but his methamphetamine use was intermittent. That changed in the spring of 2004, when he took up with a troubled woman who taught Morrison how to "cook"—manufacture meth. He and Gil-bert separated off and on for a few years, with Morrison drifting further and further away from reality. One of the women with whom he lived pummeled Morrison, forcing him to move out; another was arrested and entered a rehab center, leaving Morrison essentially homeless. He moved in with his sister Tonia, who lived in Anderson, Missouri. It was there, perhaps, that Morrison began to plot a way to get back what had slipped through his fingers, which was everything.

★ ★ ★

"Anything I do creates controversy," Tommy Morrison told the *Arizona Republic*. It was April 2006, and Morrison had chosen, aptly, it seems, Phoenix for his miracle return. For months, Morrison had been struggling in Anderson, Missouri, working odd jobs, at one point living in a barn, when his friend Stephen Bayer made a phone call on his behalf. Bayer called his mother, Susan Martin, a gallery owner who lived in Phoenix, Arizona. Martin described the conversation for NPR. "And he called me up one day and he said 'listen,' he said, 'Tommy Morrison, who is one of my best friends'—and he was with him throughout his whole boxing career—'is down and out. He has no money, he's trying to pick up odd jobs here and there, and he really wants to get back into the boxing world.' And he said, 'can you help him?' And I said, 'you bet.'"

In no time, Morrison was sharing her apartment and training vigorously at a strip mall in Phoenix, under the tutelage of a local trainer named Mike Munoz, who had given up a dental practice to coach amateurs. Although Martin had no background in boxing—she had never even seen a fight before—she accepted a role that went beyond sports management. She acted as de facto publicist, patron, and strategist. Through Martin, Morrison also met a local lawyer, Randy Lang, and together the trio sketched out his comeback.

It is unclear whether Martin and Lang knowingly participated in what can only be termed a hoax or whether they simply took Morrison at his word. And what he was saying was as absurd as it was audacious: Morrison now claimed that his 1996 test findings were inaccurate, and that he was (and had been all along) HIV-free. "I'm convinced it was a false-positive," Morrison told *Kansas City Star* writer Hearne Christopher Jr. about the NSAC result. "I've never had any signs. The only thing that's changed in my life is I have too much time on my hands, and I'm not fighting."

Every few years, in a fairly predictable cycle, Morrison would crash the public spotlight for various, sometimes conflicting, reasons. In the late '90s, it was as a tortured soul racing, full throttle, into self-immolation, refusing to take antiretrovirals, ranting about conspiracy theories, and finally hitting rock bottom in prison.

In the early 2000s, the narrative transformed into a sentimental comeback story of personal triumph. Morrison, once seemingly marked for an early grave, was now a family man (with a child on the way) who credited his turnaround to the AIDS cocktail he had been taking regularly since his release from the Central Arkansas Community Correction Center in Little Rock.

Now, in 2006, Morrison sparked his final media frenzy with his claim to have been misdiagnosed a decade earlier. It was breathtaking to see newspapers, magazines, and television journalists report such a brazen lie with nary a hint of critical analysis. For more than a decade, Morrison had been tested, retested, and treated under various auspices (including municipal ones) for HIV, and he had admitted taking antiretrovirals to the New York *Daily News*, ESPN, the Associated Press, Fox News, and the *Tennessean*. During his late '90s crackup, two of his lawyers had referenced his HIV: one to plead for leniency from the court and the other to establish mental competency before a trial.

When Morrison returned to the scene after his release from prison, he credited his HIV medication with physically stabilizing him. On an episode of the sports show *Cold Pizza*, Morrison explained his recovery to Kit Hoover. "You know, my health has been, was at one time pretty bad, but at the time when I first found out [that he had HIV], they only had a couple of different types of medication that you could take, and it was, like, DDI [didanosine] . . . basically forms of oral chemotherapy, and I just wasn't willing to do that to myself. Since then, they've come out with a lot more, much more, milder combination drug therapy treatments. So I started taking that, and everything's fine now." (In another segment for ESPN, broadcast in 2003, Morrison displayed his pillbox and blandly summarized his daily drug routine for the camera.)

There were also hundreds of pages of medical records (along with depositions from his ex-wives) that came to light during a 2016 lawsuit, revealing that Morrison had been prescribed antiretrovirals for years and that his HIV status had never been anything but positive.

Where Morrison had once been an HIV denier, influenced mainly by the crackpot theories of Peter Duesberg, he was now claiming that he had never had the virus at all. That switch underscored the pragmatic nature of his enterprise. To fight, Morrison would have to be HIV-free; otherwise, most commissions, especially those in money states such as Nevada, New York, and New Jersey, would deny him a license. The solution? Morrison would claim to have been misdiagnosed in 1996 and, according to one of his collaborators, he would do whatever it took to maintain that fiction.

★ ★ ★

Although Morrison had material reasons for claiming to be free of HIV—disability checks and memorabilia signings only went so far—he had existential ones as well. What Morrison wanted, what he needed, was the distinction he once had as a high-profile boxer and a minor celebrity, which had been central to his identity for years but had long been stripped away by his HIV diagnosis. Since Morrison had resurfaced in a series of comforting vignettes in 2002 and 2003, he had vanished into a shadow world far beyond the reach of autograph sessions, charity benefits, or celebrity interviews. This man, who had costarred in *Rocky V*, who had headlined Las Vegas, who had once earned millions of dollars, had been bouncing from motel to motel, from one meth cookhouse to another, from woman to woman, virtually forgotten. Morrison wanted to be remembered again, and he wanted to be the protagonist of an uplifting story that would counterbalance the misery of his last few years. Again and again, he repeated how his miracle return would be legendary. "This is going to be the comeback of the century," he told *HIV Plus* magazine. "Ten years ago, in the eyes of society I was given a death sentence. I saw the people stop in their tracks when they would spot me. They thought I was dead. It was even printed in some magazines. This is going to be one of the amazing stories. I think a lot of people are going to be truly inspired."

★ ★ ★

In February 2006, Morrison did an extended interview with the website Boxing Scene, where he outlined his plans to sue the Nevada State Athletic Commission. "I'm going to Phoenix to talk to this big attorney who's going to take on my case on a contingency basis against the commission," Morrison said. "He's pretty certain it'd be worth something. I'll never get the forty million dollars because they'll say, 'Well, what if you'd lost.' One thing I can get, for sure, without a doubt, and that's the amount of money that I was going to get for the first fight (against Arthur Weathers) with Don King. I can't remember what it was. Two or three million dollars. That, plus interest on that money for the last nine years is what I'll get. But you never know."

The "big attorney" turned out to be a gentleman named Randy Lang, whose relationship with Morrison would eventually implode, with Morrison himself as collateral damage. In a few years, Lang would be sued by the State Bar of Arizona for "the unauthorized practice of law." An unlicensed lawyer, Lang was just another of the frauds Morrison attracted like a UV light attracts certain insects.

But first, Morrison and his new team had to figure out how to obtain a license to fight. And how to pass an HIV test.

★ ★ ★

"I tell people I'm going to win an Oscar, and they laugh at me. I told them I was going to win a heavyweight championship, too, and they laughed. And I won two of those. A lot of people doubt that I have anything left. But one thing they're forgetting is that I haven't been fighting for 10 years. I've been resting. I'll go down in history. It's going to happen. Then I'll become a legend."
—Tommy Morrison, to Elizabeth Merrill, the *Kansas City Star*, 2006

★ ★ ★

In retrospect, had he been given an opportunity, Morrison would probably have chosen a different staging ground for his comeback. Arizona was a state with a commission, not a particularly strong one, and its dozen or so cards a year, linked to a handful of casinos, hardly made it a boxing hotbed. But Arizona had one requirement sure to bedevil Morrison: mandatory screening for HIV.

But Arizona was where both Susan Martin and Randy Lang, the high-powered lawyer, lived, and Morrison decided to try his luck there, knowing that while Arizona demanded blood work, it was no Nevada or New Jersey when it came to exacting supervision. Even so, John Montano, head of the Arizona State Boxing Commission, made it clear that there would be little room for shenanigans. "They already know, everybody knows," he told the *Arizona Republic*, "that for me to accept anything as far as blood work, I have to see the blood drawn."

During his early media blitz for his comeback, Morrison insisted that he had tested negative repeatedly for HIV and that he had been virus-free all along. Morrison also boasted about rejecting antiretrovirals since his release from prison, despite the evidence that he had been on them for years. He attributed his rippling biceps and healthy glow not to HIV cocktails (or plastic surgery) but to a higher power. "God spoke to me and told me not to take it, don't take the medication," Morrison told Elizabeth Merrill of the *Kansas City Star*. "I tell people that, I tell them God told me, they look at me like I'm from another planet. It's like people don't believe God's in the miracle business anymore. I've seen God work in my life, and I know what he's capable of, and I know what he does for his people that love him."

According to Susan Martin, the original plan did not call for Morrison to profess to be clear or cured. "For Tommy to say that he never had HIV is an absolute slap in the face of the Morrison team members that helped him find a doctor to give him the right medication to bring the HIV viral loads down to undetectable," Martin told the *Kansas City Star* in 2007. "Our premise was never to say he never had HIV. That's wrong. What we were saying is that if the HIV levels were undetectable in the person that had HIV, how is it possible that they could pass it on to someone else in a boxing ring?"

In early January 2007, Morrison kick-started the application process for a license in Arizona. Local promoter Pete McKinn, a Top Rank associate, promised Morrison a slot on a January 19 card at the Dodge Theatre in Phoenix. While his entire team insisted that he had repeatedly tested negative for HIV, Morrison would now get the chance to prove his astonishing claim to the world at large. With Montano present, Morrison provided a blood sample to a lab in Phoenix. That should have been the first step toward ending his seemingly endless nightmare.

Before Morrison could be approved or rejected, however, he withdrew from the card, citing an injury. By canceling his fight, Morrison also put an end to the licensing process in Arizona. Because of privacy laws, it is doubtful that a public announcement concerning HIV would have been made once the test results had been received. There would be no replay of what had happened in Las Vegas a decade earlier.

Naturally, it was nothing but a coincidence that Morrison suffered an injury a few days before his fight would occur.

The day after Morrison canceled his first match in over ten years, Randy Lang told the *Arizona Republic* that Morrison "will continue to seek an Arizona license." Instead, Morrison hit the road, traveling more than 2,000 miles to pursue his quixotic aspirations . . . and a less stringent commission.

★ ★ ★

In 1994, a talented young middleweight from South Carolina named Lamar "Kidfire" Parks was only days away from a title shot against Gerald McClellan when he withdrew from the bout (and a $250,000 purse), claiming that he had injured his shoulder. But it was an HIV test that knocked Parks out of boxing. He had tested positive while training in Florida. Despite the results, Parks decided that, somehow, he would keep his date with McClellan. With the title fight scheduled for Las Vegas, Parks would have to figure out a way to deceive the Nevada State Athletic Commission. "He had someone take the test for him in South Carolina, and we refused to accept it," Marc Ratner told the Associated Press. "He pulled out of the fight knowing we were going to test him if he came here." Parks never took the mandatory blood work; he quietly retired instead.

★ ★ ★

"It is not just a sport without ethics, it is one without rules. Or much logic to it, ever."
—Mike Lupica

★ ★ ★

Less than a month after his Arizona gambit, Morrison wound up in Chester, West Virginia, his injury apparently healed, approved to fight for the first time since November 3, 1996. His return to the ring would take place at The Harv, located in the Mountaineer Casino Racetrack and Resort. The West Virginia Boxing Commission, headed by Steve Allred (who also held down a day job as the executive director of the West Virginia–Ohio Valley Chapter, National Electrical Contractors Association), ran on an annual budget of $20,000.

Morrison would appear on the undercard of a February 22 Versus broadcast along with another medical conundrum, "Baby" Joe Mesi, a heavyweight who had been suspended in 2004 after suffering a subdural hematoma during a fight. "We're doing due diligence to the best of our ability to try to ensure the safety and well-being of everybody involved in this event," said Allred, who then alluded to neglecting his union job because of the controversy surrounding Morrison and Mesi. "My secretary is going to beat me up. I have devoted entirely too much time to boxing the past five weeks."

Acknowledging that privacy laws prevented him from transparency, Allred would not divulge specifics about the test results he obtained from

Team Morrison, and neither would Randy Lang. When Morrison sat for an interview with Versus analyst Wallace Matthews before the fight, Lang prevented Morrison from answering a simple question: "Who did these blood tests?"

This unseemly double feature once again reflected the vulgar match-making philosophy of Bob Arum and Top Rank, who had signed Morrison to a contract, hoping, no doubt, to exploit the sensationalized publicity of yet another peculiar boxing affair. "Tommy approached us," Bruce Trampler, matchmaker for Top Rank, told *The Ring*. "He had been romanced by other promoters, but we had some success with him some years back, so there was that comfort level already. He came up clean on his tests, so we had no reservations. Plus, Tommy has name recognition with the fans."

Despite cutting ties with Morrison in 1993 and being sued by him in 1995 over the "Hong Kong in High Noon" debacle, Top Rank still hungered and hankered after scandal—even after the FBI had raided its offices in 2004 for suspected fight-fixing—and Morrison had epitomized chaos for years. It is worth noting that when Morrison announced his first comeback, in September 1996, Arum bitterly opposed it. But things had changed in the last ten years. Now, as a potential moneymaker, Morrison represented a future commodity to Arum, who was, as always, willing to gamble that the maxim "There is no such thing as bad publicity" would prove true.

Not everyone in boxing was willing to turn a blind eye. "The idea that in the United States you have a guy with a hematoma stepping into the ring and the guy on the undercard has HIV is a disgusting travesty. What kind of barbarism is this?" said Lou DiBella, a rival promoter who had once been head of programming at HBO Sports. "It screams for unified health and safety standards in the sport throughout the country. Would you want your kid in the ring with Tommy Morrison?"

Even after more than a decade away from the ring, Morrison had not forgotten the ballyhoo end of the sport. "I'm going to hit him so hard, his grandchildren will have headaches," Morrison said about his opponent before the fight. "But I don't want to look overanxious. I don't want to look like I haven't fought in ten and a half years. This is the first leg of a journey that's going to be the greatest adventure I've ever been on."

His springboard to this great adventure was a man named John Castle, aptly described by the *Pittsburgh Post-Gazette* as a "rent-a-body," a thirty-five-year-old plugger who sported a record of 4-2 and overwhelming doubts about facing Morrison in the ring. Until a few hours before the opening bell, Castle was wavering about fighting at all. After being shown some paperwork that revealed Morrison was "negative," Castle decided to proceed. There is no telling what kind of paperwork he saw. The likeliest option is that Castle was shown documentation that Morrison had such a low viral load (due to his regimen of antiretroviral pills) that his HIV was undetectable. Since it had been well-documented for years that Morrison, by his own admission, had been HIV-positive, his duping of Castle was one of the lowlights of a life overrun by them.

★ ★ ★

Wallace Matthews: "John, you're in a position that a lot of fighters might not want to be in and might be afraid to be in: fighting Tommy Morrison in his first fight back [sic] after being diagnosed with HIV. Are you worried about it?"

John Castle: "To an extent, yeah, because I've got two kids that are young that I want to see grow old. So, yeah."

Wallace Matthews: "What were you told when you were offered this fight? Were you assured that he is now HIV-free?"

John Castle: "I was told that he had it, now he doesn't have it. And the medical association, or something, says that I can't get it even if he did."

★ ★ ★

"Let's get on with it," Morrison said before his first fight in over a decade. "I think I'll be a better fighter this time. The last ten years I've been healthy while everybody else was getting beat up. I'm like the girl at the prom. I'm just happy to be here."

As for the fight itself, it was just the first of a handful of farces Morrison had left to offer the curious public. Castle, tall, awkward, and slow, landed a pair of left hooks in the first round and a right cross that forced Morrison to clinch. In the second, a single left hook from a visibly winded Morrison sent Castle sprawling to the canvas. Despite beating the count, Castle had a groggy look that prompted referee Dave Johnson to stop the fight 1:49 into the round.

Convinced he had achieved his miracle, Morrison dropped to his knees, raised his hands to the rafters, his sweat-sheened face reflecting ecstasy, relief, and, perhaps, self-satisfaction. "I was a little apprehensive, a little jittery, which I think is to be expected," Morrison said after the fight. "I think I got a little lazy with a couple of right hands, but I think I was able to come back from it. It knocked me off balance, but I wasn't in trouble. But hey, it was my first fight in eleven years. My defense is going to improve as time goes on."

A strange evening in West Virginia was made even stranger for television viewers at home when Top Rank decided to keep Morrison off the air. Although most of the Versus broadcast centered around Morrison and Mesi (who scored a first-round KO over George Linberger), only stills were shown of the Morrison–Castle bout. According to Bob Raissman of the New York *Daily News*, it was Bob Arum who decided to nix televising Morrison. "If Arum does have final say on what fights air on Versus," Raissman wrote, "he showed his priority is all about being a lousy partner. He put his own promotional self-interest ahead of a network (which is paying him a rights fee) in desperate need of attention." In a few years, Versus would essentially fire Top Rank Promotions as its boxing provider.

In some ways, it was probably a good thing for Morrison to remain off the screen. For one thing, the fight was a travesty. For another, Morrison was clearly sporting an artificial physique, not the one from his early career, which was a product of steroids, but literally a synthetic body. His pectoral muscles were implants, and his biceps were likely also surgically modified. In contrast to his hulking torso, his legs were spindly, seemingly incapable of supporting his top-heavy bulk. Morrison took deception to the very surface.

★ ★ ★

"Mirror, mirror on the wall.
Who's the fairest of them all? . . .
Not you, motherfucker!"
—Chet Baker

★ ★ ★

On April 25, 2007, the Associated Press reported that Morrison had been added to the undercard of a Top Rank show in Houston, Texas, set to air on Telefutura and headlined by Sergio "Maravilla" Martinez. First, of course, Morrison would have to obtain a license from the Texas Department of Licensing and Regulations. As he had in Arizona, Morrison would have to submit to a blood test, and just as he had in Arizona, Morrison would eventually withdraw his application under murky circumstances.

On April 27, wire reports disclosed that Texas officials had asked Morrison for more medical information, and a day later, Texas announced that Morrison had been granted a license. This license was essentially provisional, contingent on receiving test results before the fight, a four-rounder against Dale Ortiz. Those results never arrived, and the fight was canceled at the last moment. "As soon as we get that in, he'll be licensed," said Dickie Cole, Combative Sports program manager for Texas. "They say he's OK. But we can't afford to just assume like that. I'm sure he is fine. But we need to have certain forms to prove it, and we don't have those."

Cole would never have those forms. Less than a week later, Morrison withdrew from the licensing process altogether. Texas Department of Licensing and Regulation spokesman Patrick Shaughnessy: "His application was never complete. We asked for additional information and never received it." In four months, Morrison had twice bowed out of the administrative procedures required to box, procedures all fighters went through in Arizona and Texas.

★ ★ ★

All the fame and glory that drove Morrison to pursue his career against seemingly overwhelming odds did not instantly materialize after his miracle comeback. The biopic, the talk-show circuit, the *New York Times* bestseller—none of that seemed any closer to becoming a reality after the ludicrous events surrounding his KO of John Castle. If, as P. T. Barnum once famously noted, "The American people liked to be humbugged," they seemed to shy away from Morrison. There was something grotesque about his comeback, about the obnoxious desperation that underlined it, the twisted conspiracy theories he spouted, the bizarre physical appearance that fooled one sportswriter after another into proclaiming him fit.

And the dubious crew that he had assembled alternated between incompetence (Morrison berated both Cheatham and Munoz for their inability to work the pads during warm-ups) and sleaziness (Peter McKinn had already committed an act of fraud that would eventually send him to prison).

Even with the ham-fisted reporting of the media, which repeated what Morrison and his accomplices declared about his HIV status, there was an air of incredulity surrounding him. Who could believe his absurd claims? After all, Morrison could not even keep his conspiracy theories straight. He fluctuated between claiming that he had been misdiagnosed by the Nevada State Athletic Commission in 1996 and that he had been the victim of a plot devised by Don King, who had signed Morrison to a contract that would culminate in a matchup against Mike Tyson. Why would a boxing promoter recruit a fighter to face Tyson just to sabotage the event? (It should be noted that King had been pursuing Morrison since the late 1980s.) According to Morrison, King was afraid that Tyson would lose. This ridiculous line of thinking underscored just how delusional Morrison had become over the years. King stood to make tens of millions of dollars with the first white American heavyweight champion since Rocky Marciano. Not only would King have made millions of dollars on the Tyson–Morrison pay-per-view as a stand-alone affair, but he would also have made millions more if Morrison had pulled off the unlikely upset. A rematch would have been twice as profitable as the first fight, and a blockbuster trilogy was also a possibility. That Morrison, who had not won a millisecond of his fight against Lennox Lewis and who had been steamrolled by Michael Bentt, considered himself such a threat to King that broad cloak-and-dagger machinations were necessary to prevent a Tyson matchup suggests a dissociative disorder.

In his mind, Morrison found himself at the center of not one, not two, but several vast conspiracies that spread across the globe. The Nevada State Athletic Commission, the medical community, Don King, the pharmaceutical industry, the U.S. government—all of them combining forces at one time or another to stifle, subdue, sabotage Tommy Morrison, ex–heavyweight contender now on the skids, looking for a way to relive his past. At the heart of these elaborate delusions is a narcissism at odds with the notion of powerful forces arrayed against a helpless everyman. Morrison was too famous, too important, too talented to be held back by an international cabal. "I would've beat Tyson," Morrison told the web-site Boxing Scene in 2007. "I have no doubt about that. Everything was clicking. I worked eight years of my life to get to that one pinnacle fight, and they yanked the damn rug out from under me."

★ ★ ★

Maybe it was another conspiracy that forced Morrison into a parody MMA fight in Arizona on June 9. When Chuck Liddell, the charismatic but already washed-up UFC legend, joked during an interview about wanting to face Morrison, he set a new hustle in motion. No sooner had Liddell uttered his last syllable than Team Morrison envisioned a lucrative pay-per-view against an athlete with name recognition. Sensing a possible quick-strike opportunity, Morrison responded, showbiz style, in a state-ment released to the media. "He is crazy to want to get into the cage with me," Morrison announced. "I beat George Foreman. Nobody in the his-tory of boxing hit harder than George Foreman. So why would I be afraid to get hit by Chuck Liddell? He should be the one to be afraid. Liddell has never been hit by anyone like me."

To ratchet up interest further, Peter McKinn arranged a fast-track MMA bout that, impossible as it might seem, doubled the circus-like atmosphere of the John Castle debacle. In an unsanctioned fight at the Cliff Castle Casino in Camp Verde, Arizona, Morrison would, under MMA rules, face a part-time sheetrock worker named John Stover. Although Morrison had mysteriously dropped out of the licensing process in Arizona a few months earlier, the Cliff Castle Casino was on Yavapai-Apache Nation land, beyond the jurisdiction of the state commission due to Native Amer-ican sovereignty. There would be no blood work necessary for Morri-son to compete in a discipline with which he was largely unfamiliar. His primary focus during the buildup of the fight concerned the four-ounce gloves he would be wearing. "I'm a little nervous about that, not for myself, but for the other guy. To me, it just seems like someone signing up for assassination class. He must be out of his mind. I'm just going to walk out and hit him on the chin. I'm concerned about killing someone. I'm not kidding."

★ ★ ★

Soon, Morrison would have far more serious worries. It was inevitable that this scam would crumble, that this gathering of rogues would eventually fall out. The day before Morrison was scheduled to fight Stover, Randy Lang double-crossed him. In a bombshell report in the *Arizona Republic*, Lang revealed what had been obvious all along: "Tommy has tested positive for HIV antibodies, and he always has," he told writer Norm Frauenheim.

If scientific consensus about HIV was not enough for some to see through the Morrison comeback, if years of documentation that Morrison had been taking antiretrovirals was not enough, then the abbreviated licensing procedures in Arizona and Texas should have made everything clear. But Randy Lang, an insider, someone who hoped to profit from Morrison, the man who facilitated the tests in February, delivered the final, crippling blow. Elizabeth Merrill of ESPN.com expanded on the initial report: "Lang said he cut ties with Morrison February 25th when he suspected the Morrison Camp was either doctoring blood tests or falsifying documents."

In response to having been exposed, Morrison pointed a crooked finger right back at Lang. "Randy Lang had planned his whole future—with me," he said on Kush TV. "He had this plan in his mind that he was going to take me . . . he was going to become this promoter extraordinaire and, really, he doesn't know anything about boxing. Accusing Peter and everybody of doing all this fraudulent stuff . . . and if there was ever any fraudulent stuff going on, it was him that was doing it."

According to Morrison, Lang had been passing himself off as a lawyer despite not having a license to practice. (In 2014, Lang would be enjoined from practicing law by the State Bar of Arizona.) To that, Lang countered swiftly and cleanly: "I'm not the issue," he told Elizabeth Merrill. "The issue is, does Tommy Morrison have HIV?"

Whatever drove Morrison to continue his denialist act, he never thought about yielding to reality. Why would he give in to public charges of dishonesty from Susan Martin and outright accusations of fraud from Randy Lang? "I only know what the doctor told me and what Randy told me—I am negative," Morrison insisted. "I went and took all the tests. They told me I am fine, the doctor and Randy. Randy is a greedy person. He got exposed, and now he's trying to hurt me."

Peter McKinn seemed to contradict himself in the media when asked to comment on Lang. "All the blood tests came from Randy Lang," he said, "and, as far as I saw on the paperwork sent by Lang, the results were zero-negative." Later, McKinn would inadvertently highlight just how deceptive the Tommy Morrison comeback was when he said about Lang: "If he's not a real lawyer, then how could you believe the paperwork?"

★ ★ ★

The skeptical public was not the only target for Morrison. John Stover, the struggling cage part-timer, became a victim less than an hour before the opening bell rang at the Cliff Castle Casino. That was when Stover learned he would be participating in a boxing match and not a mixed martial arts contest. "Yeah, they switched up the rules," Stover said after the fight. "At first it was strikes, knees, elbows, and kicks. They switched them up about a half hour before the show. We tried to barter around it, but Tommy, he doesn't want to do MMA. He needs to get paid. He needs his money. He needs to get his name back out there and this is basically all he's doing."

Stover, thirty-six years old and over 340 pounds, risked his life in more ways than one that night. Despite his age and inactivity, Morrison could batter any second-rate MMA grappler in fisticuffs, but Stover had never made a fraction of the money he would earn at the Cliff Castle Casino, especially since his compensation had been increased as an incentive to accept the last-minute stipulations. Ultimately, Stover agreed to the rules that guaranteed a painful beating. Weeks earlier, he had accepted the risk of battling an HIV-positive opponent with similar sangfroid. "I don't know how many times I've heard from people that they were afraid to fight him because they don't want to risk it," said Stover. "Well, the only thing we are risking are rumors. Some people would be terrified of rumors, but I gave him a shot."

Before the fight, Kush TV cameras captured Tommy Morrison in the parking lot of the Cliff Castle Casino at a meeting to review the stipulations, enraged at the uncertainty of the event. "If somebody knows what the fuck's going on," he shouted, "come over here and tell me what the fuck's going on!" With the rules finally settled, Morrison returned to his room to warm up but found himself further agitated with the incompetent cornermen with which he had surrounded himself. These were men incapable of holding punch mitts, wrapping hands, taping gloves.

After a delay of more than ten minutes, Morrison finally entered the cage, dressed in his boxing trunks (black with red stars down the sides and "Duke" stitched on the beltline) and shoes, normally prohibited in MMA. Since his fight against John Castle in February, Morrison appeared to be deteriorating physically, and his chest implants were further emphasized by his slackness and weight loss.

In the end, the four-ounce gloves Morrison worried about proved to be deadly weapons. After Stover drove Morrison to the cage, where he threw a series of ineffective noogies, Morrison worked his way mat-center and opened up with a combination punctuated by a pinpoint left hook. Stover pulled away, his nose bloodied and misshapen. "I knew that my nose was broke," he later said, "and I thought, well, I can deal with that. The first thing that happens is your eyes close and start watering. He couldn't knock me down; he couldn't knock me out." That moral victory was all Stover could count on; another vicious combination left him flinching and forced the referee to intervene 2:09 into the first round. The crowd, estimated to have been around 2,500, booed Morrison lustily.

When it was all over, Stover had the final, fitting word on Morrison. "Obviously, he's got a different attitude towards everything," Stover told ESPN. "He's rude. He's obnoxious. He's got a lot over his head right now."

★ ★ ★

One of the lies Morrison and his team repeated ad nauseam was his intention to take a blood test in Nevada to prove, once and for all, that the 1996 results were fraudulent. At times, Morrison even claimed that he would undergo blood work publicly. "I'm getting tired of having to answer all these questions and people casting doubts," Morrison told *USA TODAY* two weeks after annihilating Stover. "I've got a fight scheduled for July 27 in Albuquerque, but they want me to get this over with first. In the next week to 10 days, I'm going to Nevada, and I'll test again . . . to clear this up."

Elizabeth Merrill of ESPN.com also reported that Team Morrison was planning to visit Nevada. "Later this month, Morrison and promoter Peter McKinn hope to conduct the public blood test in Las Vegas complete with doctors and a press conference. 'We're going to try to kill this issue so that Tom can move on.'"

But Morrison never kept his word about Nevada. In fact, Morrison would never box again in the United States.

★ ★ ★

Even after Morrison had been outed by Randy Lang, the *New York Times* ran a feature on the possibility that Morrison was HIV-free. Using the same paperwork that Morrison had sent to West Virginia, the *Times* asked a slew of doctors to interpret the results. To its credit, the *Times* added an important caveat to the process: "Two nationally renowned HIV experts reviewed those and a third blood test for *the New York Times*, and said they suggested Morrison had been knocked out of the ring by false positive tests—if, indeed, the new tests are his blood."

If Morrison had been miraculously cured of HIV, he would have been the dream/desire of every scientist in the world. Morrison would have been invited to conferences, to *20/20* or *60 Minutes*, to fund drives, to gala affairs. He would have been the cover story for *Time*, *Newsweek*, *Scientific American*, *Discover*. But most scientists know better, and for them to have given Morrison a platform based solely on his word would have been insane.

To be as famous as he wanted to be, to be the inspiration that he hoped he could be, to be the subject of a Hollywood film or a blockbuster biography, all he had to do was take a supervised test at a reputable academic medical center and release the results to the public. He did not. He would not. He could not.

★ ★ ★

Around the time Tommy Morrison was submitting "negative" results to lax commissions in West Virginia, the public spotlight shined on the boxing world and its amoral protocols. In fact, a little over a week after the *New York Times* printed its credulous piece about Morrison possibly being HIV-free—and having his custom-made medical results examined by physicians from a distance—the newspaper ran an exposé of phony records inundating the sport. "At least eight states have let fighters enter the ring with fraudulent or insufficient medical examinations in recent years, interviews and records show, a pattern of neglect nurtured by a patchwork system of safety. Boxing has a sordid history of corruption, including the use of aliases to evade taxes, avoid suspensions, and fix fights. The falsification of medical exams, though, undermines laws written to protect boxers, as well as ringside workers and fans who could be splattered with blood."

That anyone would take what Morrison or his team said at face value is an indictment of a substandard mediascape. Because boxing had slipped so far in the public consciousness since the 1980s and '90s, it became an afterthought to editors across the country and a subject largely covered by wire press reports and general sportswriters, who knew little about the corrupt underpinnings of a barely regulated sport overrun by scammers, schemers, and scoffers.

If the pervasive atmosphere of fraudulence in boxing was not enough to raise suspicions, then there was always Tommy Morrison himself: an ex-con, a drug addict, a bigamist, an alcoholic, a conspiracy theorist, a Y2K/End Times believer, and a man given to distortion and dissimulation, with a fake lawyer pressing his case, a promoter (Pete McKinn) a few years from becoming a felon, and a co-trainer who had once been a dentist. Morrison repeatedly lied about never taking HIV medication outside of prison, lied blatantly about his marriage and relationships, lied over and over about having had only one HIV test, lied almost every time he opened his mouth.

His unhinged worldview was reflected in the fact that he ran an AIDS foundation for children while simultaneously denying that HIV posed any danger. It was all a government conspiracy, he had said; it was a plot to control the population, he had said; HIV medicine was designed to kill people, he had said. Despair may have driven him to drugs and alcohol, and his boxing career and meth use may have combined to cause a certain amount of neurological damage, but Morrison seemed purposeful in his last public deception. He was no less loathsome for that.

On a low-rent reality show chronicling his comeback (broadcast by the now-defunct Kush TV), Morrison expressed his homophobia openly to a micro-community of viewers. "It (HIV) can't pass through sex from man to woman, anyway. It cannot happen. I don't care what people tell you, it cannot happen. It happens from man to man because that's forbidden of God. You know, it's an abomination, you're gonna pay the price. What causes AIDS is drugs."

In a June 2007 *Details* magazine feature, Morrison, unprompted, shared his racism as well. First, he offered his opinion on African American fighters ("All so tough till you hurt 'em once. Then you own 'em.") and then, when asked what he had learned from his time in prison, Morrison expounded on his lessons: "I learned patience in prison," he said. "Learned the value of time there, too, and that I really don't like black people."

A racist, homophobic, mendacious felon with a history of delusional thinking, Morrison could hardly be considered a reputable character, but it was enough for him to say that he was HIV negative to spark gullible coverage in every form of media, especially the internet, where critical analysis was as rare as a website without pop-ups.

There was also his open hypocrisy, designed to make him sound virtuous in public. Over and over, Morrison bragged about living a healthy lifestyle to combat HIV naturally, repeatedly saying that he would never even take an aspirin. At the same time, he was consuming methamphetamine, shooting up Adderall, snorting cocaine, smoking cigarettes and cigars, getting arrested frequently for DUIs, and once, to the horror of Dawn Gilbert, even taking Special K, a horse tranquilizer that left him in shambles.

★ ★ ★

For the rest of the year, Morrison keeps a low profile. He moves to California to live with Lisa Woodard, who had been billed, falsely, as his wife on Kush TV. Woodard is a publicist who has fallen for the HIV claims that Morrison repeats ad infinitum. In her 2016 deposition, Dawn Gilbert claims that Woodard had been paying for HIV medication under false pretenses—Morrison had contended that the prescriptions were for hepatitis C.

In January 2008, Dawn Gilbert finally receives her divorce from Morrison, years after he drifted away from her life.

Morrison resurfaces in early 2008, in an interview with Brian Doogan of the *Sunday Times*, where he claims, yet again, that he is preparing to take a blood test in Nevada to prove, once and for all, that he is HIV-free. Leery of revealing too much about his seropositive status, Morrison and Woodard emerge from a huddle and put an end to that line of questioning.

"He's not a doctor," Woodard says about Morrison. "He doesn't have it and he can't really explain it, because he's not a doctor. All the things about HIV and AIDS, he doesn't have it, and hopefully, you'll believe it. He's going to pass a test and move on to a bright future."

★ ★ ★

If a bright future awaited Morrison, it would not be in America, and it would not be as a professional boxer. His next fight would merit all the publicity of a prelim between two ham-and-eggers milling in a bingo hall. On February 9, 2008, Morrison faced an unknown pug named Matt Weishaar in Leon, Mexico, on the undercard of a pay-per-view headlined by Julio Cesar Chavez Jr.

What little attention the fight drew came from Tim Lueckenhoff, president of the Association of Boxing Commissions. "The ABC is very concerned that Mr. Morrison is being allowed to participate in a boxing match," Lueckenhoff told the *Arizona Republic*. "We will encourage the Mexican Boxing Commission overseeing the match, as well as Top Rank, to present Mr. Morrison for a supervised blood draw."

Mexico, notoriously hands-off when it came to regulation, did not require a blood test, and Morrison once again avoided proving his HIV status. There would be no more opportunities in the future. "All of our commissions are on notice that Mr. Morrison would have to go through a supervised blood draw if he wants to box in the U.S.," Lueckenhoff said. That was enough to end the Tommy Morrison miracle.

★ ★ ★

Looking far bulkier than he had against John Stover in June 2007, Morrison stopped Weishaar in three rounds. As in his first comeback bout on Versus more than a year earlier, his scheduled appearance on the pay-per-view broadcast, another bait-and-switch, was scotched at the last moment.

★ ★ ★

Nearly another year would pass before Morrison resurfaced, this time without Top Rank, without Woodard, without even a semblance of that bright future ahead of him. In yet another farce, in yet another state without regulatory oversight, Morrison would battle the promoter of a tawdry MMA show in Laramie, Wyoming. For his latest outing, against a flabby local pro named Corey "Whiz Kid" Williams, Morrison agreed to modified Muay Thai rules, which included knees and elbows. "The Last Stand: Ultimate Explosion 12" would take place on January 31, 2009, at the Albany County Fairgrounds. No one cared. Although Morrison tried generating publicity for the Williams fight on radio and via the friendly if incompetent stenographers at clickbait websites, his appeal had faded long ago. Once a soft-spoken charmer with a ready smile, Morrison was now a bitter, booming braggart, hoarsely repeating the same conspiracy theories, the same lies, the same promises of a sensational run at the heavyweight title.

Morrison was no longer mainstream news. Not even the bizarre trappings of his latest materialization could generate bylines at reputable outlets. With a few notable exceptions, Morrison would now become a permanent fixture of the internet shadowland, where semiliterate bloggers, for negligible traffic, would run hero-worship puff pieces and press releases (composed by Morrison himself, or one of his latest factotums) without even a pretense of editorial standards.

Two weeks before the Wyoming fight, the main event still lacked half of its marquee—no opponent had been named in the marketing materials. Eventually, Williams, head of Who's Your Daddy Productions, the promoter of the fight, named himself as the opponent. "Well, I promise you one thing: I might lose January 31, but the world's going to know where the state of Wyoming is," Williams told the *Laramie Boomerang*. "I will make sure they respect the state by the time I step out of the ring. That's what this is about for me, it's respect and notoriety for the state. I'm tired of getting questions like, 'What state is Wyoming in?' or 'Where is that at?'"

If it was notoriety Williams wanted, it was notoriety he got when Morrison knocked him out in the first round and sparked allegations of a fix. The kayfabe began immediately, when Morrison uncharacteristically shoved Williams before the opening bell, a WWE maneuver that set the tone for what would follow. When Williams hit the deck from an innocuous-looking right hand, he did so with the aplomb of a slapstick comedian. After energetically flopping around the canvas for a few seconds,

Williams beat the count only to free-fall flat onto his back following a nonchalant left hook.

In a dimly lit auditorium, with only a few hundred spectators in attendance, and a ring announcer dressed as a rodeo official, Morrison would pantomime his beginnings as a professional boxer, when he was a teenager hoping to leave the piddling world of Jay, Oklahoma, behind. But, on the heels of three previous fiascos, the Williams fight would solidify Morrison as a sideshow specialist. No matter what he said, his days as anything but a curiosity were over. And even that unenviable distinction would soon be lost to him.

★ ★ ★

About the charge that his fight against Williams was bogus, Morrison told Top Class Boxing: "He could have gone on another two or three rounds, but he was too worried about spending the money he ripped me off for the fight and pay-per-view. His check bounced on me and he emptied the pay-per-view account and I am still hunting him down . . . and so are others."

★ ★ ★

January 2011. He will make one last pell-mell effort. At a press conference in Montreal, Morrison poses with his future opponent, Eric Barrak. A bandana obscures Morrison's bald head, his eyeliner enhances his manic look, his hands are dotted with lesions. Morrison expects to headline a card on February 25 at the Pierre Charbonneau Centre. His old foe, Ray Mercer, now fifty, is scheduled for the co-feature. "I'm living proof that HIV is a myth," Morrison said. "All the things that were going to happen, they didn't. Medical mistakes happen all the time and people are misdiagnosed. I don't see any reason why this fight won't happen. It's not like I weigh ninety-five pounds and my eyes are sunk back. That's not the case."

The governing body of Quebec (La Régie des Alcools, des Courses et des Jeux), known as the RACJ, soon runs afoul of Morrison, whose optimism about fighting in "The City of Festivals" is ultimately misplaced. Because Morrison refuses to take the blood test necessary for a license, his first main event (as a boxer) in more than fourteen years is jeopardized.

"The only thing I'm asking is for him to pass the test. He's making a fuss and it has become a big story," said Michel Hamelin, director of the RACJ. "Our doctors require the blood test because they're not sure. This isn't the first time we use the rules we have. He requires a blood test that's supervised. We're not making an example of Tommy Morrison. . . . He's making a fuss."

Instead of submitting to the common procedures of the RACJ, Morrison chooses to grandstand. He issues a statement to his favorite internet outlet, part gibberish, part deliberate obfuscation, all lies. From his nonsense press release: "IF the HIV VIRUS EXISTS then there should be an HIV VIRUS TEST and one that is approved by the CDC and FDA and where the manufacturers of the test CONFIRM the presence or absence of the HIV VIRUS itself—100%." To his dwindling supporters—mostly gullible readers of risible websites—Morrison is fighting for his career, but in truth, he is fighting reality, feverishly, foolishly, futilely.

Morrison, already starting to look skeletal, ultimately loses his spot on the card. He will never attempt another comeback.

★ ★ ★

Unwilling (and unable) to provide a reputable commission with a supervised blood test, Morrison knew his days as a prizefighter—even one with a sideshow bent—were over. His career, which began in 1988, ended with a record of 48-3, with 42 knockouts. On the surface, this ledger is impressive, but boxing is a sport in which nothing should be taken at face value. From the day he turned pro, Morrison epitomized the smoke-and-mirror world of boxing, where the line between athletic event and consumer fraud is often thinner than a lightbulb filament. In his only signature win, Morrison scored a unanimous decision over George Foreman in 1993, which earned him the negligible WBO heavyweight title. Two or three other results shine: KOs over Joe Hipp, a bruising club fighter; and Razor Ruddock, an ex-contender well past his expiration date; and a draw against Ross Puritty, who would go on to become a fair journeyman.

But Morrison could not overcome a slew of technical (as well as personal) flaws. First, his defense was mediocre. Morrison was especially susceptible to right hands, and when he opened fire, he often did so squared up to his opponent, which made him a big target and left him exposed to counterpunches. More than once, Tommy Virgets noted how robotic Morrison could be, how his style was neither natural nor spontaneous, but the result of constant drilling in the gym. Certainly, Morrison had difficulty combining offense and defense, and it was the latter that caused him the most trouble. In addition, his bob-and-weave style was erratic: Sometimes he bobbed, sometimes he weaved, and sometimes, caught up in the moment, he did neither. This inconsistency also left him comically open to uppercuts, a blow that repeatedly left him on the canvas, trying to reassemble his scattered neurons.

Morrison also suffered from nerves. Being anxious before a fight would deplete his already limited stamina (from a dedicated nightlife), even while waiting for the opening bell to ring. That left Morrison exhausted, flagging at critical points during fights. "The problem with Tommy is that he's a very shy kid," John Brown told *Boxing World*. "He's so shy that he has to train in private. It's like a person who's afraid to speak in public. When Tommy is working out, and a few extra people come into the gym, he can't train in front of them. We've discussed this with him. We've applied logic in gargantuan portions, and he knows there's no reason for him to act this way, but he does. And when he gets in a big fight, he's scared."

Temperament and a lack of discipline exacerbated his shortcomings, which were considerable to begin with, but had he been able to curtail his excesses, Morrison might have made more than a single farcical defense of his equally farcical WBO title. Holyfield, Bowe, and Lewis were one step beyond him, but he defeated Foreman convincingly, and had a fair shot at denting Michael Moorer, whose chin never matched his technique, and stopping some of the lesser Alphabet Soup champions of the '90s: Herbie Hide, Frank Bruno, and Bruce Seldon. Of course, the possibility that any of these men would have flattened Morrison is just as feasible. (When focused and in condition, for example, Moorer was a slashing boxer-puncher, whose sharpshooting southpaw approach would have been a nightmarish style matchup for Morrison.) The sturdier second-tier pros of the early to mid-1990s, such as Oliver McCall and the gangly Henry Akinwande, would likely have forced Morrison into the late rounds, where he was most vulnerable, and stopped him from a combination of accrued punishment and exhaustion.

But Morrison also had talent to go along with certain intangibles essential for a prizefighter. Because of the varying quality of fighters a professional faces throughout his career, statistics in boxing are virtually useless, but the 80 percent knockout rate Morrison boasted is notable if not exactly remarkable. Of course, given the low level of opposition Morrison faced, most of these knockouts had a comical air to them, a fact that solidified the blanket skepticism he attracted from a media corps long exposed to fraudulence in boxing. To them, Morrison was nothing more than another Great White Hope manufactured in the mold of Gerry Cooney, a limited fighter matched solely to build a deceptive record and cash in on a championship fight he had no chance of winning.

But was that all Morrison was? After all, the sporting world had been familiar with fugazi White Hopes for years. Yet Morrison bore little resemblance to his lumbering predecessors (Jim Beattie, retired by the New York State Athletic Commission in 1966 as a hazard to himself; Ron Stander, brutalized by Joe Frazier in two rounds) or to his contemporaries (Richie Melito, whose matchmaker went to prison for fixing his fights; Peter McNeeley, first-round KO loser to a comebacking Mike Tyson under unusual circumstances). A fine athlete, Morrison had, along with Evander Holyfield, the fastest hands of any heavyweight since a prime Tyson. And while the improvisational skill most elite fighters rely upon was beyond him, Morrison often assembled his rapid-fire combinations with precision. The finishing barrage that left Joe Hipp bloodied, empurpled with bruises, and teetering on his feet was a blistering sequence only a few big men of that era could have replicated.

Because heavyweights throw far fewer punches than fighters in smaller divisions, they rarely mount a sustained body attack. But Morrison worked the body with zeal, often doubling up hooks with either hand after landing to the rib cage. His signature right-to-the-body/right uppercut combination—lifted from Mike Tyson videotapes—was both lethal and often unexpected. In close, Morrison could surprise an opponent from either side with damaging shots, an unusual skill at any weight but more so among men who weighed 220 to 250 pounds and who were mostly stationary. There was also the undeniable potency of his left hook. "Tommy's hook is the best single punch in boxing, ABC analyst Alex Wallau told Boxing 93. "No matter what else he does, it's still his key. I wouldn't be surprised if anyone in the division knocked him out. Put him in with Bowe or Lewis, and he should be the underdog—an absolutely decisive one. But can he beat these guys? Sure, he can. And you can't say that about too many heavyweights."

Finally, Morrison showed the kind of heart often lacking among his peers. Where Buster Douglas, Henry Akinwande, Phil Jackson, and others had demonstrated something less than uncommon valor in some of their fights, Morrison was someone who had to be nailed to the canvas before he lost. Morrison epitomized the archaic phrase "dead game." Before fights, he was unfocused, cavalier, bacchanalian—and that, to be sure, counts as unprofessional—but Morrison scored a slew of come-from-behind wins and rose from multiple knockdowns in fights against Carl Williams, Michael Bentt, Ross Puritty, and Lennox Lewis. Against Bentt, Morrison was clearly in no condition to continue after hitting the canvas for the second time, and yet, there he was, dead game, willing, if not necessarily ready, to take more. He also battled through various injuries—including a broken jaw—to stop a rallying Joe Hipp.

What made Morrison significant was not his accomplishments in the ring, however, but his standing as a legitimate box-office and pay-per-view attraction. At the heart of his popularity was his grassroots support, and, yes, his skin color was also an asset in a sport that was 95 percent Black and Latino. But Morrison also had a style guaranteed to quicken pulses. And it was calculated. "I have an exciting style," Morrison told *Boxing Scene*. "People pay to watch me because regardless of the outcome, something exciting is going to happen. That's what made Mike Tyson the most popular athlete around when he was fighting." That wrecking-ball approach produced forty-five knockouts in fifty-two fights, a virtual guarantee to the paying audience that a memorable moment would take place whenever Morrison fought. Even run-of-the-mill decisions were marked by tumbles. Except for his points wins over Lorenzo Canady and George Foreman, Morrison scored knockdowns in every distance fight he had, and, as in the case of his draw against Ross Puritty, suffered some of his own. In a 1989 interview with the *Salina Journal*, Morrison made his ring philosophy clear. "People don't like to see a sloppy fight," he said, "to see heavyweights wallowing around. They like to see exciting fighters." This combative attitude, a conscious decision to heighten the performative aspect of boxing, is what made Morrison a hero in Middle America and a television staple for years.

★ ★ ★

"Master of my own defeat!"
—Paw

★ ★ ★

Having failed at his latest return to the ring, Morrison sparked publicity the only other ways he knew how: by providing an interview that made him sound insane and by getting arrested. Once again, the *Kansas City Star* served as a portal into a disintegrating mind. Columnist Sam Mellinger related how Morrison had "teleported" out of danger from a Springfield bar where "an overwhelming feeling of evil" predominated. "I know it sounds [fucked] up," Morrison said. "But I'll tell you what, it happened to me. It's real. But things like this don't work for anybody that doesn't believe it."

For years Morrison said that he would take a test in Nevada (publicly, if necessary) to prove his HIV-free status, but now it was a different story. No, Morrison told Mellinger, he was disinclined to undergo blood work. "If I do that, that's letting them win, don't you think?"

★ ★ ★

Negativity followed Morrison wherever he went. But even someone so flawed cannot be reduced to his worst moments. He was generous to his friends and his fans. His handshake agreement with Tony Holden, a rare bond in a sport dominated by lawyers, contracts, and litigants, reflected his belief in friendship beyond the limitations of business. "If he considered you a friend," Troy Morrison says, "and you were loyal . . . he had your back for life. He was not a traitor; he was a very loyal friend, and he was there for you through thick and thin."

His benevolence included attending several charitable events to raise money for various causes. If he sometimes showed up to these affairs high or drunk, it was not an indictment of his goodwill. "Tommy couldn't stay away from bad influences, but he also did some tremendously generous things for a lot of people," Holden told the *Tulsa World* in 2013. "He would read the paper and see that someone was in an accident or having a tough time, and he'd give them $10,000 without even thinking about it."

In 1995, he donated a percentage of the gate receipts of a fight to Oklahoma City disaster relief, and there are countless stories of Morrison handing out hundreds if not thousands of dollars to homeless people on the street. He helped pay for a church fellowship. He founded the Knock-Out AIDS Foundation in 1996. His entourage, mostly moochers and party animals, was well provided for until the money started running out.

The things he did, the things he said, the life he led at the end—all seemingly incompatible with virtue. But Morrison was born on a moral crossroads. "Anyone in the same circumstances, given what he was given, probably would have made a lot of the same foolish mistakes that he did," Troy Morrison says. "I pity Tommy in a lot of ways."

★ ★ ★

On Thursday, February 17, 2011, only four days after his appearance in the *Kansas City Star*, Morrison was arrested on milepost 131 of the Kansas Turnpike, a few miles north of Emporia, and charged with possession of marijuana. After posting bail of $2,500, Morrison was released from Lyon County Jail to await a hearing. Because Morrison had already been convicted twice for drug-related offenses, he was at risk of another jail sentence. But when the arresting officer, Highway Patrolman Beau Wallace, died in a motorcycle accident on May 26, charges against Morrison were dropped.

A few months passed before Morrison found himself in court again. In September, he was extradited from his home in Pigeon Forge, Tennessee, back to Kansas to face charges on a March 2010 drug charge that had gone under the radar in Wichita. This time the counts included felony possession of controlled substances and misdemeanor possession of paraphernalia for use.

★ ★ ★

The sports world is shocked to see the latest mug shot of Tommy Morrison, an image that seems to foreshadow death. Only forty-two years old, Morrison resembles a vagrant who has just returned from a harrowing ordeal. A video of his court appearance, filmed at the Sedgwick County Jail, is even more disturbing. Morrison looks like a cross between a confused little boy and a senile old man. He is wearing a colorful polo sweater with the word TOMMY stitched across a horizontal stripe. He is haggard, ashen, bewildered. "We're in Kansas, aren't we?" he asks.

When Kansas officials eventually drop their case against Morrison, they offer no explanation. But the sight of Morrison—emaciated, rambling, seemingly helpless—provides a clue that cannot be ignored. Just as Oklahoma District Judge Robert Haney released Morrison from Delaware County Jail in 1999 because of his declining health, so, too, did Kansas officials apply pragmatic mercy in 2011. Simply put, Morrison is unfit for prison. He is, by then, unfit for anything. In less than two years, he will be dead.

★ ★ ★

Troy Morrison wept for hours when he saw the mug shot of his nephew.

★ ★ ★

During the social media age, when it became possible to connect, digitally at least, with a seemingly infinite number of people, Morrison remained close to his fans. Part of his appeal had always been his approachability. "I've read that Muhammad Ali and Elvis Presley never turned down an autograph request," Morrison told *POZ* magazine, "and I try to be the same way." Charitable events, auctions, memorabilia shows, boxing matches, personal appearances—Morrison was always generous with his time. Fans would line up for a signature and the chance to exchange pleasantries with the man who had beaten George Foreman and who had costarred in *Rocky V*. In the aughts, he ran a website that featured a forum in which he would exchange posts with various members, and he regularly chatted with admirers on Facebook. Although interviews rarely reflected well on him, Morrison granted several of them to smaller websites, often with writers he had befriended.

And then, one day, Tommy Morrison vanished.

★ ★ ★

"Being ill like this combines shock—this time I *will* die—with a pain and agony that are unfamiliar, that wrench me out of myself. It is like visiting one's funeral, like visiting loss in its purest and most monumental form, this wild darkness, which is not only unknown but which one cannot enter as oneself. Now one belongs entirely to nature, to time: identity was a game."
—Harold Brodkey

★ ★ ★

Now is the time of CT scans, VACs, CPAPs. The memories of Rocky V fame, of heavyweight KOs, of a million-dollar bank account, of a spotlit name on one marquee after another, of all the willing redheads, blondes, brunettes—that life of revel, far removed from Highway 59 in Jay, yields to the hell of a body in riot. From ICU to ICU, Morrison becomes weaker and weaker, finally bedridden, a fading silhouette, unable to speak, kept alive by ventilators in a world of catheters and monitors. Until September 1, 2013, in an Omaha, Nebraska, hospital: flatline. That fantastical, fanatical lie—no HIV—finally proving fatal. "All the things that were going to happen," Morrison once said, "they never will."

ACKNOWLEDGMENTS

Thanks to John Brown, Tony Holden, Dr. Stuart Kirschenbaum, Lindy Lindell, Troy Morrison, and Sean Newman.

SOURCES

Court Records
Court documents available on PacerMonitor.com include hundreds
of pages of medical records, memorandums written by physicians,
depositions (all given under oath), notes, and bills that confirm Tommy
Morrison had HIV and was treated for it, on and off, for more than a
decade.

Morrison v. Quest Diagnostics Inc.
Case No. 2:14-cv-01207-RFB-BNW, (D. Nev. June 8, 2016)
https://www.pacermonitor.com/public/case/4115422/
Morrison_v_Quest_Diagnostics_Incorporated_et_al

Books
Andersen, Kurt. *Fantasyland. How America Went Haywire: A 500-Year
    History.* New York: Random House, 2017.
Batchelor, Bob and Scott Stoddard. *The 1980s* (American Popular
    Culture Through History). Westport: Greenwood Press, 2007.
Berger, Phil. *Punchlines: Berger on Boxing.* New York: Da Capo, 1993.
Brady, Dawn Morrison and Charles Hood. The Tommy "The Duke"
    Morrison Story. Kosciusko: Touchpoint Press, 2014.

Brodkey, Harold. *This Wild Darkness: The Story of My Death*. New York: Henry Holt & Co., 1996.

Dent, Tory. *HIV, Mon Amour: Poems*. New York: Sheep Meadow Press, 1999.

Engel, Jonathan. *The Epidemic: A Global History of AIDS*. New York: HarperCollins, 2007.

Evans, Gavin. *Mama's Boy: Lennox Lewis and the Heavyweight Crown*. Berkshire: Highdown, 2004

Foreman, George and Joe Engel. *By George, The Autobiography of George Foreman*. New York: Villard Books, 1995

Friend, David. *The Naughty Nineties: The Triumph of the American Libido*. New York: Twelve, 2017.

Goldwag, Arthur. *Cults, Conspiracies, and Secret Societies: The Straight Scoop on Freemasons, The Illuminati, Skull and Bones, Black Helicopters, The New World Order, and many, many more*. New York: Vintage, 2009.

Heller, Peter. *Bad Intentions: The Mike Tyson Story*. New York: Da Capo, 1995.

Hoffer, Richard. *A Savage Business: The Comeback and Comedown of Mike Tyson*. New York: Simon and Schuster, 1998.

Kalichman, Seth. *Denying AIDS: Conspiracy Theories, Pseudoscience, and Human Tragedy*. New York: Copernicus Books, 2009.

Lardner, John. *White Hopes and Other Tigers*. Philadelphia: J. B. Lippincott, 1951.

Merlan, Anna. *Republic of Lies: American Conspiracy Theorists and Their Surprising Rise to Power*. New York: Metropolitan Books, 2020.

Newfield, Jack. *Only in America: The Life and Crimes of Don King*. Sag Harbor: Harbor Electronic Publishing, 2003.

Padgett, Ron. *Oklahoma Tough: My Father, King of the Tulsa Bootleggers*. Norman: University of Oklahoma Press, 2005.

Reding, Nick. *Methland: The Death and Life of an American Small Town*. New York: Bloomsbury, 2009.

Roiphe, Katie. *Last Night in Paradise: Sex and Morals at the Century's End*. New York: Vintage Books, 1997.

Sagan, Carl. *The Demon-Haunted World: Science as a Candle in the Dark*. New York: Ballantine Books, 1997.

Shukla, Rashi K. *Methamphetamine: A Love Story*. Oakland: University of California Press, 2016.

Sontag, Susan. *AIDs and Its Metaphors*. New York: Farrar, Straus, Giroux, 1989.

Ward, Geoffrey C. *Unforgivable Blackness: The Rise and Fall of Jack Johnson*. New York: Knopf, 2004.

Whiteside, Alan. *HIV/AIDS: A Very Short Introduction*. Oxford: Oxford University Press, 2017.

Periodicals

Boxing 91–Boxing 95

Boxing Monthly

Boxing News

Boxing Scene

Details

ESPN The Magazine

GQ

HIV Plus

KO

New Scientist

New York Review of Books

New Yorker

Newsweek

People

POZ

The Ring

Sports Illustrated

Time

World Boxing

Newspapers

Arizona Republic

Bonner Springs-Edwardsville Examiner

Boston Globe

Californian

Central New Jersey Home News

Daily Oklahoman

Detroit Free Press

Great Falls Tribune

Green Bay Press-Gazette

Guardian

Independent

Ithaca Journal

Joplin Globe

Kansas City Star

Leaf Chronicle

Los Angeles Times

Manhattan Mercury

Miami Herald

Montana Standard

Morning Call

New York Daily News

New York Times

Newsday

Philadelphia Daily News

Philadelphia Inquirer

Pittsburgh Post-Gazette

Quad City Times

Reno-Gazette Journal

Sacramento Bee

Salina Journal
San Bernadino County Sun
San Francisco Examiner
Sapulpa Daily Herald
Sedalia Democrat
Signal
Sonoran News
South China Morning Post

South Florida Sentinel
Springfield News-Leader
St. Louis Post-Dispatch
Sunday Times
Tampa Tribune
Tulsa World
USA Today

Interviews
John Brown
Lindy Lindell

Troy Morrison

Websites
AIDStruth.org
Associated Press
KC Confidential
PacerMonitor
Psychology Today

Salon
Scientific American
Slate
Smithsonian
Top Class Boxing

Videos/Documentaries
60 Minutes
Boulevard of Broken Dreams
Cold Pizza
*The Comeback: The Tommy
    Morrison Story*
Dateline

ESPN 30 for 30—Tommy
Frontline
Hardcopy
Larry King Live
Maury Povich Show
Outside the Lines

The Duke is set in 10-point Sabon, which was designed by the German-born typographer and designer Jan Tschichold (1902–1974) in the period 1964–1967. It was released jointly by the Linotype, Mono-type, and Stempel type foundries in 1967. Copyeditor for this project was Shannon LeMay-Finn. The book was designed by Brad Norr Design, Minneapolis, Minnesota, and typeset by New Best-set Typesetters Ltd.